POWER

Nonviolent Transformation from the Transpersonal to the Transnational

Tom H. Hastings

Hamilton Books
an imprint of
University Press of America,® Inc.
Dallas · Lanham · Boulder · New York · Oxford

Copyright © 2005 by
Hamilton Books
4501 Forbes Boulevard
Suite 200
Lanham, Maryland 20706
UPA Acquisitions Department (301) 459-3366

PO Box 317
Oxford
OX2 9RU, UK

All rights reserved
Printed in the United States of America
British Library Cataloging in Publication Information Available

Library of Congress Control Number: 2004106894
ISBN 0-7618-2909-1 (paperback : alk. ppr.)

⊖™ The paper used in this publication meets the minimum requirements of American National Standard for Information Sciences—Permanence of Paper for Printed Library Materials, ANSI Z39.48—1984

*Dedicated to Philip Berrigan
— the Sargent Rock of the nonviolent peace movement—
and to Wally Nelson & Ladon Sheats,
the best male role models we had,
and to all the quiet and heroic
practitioners of risky nonviolence
—from the children who stop other children from fighting,
to the accompaniers of indigenous human rights leaders,
to the sheroic women who,
with burning and undefeatable love,
confront those who torture and make war—
these are the people who make daily life more secure
and who struggle to end violence*

Table of Contents

Preface	*vii*
Acknowledgments	*xiii*
Definitions	*xv*
Acronyms	*xvii*

Section one:
transformation: transpersonal and group-to-group — 1

chapter one: **Domestic transformation**	5
chapter two: **Neighborly nonviolence: schools, streets & workplaces**	17
Transforming schools	22
Rapists and robbers: more evidence	35
On the job	41
chapter three: **Identity violence**	45
Alarmingly normal: identity conflict pervasive, natural, destructive	49
Killing the spirit in the name of religion: oil and identity in the Mideast	60
chapter four: **Civil strife**	71
Interposition in intrastate conflict	76
We don't negotiate with terrorists (until we do)	90
chapter five: **International conflict**	97
Vom Krieg: why?	101
Against war, for nonviolence	104
Sexism and the war system: feminism and peace	113

Section two:
planetary nonviolent transformation — 125

Peace: a movement, a tradition	129
The art of peace: facing the music	131
chapter six: **Nonviolent histories, transformative training**	135
Human capabilities	135
India	144
From Reconstruction to Civil Rights	146
chapter seven: **Drill it in: training like the nonviolent military**	155
Nonviolent citizen soldiers: civilian-based defense	158
The law of the nonviolent jungle	162
Sample nonviolence training	168
chapter eight: **National liberation**	183
Terrorism, military action, or law enforcement?	185
Empires and nonviolent resistance	206
chapter nine: **Defense of Creation**	213

War on Mother Earth: military attacks planet	224
Resource wars	229
bibliography	239
index	251

Preface

Dulce et decorum est, pro patria mori.

— ancient Romans and most other powerlovers since. *It is sweet and fitting to die for the Fatherland.*

One of the eternal truths is that happiness is created and developed in peace, and one of the eternal rights is the individual's right to live. The strongest of all instincts, that of self-preservation, is an assertion of this right, affirmed and sanctified by the ancient commandment: "Thou shalt not kill."

—Bertha Sophie Felicia von Suttner, Austrian pacifist, writer, Nobel Peace Prize Laureate in 1905 (von Suttner: 213)

Two others and I stood in the lightly falling snow at about 2 a.m. in January of 1985 in a farmer's field in Missouri. Headlights jounced around the freeway exit onto the county road and tore across the bridge toward the three of us. "They're going fast," I remember thinking. "What's the rush?"

Sure enough, the vehicle swung swiftly around the corner onto the access road and then churned right onto the little gravel apron on which we vigilers stood, clattering to a sudden halt amidst a smack of spun pebbles. We were the peaceniks in the headlights, caught with no thought of consequence.

Two air force boys leapt out of the military vehicle. One hung back and wasn't really visible. Presumably, he was covering the other, who strode up to the three of us, sized us up and raised his automatic weapon, pointing it directly at my chest.

I looked at the lad and realized he was perhaps all of 19 or 20 years old. Was he shaking? Hard to tell in the lambent light at 2 a.m. in the swirling snow. He may have been cold. He may have been cold-blooded. But I didn't think so. Just an American kid who was told in high school how great the air force would be, and now here he was, weapon drawn not on some alien threat but on three positively unimposing citizens of his own nation.

Standing in the company of a short portly woman and an elderly man with Coke-bottle glasses, I seemed to be the default danger, or the closest thing to it, as a relatively young man. That was almost certainly why he chose to level his gun at me.

My reaction was easy, almost natural, as a result of years of participation in nonviolence training and in nonviolent witness—and also not unrelated to the steady company in which I stood. I calmly told him, "I respect you, brother, but I don't respect your weapon. You can stop pointing it at us."

He thought about it momentarily and then lowered the muzzle. The tense moment was over and we could talk, which we did. Sam Day, the elderly man alongside me, explored several subjects with the air force men that night, establishing a commonality with them and educating them about the nuclear missile in the silo in the field just a couple of hundred feet from where we were standing in witness. Not surprisingly, the young men had no real notion of geopolitics and how the nuclear arsenal affected everything. We kept each other awake.

I am in favor of nonviolence under all situations, by everyone, toward any human being. I have not been in all situations, I am not every other human being, and thus I cannot judge others by their philosophies, their actions, their strategic plans or their tactical decisions. I can only judge myself.

I teach Conflict Resolution to graduate students and Peace Studies to undergrads. Thus I can, and must, at least attempt to analyze the effectiveness of certain responses to tension, to crisis, to threat, and to attack. And I can argue for the philosophy, strategic cohesion and efficacy of total nonviolence. That is what this book is about, from reducing the violence in the smallest interpersonal interaction to stopping war between nation-states. To borrow Jonathan Swift's phrase, a Modest Proposal. What works? What doesn't work? Says who? It's a matter of perspective, as Freeman Dyson pointed out in his masterful understatement of the difference by which the British empire—at the pacifist prodding of the Quakers and others—ended their slavery nonviolently in 1833 and the way the US ended it by a civil war. The UK passed no judgment on its slaveowners and offered compensation, removing all the resolve-producing elements that might have caused the slaveowners to rebel in places like the West Indies. "The British government paid the slave-owners twenty million pounds. The cost of the American Civil War was considerably higher." (Dyson: 201) How may we reframe these kinds of problems and solutions? How can we use nonviolence to make our neighborhoods, our schools and our homes safer? How may we incorporate nonviolence into a war on terrorism or a battle against globalization of human

Preface

and natural resources by transnational corporate interests? And how do individuals play a role or initiate a movement that might work?

A word about my style: I'm a professor but not an academic. My background is as a writer and activist, two trades that stress persuasion, not aloof (and some would say truly impossible) objectivity. Indian novelist, activist and essayist Arundhati Roy addresses this issue of objectivity searingly:

> *But is it mandatory for a writer to be ambiguous about everything? Isn't it true that there have been fearful episodes in human history when prudence and discretion would have just been euphemisms for pusillanimity? When caution was actually cowardice? When sophistication was disguised decadence? When circumspection was really a kind of espousal?* (Roy: online)

Like one of my writing heroes, Colman McCarthy, I try not to be shrill—"Scream too loudly and they are turned off by the noise. Write softly and they ask, *Where's the passion?* Perhaps the soft scream is the ideal tone." (McCarthy: xiii)

This book is a soft scream for nonviolence. Bertha von Suttner made the call in 1905 for the recognition that nonviolence was not only a nice option, but the most adaptive strategy for self-preservation too. It was two years later that Mohandas Gandhi began his own version of that call—with action—in South Africa and then in India. Their wisdom was both tempered and annealed in the bloody yet liberatory 20th century. We are rolling along in a new century, many say, of the terrorist, the final contest of civilization versus the urge to destroy the good. Perhaps. But if we fail to use nonviolence, we lose the good in the very war we fight against evil. The danger is palpable; will we open our souls to the possession of the forces of evil in our hatred of them, or will we act for self-preservation with the ancient spirit of the Fifth Commandment and defeat evil where it does its worst work, in our hearts?

> *As long as war is regarded as wicked, it will always have its fascination. When it is looked upon as vulgar, it will cease to be popular.*
>
> —Oscar Wilde, *The Critic as Artist* (Wilde: 14)

When we honestly look at the costs of violence and the effectiveness of nonviolence, we will see just how vulgar war and indeed all violence truly is. If Wilde was right, our work is to learn about these things with authority, speak and write about them throughout society, demonstrate mass opposition to such gross and dishonorable behavior and slowly turn the consciousness of the citizenry toward working for peace and nonviolence as vastly preferable means and ends.

The puck has been dropped, as we say in hockey country. The game may get rough, but when we fly fast and retain the grace of nonviolence, we get nearer to the goal with much less bloodshed than those who revel in brutish and dirty fighting. The innocents living in villages in the vast majority of the world deserve our best game, as do the unborn—another constituency who cannot vote but who can speak to us if we listen closely to our own hearts and our vision of a world without war. From our families to our neighborhoods to our country to our world, the natural rules are the same even if the laws of mankind are inconsistent. *Thou shalt not kill* is a simple dictum; what part of it don't we understand? That commandment is not a shout into the void or a spit into the wind; humans are wired for violence *and* nonviolence. Some experts insist it is all one way or another; some say that we will naturally be warlike under many common circumstances. Others see that "People in the mold of the September 11th hijackers are a precious resource for an insurgency, because few people are naturally violent." (Lemann: 39) Indeed, most of us desperately wish for nonviolent solutions, for the power, protection, civilization and security that nonviolence can promise.

And so, our side—if we wish for nonviolence—also needs those precious resources, those willing to commit at least a portion of their lives to causes much larger than themselves, causes which can be overwhelming for the individual yet, in the estimation of at least some philosophers, a duty for all of us and each one of us. Scottish philosopher Adam Ferguson gave us "his 1767 **Essay on the History of Civil Society**, in which he warns repeatedly against the development of a professional political class who will take over the functions of government, while the rest of us lapse into political passivity, and a narrow preoccupation with our own private concerns." (McMillan)

The scenes: of the dead boy in a pool of blood in a school shooting; or of a woman with emaciated children in a refugee camp following desperate flight in front of a war machine that eats people; or of people dropping in existential terror from 100 stories rather than face the lethal iron-twisting fire behind them—these are the scenes of vengeance, the unlearned lessons from millennia of war, the wages of sin and the *quid pro quo* of Faustian bargains with the venal principles and practices of imperialism, of the dance with the devil of global pillage. That governments don't acknowledge that and act accordingly is the "unending cycle of stupidity." (Zinn: 7)

On being nonviolent: nobody is perfect, especially if we attempt to equate nonviolence with thought and emotion, not merely deed. Kathy Kelly—brave and persistent international practitioner of nonviolence—writes

Preface

of talking to classes of students on what nonviolence really is:

> I quote Rabbi Abraham Heschel on pacifism: "There are no absolute pacifists, only biographical ones." (Kelly: 168)

Kathy—as graceful a person under pressure as I've ever seen on the front lines—knows the mandatory pull of conscience and the discipline of obligatory love under duress. She understands as well as anyone I've ever worked with just how impossible pure love and uncontaminated nonviolence are if we look at our emotional reactions to killers or to those who preach hatred. When we fail to feel nonviolence in our hearts we so very much need to accept, embrace, fully know and compartmentalize our negative feelings. There may be no absolutely nonviolent humans, but to act absolutely nonviolently even as we feel outrage at someone who is hurting others is to be as fully human as possible.

Gandhi, of course, appeared to disagree with this assessment entirely in his description of what nonviolence is. His roots—at least on his mother's side—were partly in Jainist spirituality, which looked deeply into *himsa*—violence—and its corresponding *ahimsa*—nonviolence. Gandhi noted his truth, which was that we invariably act with violence, even if it takes the form of walking across the ground and inevitably stepping on insects and thus ending lives violently. What Gandhi saw as the duty of the student of nonviolence, then, was to attempt to reduce the level of *himsa* committed by developing an attitude of constant compassion and attention. (Gandhi: 312) Heschel's truth and Gandhi's truth conspire to both forgive us all and challenge us every moment, a recipe for growth and goodness.

Two items regarding using this book as a study tool: I reiterate my lack of objectivity. I detest violence and regard violent warriors as usually well meaning but generally immature. Second, I've tried to make the chapters roughly the same length (with mixed success) and have kept them to a total of nine, on the theory that many courses are ten-week quarters (with no reading assigned for the first week). But professors who choose to use any text will select what they regard as valuable to their learning goals and I invite feedback from them, from students and from any reader: hastings@pdx.edu.

Nonviolence can succeed. We know that because it has been the method used by millions to gain liberation and basic human rights. We know that because we've all seen a variant of an uncommon but occasional interposition: a little girl steps in between a bully and a potential victim and halts the abuse with her strong presence. Let us explore a few of the ways in which we can make nonviolence more likely to work to everyone's benefit. That little girl is our role model.

sources:

Dyson, Freeman, ***Weapons and Hope***. NYC: Harper Colophon Books, 1984.

Gandhi, Mohandas K., ***Autobiography: The Story of My Experiments with Truth***. NYC: Dover Publications, Inc., 1983. (original Public Affairs Press, 1948)

Kelly, Kathy, "Nonviolence and the ongoing war against Iraq," in: Harak, S. J., G. Simon, ed., ***Nonviolence for the Third Millennium: Its Legacy and Future***. Macon GA: Mercer University Press, 2000.

Lemann, Nicholas, "What terrorists want," *The New Yorker*, 29 October 2001 (36-41)

McCarthy, Colman, ***All of One Peace: Essays on Nonviolence***. New Brunswick NJ: Rutgers University Press, 1994.

McMillan, Joyce, "On the slippery slope of disengagement," *The Scotsman*, 21 November 2001. http://www.thescotsman.co.uk/index.cfm?id=124472

Roy, Arundhati, "Shall We Leave It to the Experts?," http://www.outlookindia.com/full.asp?sid=1&fname=Arundhati+Roy+%28F%29&fodname=20020114&secname=

von Suttner, Bertha Sophie Felicia, "The evolution of the peace movement," in: Thee, Marek, ***Peace! By the Nobel Peace Prize Laureates: An Anthology***. Paris: UNESCO Publishing, 1995.

Zinn, Howard, "Not vengeance but compassion," *Peacework*, October 2001. (7-8)

Acknowledgments

Nonviolence is a normal human activity, and for that perspective, I thank Dr. Gene Sharp, who continues to point that out to the rest of us who somehow fail to internalize that truth—and to Jack DuVall of the International Center on Nonviolent Conflict for his tireless work. But putting our collective finger on just how that power is generated most effectively depends on experiments, as Gandhi told us. That's why I am so grateful to those who continue to try, to learn, to admit mistakes, to claim that we *can* protect each other using nonviolence. This means I am grateful to Dr. King and to the nameless woman in her burqa in Afghanistan who confronts her oppressors with nonviolence, and I am grateful to each equally; he and she each reveal such strength, knowledge and faith to those who will learn. To the SoA resisters, Plowshares resisters, the International Solidarity Movement, Kathy Kelly, the Nonviolent Peaceforce and to each human on Earth who tried to stop the latest immoral, obscene invasion of Iraq.

I thank each person who read and commented on all or part of this work (each improving on it)—Shari Bandes, Amanda Byron, Isbel Ingham, Loreene O'Neill, Richard Powers, David Westbrook—and I remain in firm ownership of any remaining errors, insensitivities, unwarranted assertions, political incorrectness, prolixity and sentimentality.

The Peace and Justice Studies Association, the Oregon Peace Institute, Oregon PeaceWorks, Portland State University and Portland Community College all contribute to my ongoing education about nonviolent power. Important individuals are very many indeed, but I will offer thanks to my Catholic Worker community mates Lisa Hughes, Gail Skenandore and Mary Kay McDermott; Jan Abu-Shakrah, Rhonda Baseler, Medea Benjamin, Dick Bennett, Peter Bergel, Michael Carrigan, Barb Cass, Rob Gould, my feisty father— Thomas J. Hastings, Altaira Hatton, Tina Hulbe, Ann Huntwork, Regena Jones, Kathy Kelly, Lori Loftin, Mike Miles, Kent Shifferd, Michael Sonnleitner, Barbara Wien, (with a special infinite gratitude to Jennifer Dawn Terry for her nonviolent shadowboxing, her values and her impressive beliefs) and hundreds of challenging fellow students, fellow professors and fellow activists happily too numerous to mention. As Tina tells us, all of you are educators.

Definitions

These definitions are used for these words in this text; this is not meant to imply academic, dictionary or dispositive authority. Language is most effective when we all understand what the speaker or writer means by each word. The following words are not necessarily understood in this way by all, but this is what I mean.

aggression: violating another's space with insistent or hurtful demands, either verbally or physically.

assertion: being insistent and challenging without violating another's space, either physically or emotionally.

fair trade: trade, sales and barter that is predicated on economic justice, human rights and environmental good practices.

free trade: often used to describe corporate-friendly, military-defended transnational trading practices usually associated with low standards for both human rights and collective bargaining, and with no care for environmental abuse.

globalization: transnational activities that can be just, unjust, positive or negative, economic, ecological, scientific or cultural, though commonly used to describe the entire corporate-state sequelae to nation-state imperialism begun with the victory of capitalism over communism.

nonviolence: assertive action that protects humans, the Earth and principles, often involving risk to the actionist but which forswears violence.

pacifism: avoidance of conduct that harms another, either passively or actively.

peace: a condition of nonviolent justice, not gained or maintained by armed force, violence or the threat of violence.

violence: direct physical harm to another. All other forms of violence require qualifiers (e.g. verbal violence, psychological violence, emotional violence).

Acronyms & abbreviations

ACLU:	American Civil Liberties Union
ADL:	Anti Defamation League
BAe:	British Aerospace (warplane mfg.)
BCE:	Before Common Era (also called BC)
CBD:	Civilian-based defense
CE:	Common Era (also called AD)
CORE:	Congress of Racial Equality
CPT:	Christian Peacemaking Teams
CSO:	Community Service Organization (San Jose CA)
CW:	Catholic Worker
DoD:	Department of Defense
FEPC:	Federal Employment Practices Commission
HAARP:	high-frequency active auroral research project
ICC:	International Criminal Court
ICJ:	International Court of Justice
IDF:	Israeli Defense Force
IDSA:	Institute for Defence Studies & Analyses (New Delhi)
IFOR:	International Fellowship of Reconciliation
IMF:	International Monetary Fund
KLA:	Kosovo Liberation Army
MNS:	Movement for a New Society
NAACP:	National Association for the Advancement of Colored People
NAFTA:	North American Free Trade Agreement
NATO:	North Atlantic Treaty Organization
NFWA:	National Farm Workers Association (precursor to UFW)
NGO:	nongovernmental organization
OAS:	Organization of American States
OPI:	Oregon Peace Institute
PBI:	Peace Brigades International
RAWA:	Revolutionary Association of the Women of Afghanistan
RUC:	Royal Ulster Constabulary
SCLC:	Southern Christian Leadership Conference
SNCC:	Student Nonviolent Coordinating Committee
UFW:	United Farm Workers

WB:	World Bank
WMD:	weapons of mass destruction
WTO:	World Trade Organization

SECTION ONE:

Transformation:

transpersonal and group-to-group

A précis for this book:

Nonviolence can work, from the interpersonal to the international. We know that it might work in the future because it has worked in the past. Nonviolence is, for most of us, counterintuitive, yet, like a neurosurgeon who can be trained not to faint or even cringe at the sight of blood, we can train ourselves to react nonviolently to crisis, conflict and even existential danger. There are ways to learn nonviolence and every person who learns and practices nonviolence contributes toward two important goals; first, that an act of nonviolence substitutes for violence and second, we take one little step closer to creating a social norm that approves of nonviolence over violence every time. Thus, the actions of each individual are crucial to the development of societal values and thus to history, the present and the future. We are each quite important, and no one is more or less important than anyone else. We are all immensely responsible for how our world of humans works, and when we act with and advocate nonviolence we perform a service to all humankind each time. There are techniques to help us practice nonviolence more effectively and there are keys to promoting nonviolence between individuals and between groups.

Meeting the Reverend James Lawson—the man who trained the cutting edge of African-American Civil Rights Movement workers beginning in the late 1950s in Nashville, Tennessee—proves the point that he instilled in his young charges from Fisk University as they trained to offer themselves as nonviolent resistance to entrenched racial segregation in the American South. He is unassuming, unimposing, quietly telling us about the power of nonviolence as he did decades ago to black kids ready to risk it all for justice. He smiles a bit, looking like the fumbling professor, and then we realize this is the same man who told his students of nonviolence that they were ordinary people who were headed for transformation, because ordinary people who acted on conscience and took extreme risks were no longer ordinary people. (Halberstam: 62) We shake hands. He smiles from beneath his white hair, gentle, yet prophetic, a man who changed the world, an extraordinary human indeed. That is the power of nonviolence.

Historian Howard Zinn likes to point out that human advances happen quite suddenly, apparently, but that beneath those rapid and often unexpected changes is a sea of good people who "have labored patiently for a long time." (Zinn: 33) This is how good and bad changes normally happen in virtually all living environments; Harvard biologist Stephen Jay Gould proposed a theory of punctuated equilibrium that explains evolution not in terms of gradual and nearly imperceptible change but as blindingly fast, based upon a minority of a population ready to adapt to certain conditions suddenly confronted with exactly those conditions. This is how nonviolence could rapidly change human history—and indeed, said Margaret Mead, it is the small groups of thoughtful, committed humans who change the world every time. The rodomontade of the violent—the bluster and bragging and threats and noisy stick-waving—belies the quiet, deeper currents of change that can come from centered nonviolent power.

A cautionary note to those who have found nonviolence, who have found a particular issue to which nonviolent activism will apply: be aware that activism is a cyclical phenomenon. Do not be surprised or disappointed when you hit a wall of inertia, when you just get discouraged, when you want your life to be free from all this seemingly (indeed, *actually*) endless volunteering, ceaseless need for your time and your efforts. As my counselor friend Joe used to say, *Toss yourself a break*. Pause. Hike. Garden. Love. Spell yourself from this demanding, rewarding, exhausting, exhilarating, enervating, energizing work whenever necessary, for as long as needed. The bad news is that problems will still need your attention when you are ready to rejoin the battle. The excellent news is that you will be refreshed and welcomed back by friends who have missed you but who understand. Fortunately, we who believe in, practice, and promote nonviolence are generally more persistent and suffer less alienation and burnout than do our more volatile, temperamental and "by all means at our disposal" fellow activists. In addition, understanding the value of a lifelong commitment as opposed to the idea that somehow we will find a total "fix" someday contributes to a realistic and sustainable level of activism. (Downton: 132) So, understand and accept your personal and the societal cycles of activity. Stick with the hope offered by nonviolence. These traits will help you roll along with less trauma and more tolerance and self-acceptance.

Commitment is what Gandhi stressed, more than analytical intellect, more than influence. (Gandhi: 4) Persistence is necessary to success, while brilliance is merely a contributory factor. And how we are influenced is another contributory factor, but two people who have almost the same set of influences acting upon them will become vastly different people whose lives have profoundly different results. It is what we do with those influences—which includes the denial, at times, of the inner selfish influences that rule us from moment to moment—that makes a life either a positive for humanity and our planet, or a negative.

One of the reasons we write about nonviolence is that it seems so counterintuitive to so many that it needs both theoretical explication and actual histories in order to seem even remotely hopeful. When, for example, we learn that some women have stories of avoiding rape by using nonviolent skills, we gain some notion of the possible. And when we learn from conflict researchers that communication itself will not necessarily make things better, (Lulofs: 30) we are forced to sharpen our pencils, to pay attention to the details, to learn the elements of the theories that ultimately enable us to make good communication and to take effective action.

In the field of Peace Studies and Conflict Resolution, we learn to make connections; that, more than anything, is our strength. Our breadth is our depth. Thus, we ask questions such as, How can we teach our children to behave nonviolently when we send the bombers over Kosovo and Belgrade? How can we advise those in the Mideast to stop the violence when we sell them boatloads of weapons each month? How can we prepare for a peaceful world when we have invested almost $6 trillion in preparing to wage absolute nuclear annihilation? (Schwartz: *xxii*) Since it's all connected, working on tolerance with grade school children will affect how easy—or hard—it is for Congress to fund the next absurd military expenditure. Working to outlaw weapons of mass destruction will help to create a context in which nonviolence can work. This book ranges where it needs to in order to demonstrate some of those connections. The wide angle may feel distorted to the new student of nonviolence, but understanding the Big Picture is critical. It may feel frustrating to be so aware of so many facets of the larger problem of violence and the larger solution of nonviolence, but there are times—many times indeed—when simply *managing* (not resolving, not transforming) a minor conflict is a major challenge. (Deutsch: 546) Transforming the players is our goal, but weaving tolerance and principle into any social or interpersonal conflict is usually a grand contest calling all our skills and patience to bear. Grasping the essence of the theories and practices of communication, conflict resolution, history of conflict and conflict resolution, gender relations, identity conflict, the nature of a system, our psychological need to love each other and the Earth, and how we can resist evil with good, effectively all work, in the end, to fill out our understanding of the ambiance in which we will practice our arts of peace.

In order to penetrate even farther into their subject, the host of specialists narrow their field and dig down deeper and deeper till they can't see each other. But the treasures their toil brings to light they place on the ground above. A different kind of specialist should be sitting there, the one still missing. He would not go down any hole, but would stay on top and piece all of the different facts together.

—Thor Heyerdahl, writing in 1960 (Daniels: 24)

Seeing the point of precious contact in our great human diversity is the challenge to those of us who believe in nonviolence. Keystrokes, brushstrokes and psychological strokes are all part of the art, part of how we will join each other to save this wonderful, irreplaceable Creation and each of Her exquisite, equally irreplaceable creatures.

♥

CHAPTER ONE

Domestic transformation

Let all your work be rooted in love, and stay small.

—Mike Harank, Catholic Worker advice to new volunteers (Davis: 1)

In the 1999 Hollywood movie, *Girl, Interrupted,* a young woman—former patient released from a locked mental health unit—commits suicide when another young woman escapes, comes to her for shelter, and proceeds to accurately and viciously dissect her innermost and most humiliating feelings. A third young woman, played by Winona Ryder, has come along on the escape and witnesses the horrific psychological evisceration of the vulnerable released woman—their host, as they make their escape. Ryder's character does little to stop the cruelty and nothing to repair it. She finds the suicide victim. Later, she tells her therapist that "a decent person" would have done something.

She's absolutely right, of course, which is part of the point of learning nonviolence. We train to intervene, to interpose, when we see injustice being committed. We look to redirecting the attacker; we are willing to risk more personally to achieve some dignity and humanity for those being hurt unfairly. As a side benefit, we learn how to lessen the danger to ourselves when circumstances spring themselves on us. We learn to be decent and we learn to evoke the decency in others.

Part of the problem with domestic violence is that domesticity is regarded as what a person is, not who. Humanizing the Other is what nonviolent conflict management is all about and all too many still hang onto the antiquated and maladaptive notion that a woman cannot combine a role in the upbringing of children with holding down a job; that she cannot perform some of the homemaking tasks and build a career. It is, in the end, about recognizing that all people have the right to, as Mary Catherine Bateson calls it, compose a life. A whole life for a whole person. (Bateson: 162) Otherwise, a work object and sex object can be treated as can any other property, which can be dismantled without committing a crime. Since more than 90 percent of all victims of domestic abuse are women (Browne: 8), our work in preventing domestic violence is usually in part about fully humanizing women—even if that must be done on the spur of the moment, under extreme duress.

Challenging prevailing mores is part of what we are called to do, if we wish to continue the trend toward eliminating abuse. Even cross-culturally, we can prod the perpetrators to change and we can educate the youth to regard domestic violence as reprehensible. Christians of most denominations recognize that spousal and child abuse is a sin. Even the cultures that some media love to portray as particularly Neanderthal about gender and violence issues are generally more advanced than to sanction beating or other physical abuse of a family member. In Islamic law, for example, the mufti Khayr al-Din calls the abusive husband evil. He wrote that "He is forbidden to do that, and he is rebuked and enjoined from her." If it continues, wrote the mufti, she can legally kill her tormentor. (Tucker: 65) Obviously, that is not an acceptable outcome for those who would promote nonviolence, but it does demonstrate that the most maligned religion, Islam, is not as medieval as some portray, that abuse is not acceptable to most Muslims.

Of course, any culture that trends toward violent retribution in any arena can expect some blowback (reaction) into the domestic arena. Any look at how returning soldiers treat their wives and children can verify that. Soldiers are first trained to dehumanize others, to objectify them to the point where murdering them isn't a crime, it is a service. Most basic training is for men and most of it is explicitly anti-woman in that womanly traits are seen as soft, weak, harmful and corrupting. This works well when the mission is to root out al-Qaeda members from amongst bearded shepherds, summarily judge and execute them, and move on to the next target. It fails when the soldiers return home and find rumors of infidelity, financial hardship or incessant demands from those easily overpowered. Soldiers commit thousands of domestic assaults each year, and few are ever prosecuted in civilian courts. (Gegax)

Calling on the diverse community to reject domestic violence publicly and to rebuke perpetrators unconditionally—there is no excuse for domestic violence—continues to help change the social norms, which is the best way, in the long run certainly, to bring about nonviolent change and to eliminate violence from the repertoire of reaction in family life.

communication hurts and heals

When we use our unique human communications skills, we use the tools with more power than we sometimes know. When we hope to use those tools to build relationships—and not to "win" or otherwise risk tearing down relationships—we are told by the experts that there are five nested tools in that bucket:

- *information sharing*

This process—what most of us think of as normal communications, is only moderately emotional.

- *reflective listening*

If one person is exceedingly needy and emotionally charged, reflective listening can be the most helpful offering.

- *assertion*

When one is agitated over perceived injustice or injury, assertion is the appropriate style of communication. Some see assertion as a "middle ground between nonassertiveness, which is failing to stand up for your personal rights or doing so in a dysfunctional way, and aggressiveness, which is standing up for your personal rights without regard for others." (Lulofs: 216) I disagree with this schematic perception of a continuum; in my opinion, the assertive manner of dealing with conflict is at the functional end of the continuum, the physically violent reaction is at the far other, dysfunctional, end, and the passive approach (or non-approach) is much closer to the violent, maladaptive end. The point is not insignificant, since placing nonviolent assertion between the two dysfunctional methods indicates a different relationship entirely than placing it far away by comparison and contrast.

- *conflict management*

If both parties are agitated and in pressing need, conflict management is crucial.

- *problem solving*

After—and not before—the process of conflict management and mediated conflict has proceeded far enough, problem solving is most needed. (Umbreit: 12)

Within these categories, other skills are nested. Thus, self-discipline, for example, is key when using reflective listening, since the urge to assert, to problem solve, to lecture or advise is strong at times—and completely counterproductive under many circumstances. For example, when a belligerent husband has displayed his worst temper, he expects either a shrewish response or a cowering response, either of which elicit his fighting side further. Assertive challenges coupled with reflective listening are the most advantageous response under most of these kinds of circumstances. When he knows his grievances have been truly heard he will find no pressure to ratchet up the volume or intensity; when he understands that his behavior is his own and that no one else can be drawn down to his level, he may soon seek to elevate himself. Communications are critical to violence prevention and even to its cessation once it has happened.

Home to homeland: domestic security

> On January 18, the day on which John Lewis led the march, Jim Clark wore a gun and carried both a nightstick and an electric cattle prod. ...Lewis brought his people to the courthouse, only to find their way blocked by Clark. The sheriff ordered them to go back, but Lewis stood up to him. The courthouse, Lewis said, was a public place and they had a right to go inside. "We will not be turned around," he said.
>
> "Did you hear what I said?" Clark asked. "Turn around and go back." He seemed closer to an explosion than ever, some people thought, after Lewis's defiance.
>
> "Did you hear what I said?" Lewis answered. "We are not going back." And he stood his ground. Finally Clark, in some irritation, backed down and told them to go on in.
>
> —David Halberstam, *The Children* (Halberstam: 497)

Had black people turned to nationwide violence in 1965, when the above incident occurred, it would have been understandable and predictable. Indeed, how could anyone have predicted what actually did happen? A handful of courageous and visionary leaders seemed to collectively keep an ethic and strategy of nonviolence in place even under the greatest provocation in various locales and rose to meet the violence of the oppressor with increasingly bold nonviolence. Had John Lewis been even remotely suspected of a possible violent response, I suspect notorious Selma, Alabama sheriff Jim Clark would have cracked down without hesitation when Lewis defied him. But Lewis and the civil rights workers were open, transparent, nonviolent and won just enough grudging respect to keep from being beaten and bloodied at every turn. Like the pepper gel used to torture nonviolent environmental activists in the late 1990s, the cattle prods used by Clark in Selma were justified as "better than bullets," as some kind of humane alternative, supposedly, to something vastly worse. And like the rubber bullets used to drive back nonviolent demonstrators at the WTO protests in Seattle, Washington DC, Prague and elsewhere, the cattle prods were seen not as a humane alternative to lethal force because the protesters were not committing capital crimes. The public saw those weapons in those contexts for what they were—the irresponsible weapons of bullies, defied by courageous freedom-seeking, justice-loving nonviolent resisters. Sadly, by contrast, when the young man in Genoa was about to throw a fire extinguisher through a police van window, he was shot dead and it was seen as an appropriate response by a public that put itself more in the shoes of the cop about to be hit by glass shards and a metal cylinder than the kid with the ski mask who was breaking glass. John Lewis and the civil rights movement taught us these lessons a half-century ago and we continue to need to relearn them.

Is war inevitable? During the first half of the 20th century, war between nation-states was prevalent and most destructive, and thus was the focus of study by the small group of interdisciplinary scholars and activists who wished to make war unnecessary. Certainly the war to end all wars—World War I—had failed to accomplish its putative mission and the challenge to these peaceminded folks was monumental. Serious study of how to eliminate war began academically, formally, in the 1930s, by "interdisciplinary-minded scholars and activists." It continues to this day, and includes the International Peace Research Association, a large transnational group of academics that grew out of the original, older Council on Peace Research in History. (Boulding: 26) It has gone well beyond the international to the intranational, to identity conflict, to all group-to-group violence.

The long arm—or disarm—of the law

That the bombing of Dresden was a great tragedy none can deny. That it was really a military necessity few, after reading this book, will believe. It was one of those terrible things that sometimes happen in wartime, brought about by an unfortunate combination of circumstances. Those who approved it were neither wicked nor cruel.

—Air Marshal Sir Robert Saundby, deputy commander-in-chief of Bomber Command under Sir Arthur Harris (Ringler: 12)

All human beings are born free and equal in dignity and rights. They are endowed with reason and conscience and should act toward one another in a spirit of brotherhood.

—Article 1, *Universal Declaration of Human Rights*, 10 December 1948 (Center: 6)

How, if ever, can we use the institution of the law to promote nonviolent solution to group-to-group conflict? If agents of law enforcement all use or threaten to use violence to enforce the law, can those who wish to advance nonviolence logically use the law?

Yes. The law doesn't exist by necessity as a violent instrument; it is a neutral tool used by any and all sides, and international law is especially open to nonviolent enforcement since there are no official international police with true arrest and imprisonment powers, except on an ad hoc and very situational basis. We see the spectacle, for example of former Panamanian dictator Manuel Noriega now shuffling about in the US supermax prison in Colorado for his acts as military dictator in his homeland, and we witness the appearance of Serb strongman Slobodan Milosevic on trial for war crimes in Bosnia, or Saddam for his crimes against Kurds, but no one has brought Henry Kissinger to the bar for his roles in war crimes in Cambodia, Vietnam, East Timor or Chile, though much of the evidence is clear on these matters.

This doesn't mean that nonviolent activists have no use for the law. To the contrary, it may be argued that the law itself is inherently moving toward nonviolent enforcement as it wrestles over time with issues of the legality of various forms of violence. Indeed, the law has been evolving since the Code of Hammurabi and Mosaic Law mandated what we now regard as brutally retributive punishments for an assortment of crimes. Global opprobrium for the reversive perversion of the Taliban was illustrative of that advancement; our challenge is to reduce the inconsistencies in our application of international law; at times we are called to break the law in order to seek its advancement. Thus, if an "illegal" blockade of arms to Afghanistan precipitated first the arrest of the blockaders and then their acquittal on the basis of dispositive international humanitarian law, the law evolves one tiny step. Each accreted ruling makes a difference in the preponderance of the opinion of legal scholars—either toward peace and justice or away from it.

If the law is searching for perfection, it will eventually mandate its own nonviolent means of enforcement. The international rules of the conduct of warfare and the various international human rights laws have offered nonviolent activists an entrée; if we can convince the judges and juries, the public and the politicians, that certain classes of weapons are illegal under current laws, we can further the process of disarmament. If we can continue to bring pressure upon violators of basic human rights, we can move the law forward. Each time disarmament occurs nowadays, it is met with great resistance by those who cite historical examples of the inadvisability of such measures, thus forcing those in the nonviolent community to sharpen arguments that go to the pragmatism of good law, the effectiveness of ethical steps in the application of such international law.

The historical struggle to delimit the destructive power and insidious nature of the tools of war is ancient. The Laws of Manu—Hindu laws dating back thousands of years—forbade the use of poison arrows, as did customary

Domestic transformation

ancient Greek and Roman rules of warfare. In a fleeting attempt to stem the historical trend toward longer range projectiles, the Lateran Council of 1132 declared the crossbow "unchristian." The first modern law on weaponry was issued in 1868 in St. Petersburg and outlawed explosive bullets under the weight of 400 grams. (Roberts: 53) Whatever humanitarian arguments are accepted in the creation of international law can be used and furthered by those who wish to ultimately convert armies to disarmies. For example, if the bullets outlawed in 1868 were not humane because they were designed to explode inside the soldier's body, why do we not outlaw napalm and other weapons designed to burn the skin and tissues of soldier and civilian alike? A first modest goal: to outlaw any and all indiscriminate weaponry and its components.

Part of our mission is to engage the human heart and mind, which ultimately will engage the lawmakers. "Compassionate people can only shudder when they consider the combined horrors of military insecurity and human desperation in Russia," writes Nobel Peace Laureate and past president of Costa Rica, Oscar Arias. Arias notes that, while the Russians continue to attempt to maintain a huge nuclear arsenal, life expectancy for males declined from a pre-reform 65.6 years to 57 years. Can we afford weapons that take from the coffers of health care systems even as health deteriorates? Arias calls for new ethics and new laws governing sales of weaponry, naming those priorities (military first, welfare last) as "evils." He wants international agreements with the force of international law to slow, stop and reverse the condition of hyperarmed developing nations. (Arias: 121+)

The international community is generally ahead of the individual nation-states in human rights law. For example, the US lags behind in failure to observe the 1989 Protocol concerning the abolition of the death penalty. Several Islamic nations violate elements of the 1990 Cairo Declaration on Human Rights in Islam. (Center: 190) How would the Taliban have answered to Article 1, which declares: "All men are equal in terms of basic human dignity and basic obligations and responsibilities, without any discrimination on the grounds of race, colour, language, sex, religious belief, political affiliation, social status or the other considerations." And how can the Saudis—a regime propped up by the US—answer to that accepted law now? How would Palestinian suicide bombers, Ariel Sharon—or US bomber pilots over Afghanistan or al-Qaeda operatives—answer Article 3, which states in part: "In the event of the use of force and in case of armed conflict, it is not permissible to kill non-belligerents such as old men, women and children." (Center: 190) Similarly, how can Israel justify breaking numerous UN resolutions and international laws in its treatment of the Palestinians? The belligerents themselves are accountable to the law only if the citizenry demands it.

We can use the law; we can build it toward nonviolence. A pax on both their houses. All their houses.

Superauthority, sovereignty and nonviolence

When "the international authorities" decide to intervene in a conflict—UN in Iraq and Kuwait, UN and then NATO in the former Yugoslavia, UN in Rwanda, OAS and UN in Haiti, UN in Somalia, all in the 1990s—they do so with no clear record success in hand. Most regard the Haiti experience as a victory, the Northern Iraq interdiction as a qualified win, and the others as mixed at best. Obviously, violence offers no guarantees, even when undertaken by US-led coalitions of the world's most highly trained militaries against the forces of "backward" or even collapsed nations. (Weiss, 1999: 194) So-called "humanitarian interventions" may be well-meaning, but are even more naïve than the most Pollyannaish ideas about nonviolence.

Massive interposition, smart sanctions, overwhelming aid and other possible tactics are experiments that cry out to those who look at intervention. Instead of a few hundred faith-based witnesses, what might have happened in Haiti had 40,000 nonviolent shock troops landed bearing aid and a "deal" similar to that struck with military coup leader Raoul Cedras? Perhaps the state of the state would have improved permanently instead of its current devolved condition. We will never know. What if 200,000 reasonably paid and highly trained nonviolent conflict workers had arrived in Rwanda as signs of impending genocide were flaring and flashing in early 1994—and well before? What if they brought gifts from a planet's population concerned with the well-being of Hutus and Tutsis? What if they also brought assurances that any internal acts of oppression would bring criminal charges against all participants?

Far-fetched? Tell that to a nation beaten and oppressed, ready for relief; they will try anything. Somalia didn't hate the peacekeepers, they hated the guns and helicopters clearly meant to impose the will of others or else. When demagogues see blue helmets and "light arms," they have license to appeal to the xenophobe in every human, the fear of the stranger. That fear seems logical when the stranger shows up in a flak jacket carrying an automatic weapon. Instead of regarding nonviolence as naive, the UN might think about its so-called humanitarian interventions as naïve. They experimented with peoples' lives in the immediate post-Cold War; why can't mass nonviolence be the next experiment? Results were so poor in at least 60 percent of the cases, maybe nonviolent troops could do better. It would take commitment—financially, politically and philosophically. But the potential for saving lives is a stark reminder that we have so much to gain. The history of these military interventions suggests we need to try something new; nonviolence demands commitment and creativity, something humans have when they are at their finest, which will be necessary to replace the violent model of conflict management. Let us always remember that the greatest nonviolent warrior ever, Mohan Gandhi, never felt as though his campaigns were necessarily the best model; indeed, he suffered from great doubts at the conclusion of each one, despite public and pundit acclaim. (Erikson: 365) This spirit of endless experiment—used to help us evolve so quickly and to such great effect by Gandhi—ought to continue to be our methodology. More, not fewer, experiments with nonviolence will teach us, prepare us, offer ideas never before contemplated by a species too linked and locked to the war model.

As the nonviolent commitment grows globally, perhaps we will listen to peace scholars who tell us where we can likely have some effect. For example, Johan Galtung was telling the too-small and overcommitted nonviolent community back in the early 1990s that we ought to pay attention to ways to help the nonviolent liberation struggle underway in Kosovo. We failed. Ibrahim Rugova and Albanian Kosovars had undertaken and constructed such a parallel infrastructure that they had their own clinics, their own universities and even a self-imposed income tax to fund these services. Every time Slobodan Milošević ordered another act of oppression against the non-Serbs in Kosovo, the Albanian Kosovars responded with another nonviolent initiative while they waited for some nonviolent help from the outside. They never got that help.

Serbs, a less-than-10 percent minority in Kosovo, felt oppressed themselves during the 1974-1989 period of Tito-approved autonomy in Kosovo. (Weiss, 2000: 94) In 1989, Slobodan Milošević proclaimed the new constitution for Kosovo, a tragic farce referred to by Kosovars as the "constitution of the tanks," indicative of its forced and non-democratic nature. When NATO left Rugova twisting in the wind both at Dayton in 1995 and at Rambouillet in February 1999, the fate of the nonviolent liberation struggle took turns for the worse. Then, when outside funders began to arm the KLA, the Serb police and military began to come under increasing violent attack and thus dramatically ratcheted up their oppression of Kosovars. Naturally, the refugee situation worsened. Finally, the bombing began in the 1999 78-day air war and ethnic cleansing replaced ethnic oppression, thus making matters infinitely worse. The warmakers ruined a promising nonviolent revolution, but those of us in the nonviolent community did virtually nothing when it was possible to actually help. When we turn that model around, perhaps we can enhance indigenous nonviolent effectiveness. Even small groups of nonviolent actionists linked to a global alert system, involved early on, might have altered public perception and involvement. As it was, an opportunity was missed and many people died because of the armed model of conflict management.

An endlessly dangerous element of international diplomacy as currently practiced is the face issue. Embarrassment, loss of dignity, disrespect or whatever terminology we wish to employ is at the heart of many conflicts.

> *Conflict literature is pretty clear in this point: The introduction of face issues into a conflict can escalate the severity of the conflict, making it very difficult for people to resolve the original issue.*
>
> —Roxane S. Lulofs of Azusa Pacific University and Dudley D. Cahn of State University of New York, New Paltz (Lulofs: 294)

This is true of conflicts from the interpersonal through the international, though the complexities of the interpersonal are merely the warm-up routines for the overwhelming set of connecting problems with a large group-to-group conflict, where face is wired to so many varying cultural constraints and so many emotional landmines. Resolving an interpersonal conflict with my German grandmother was relatively easy; toss in Hitler and a flag and the problems quickly bog down—or burst into flames. To make matters far more complex, a great deal of intercultural communication—miscommunication, in many cases—is nonverbal, with no translation or cross-cultural referential base.

avoid the ignominious to avoid violence

> *Although insiders learn to master the cultural encoding rules of these nonverbal emotional cues at a very young age, it may take outsiders many years of experience before they can accurately decode some of these complex emotional displays during a conflict.*
>
> —Stella Ting-Toomey, professor of Speech Communication at UC-Fullerton and world expert on intercultural communication (Ting-Toomey: 83)

Innumerable people have died throughout history because national leadership felt somehow slighted and were able to convince their constituents to feel the same to the point of exerting armed force upon the Other. When Richard Holbrooke writes that he and his team of negotiators "scrambled to prevent an embarrassing setback" as they negotiated with belligerents in the Balkans in 1995, we then stay alert for the other shoe, that of the armed solution. When Holbrooke writes of one of those parties that "we had not paid enough attention to the dapper and normally polite Zubak, partly because he did not speak English well, partly because he was overshadowed by extroverted people like Sacirbey and Silajdzic. He had become difficult, withdrawn, and sullen," we know that trouble is brewing. People hate being disregarded.

Domestic transformation

Holbrooke then describes bringing then-Secretary of State Warren Christopher to speak with the recalcitrant Zubak, which served to bring the Bosnian around. "Flattered," the Federation President did the bidding of the US. (Holbrooke: 263) Holbrooke perceives his work as peacemaking; some perceive it as prelude to war.

It was only a matter of time until the US used brutal force to police the area, and it started in the spring of 1999. Von Clausewitz called war "diplomacy by other means," and that is exactly what the violent forces propose during their negotiations, even if that proposal is shrouded in language designed to avoid the humiliation associated with backing down to threats. Nonviolent power is much less likely to cause fear and loss of face. Faces saved equals bloodshed reduced, and it's much easier to save face using nonviolence, since there is never a threat to hurt or kill people physically. Any armed group negotiates using veiled threats of bloody harm, which is insulting on a prima facie level, unlike nonviolence.

sources:

Arias Sánchez, President Oscar, "International Code of Conduct on Arms Transfers," in: Hopkins, Jeffrey, ed., *The Art of Peace: Nobel Peace Laureates Discuss Human Rights, Conflict and Reconciliation*. Ithaca NY: Snow Lion Publications, 2000.

Bateson, Mary Catherine, *Composing a Life*. NYC: Plume, 1990. (original: NYC: Atlantic Monthly Press, 1989).

Boulding, Elise, *Cultures of Peace: The Hidden Side of History*. Syracuse NY: Syracuse University Press, 2000.

Browne, Angela, *When Battered Women Kill*. NYC: The Free Press, 1987.

Center for the Study of Human Rights Columbia University, *Twenty-five Human Rights Documents*. NYC: 1994.

Columbia Pictures Industries, Inc., film: *Girl, Interrupted*. US: 1999.

Daniels, Steven E., and Gregg B. Walker, *Working Through Environmental Conflict: The Collaborative Learning Approach*. Westport CT: Praeger, 2001.

Davis, Murphy, "No faith in the state," *The Catholic Worker*, October-November 2001. (1+)

Deutsch, Morton, and Peter T. Coleman, eds., *The Handbook of Conflict Resolution: Theory and Practice*. San Francisco: Jossey-Bass Publishers, 2000.

Downton Jr., James, and Paul Wehr, *The Persistent Activist: How Peace Commitment Develops and Survives*. Boulder CO: Westview Press, 1997.

Erikson, Erik H., *Gandhi's Truth: On the Origins of Militant Nonviolence*. NYC: W.W. Norton & Company, Inc., 1969.

Gandhi, Arun, "Who influenced Gandhi?" in: Harak, S. J., G. Simon, ed., *Nonviolence for the Third Millennium: Its Legacy and Future*. Macon GA: Mercer University Press, 2000.

Gegax, T. Trent and John Barry, "Death in the ranks at Fort Bragg," *Newsweek*, August 5, 2002.

Halberstam, David, *The Children*. NYC: Random House, 1998.

Holbrooke, Richard, *To End a War*. NYC: Random House, Modern Library, 1999.

Lulofs, Roxane S. and Dudley D. Cahn, *Conflict: From Theory to Action*. Boston MA: Allyn and Bacon, 2000.

Ringler, Dick, ed., ***Dilemmas of War and Peace: A Sourcebook***. Madison WI: University of Wisconsin-Extension, 1993.

Roberts, Adam, and Richard Guelff, ***Documents on the Laws of War***. Third Ed. Oxford UK: Oxford University Press, 2000 (original 1982).

Schwartz, Stephen I., ed., ***Atomic Audit: The Costs and Consequences of U.S. Nuclear Weapons Since 1940***. Washington DC: Brookings Institution, 1998.

Ting-Toomey, Stella, and John G. Oetzel, ***Managing Intercultural Conflict Effectively***. Thousand Oaks CA: Sage Publications, Inc., 2001.

Tucker, Judith E., ***In the House of the Law: Gender and Islamic Law in Ottoman Syria and Palestine***. Berkeley CA: University of California Press, 1998.

Umbreit, Mark S., ***Mediating Interpersonal Conflict: A Pathway to Peace***. West Concord MN: CPI Publishing, 1995.

Weiss, Thomas G., ***Military-Civilian Interactions: Intervening in Humanitarian Crises***. Lanham MD: Rowman & Littlefield Publishers, Inc., 1999.

Weiss, Thomas G., and Cindy Collins, ***Humanitarian Challenges & Intervention***. 2nd ed. Boulder CO: Westview Press, 2000.

Zinn, Howard, ***The Future of History: Interviews with David Barsamian***. Monroe ME: Common Courage Press, 1999.

CHAPTER TWO

Neighborly nonviolence:

schools, streets & workplaces

When, in 1983, the small town of Hartland, Vermont, decided to declare themselves a sister city to a rural town in the Soviet Union, the children learned a lesson about who they were, what reality can be, and that reaching out to the reviled enemy can make us feel even better than the emotional satisfaction of hating them. Hartland was the smallest town to prepare a package for whomever their Soviet counterparts were—at the time there were only five sister city relationships between US towns and SU towns and all of them were cities of more than 100,000 and four of the five had lapsed into inactivity when the Soviets invaded Afghanistan. In Hartland, most citizen groups were brought in by "bought in," that is, they were approached and asked to participate, to help, and they did. From the Boy Scouts to the PTA, from the Ladies' Benevolent Society to the Brownies—all ages, all walks of life in the little town of 2,700—they put together scrapbooks of who they were, their group activities, their homes and their lives. While the entire town became involved, the entire project was initiated and undertaken by a group of perhaps six peace activists who doggedly pursued everyone with this idea. As they held their ceremonial send-off of the wooden box in which they had assembled the story of their town on 9 April 1983, an eight-year-old girl said, "In a hundred years, Hartland will be famous because we will have started the movement that really brings peace. We will have shown the governments how to do it." (Mather: 101) That eight-year-old—she's 28 as this is written—has, with her friends, no doubt been a part of making Hartland less vulnerable to hatred and violence. The "mere" gestures and "only" words can create a context that makes violence socially uncool to all. Beginning with the youngsters, we create a new world in which violence is the aberrant behavior, not the default setting for those with "justifiable" rage. We begin with the youth in a million ways large and small.

Our local academic and activist organization, the Oregon Peace Institute (on whose board of directors this author sits), worked with youth from our state and with Green Fire Productions—a progressive video company—to produce "Peace by Piece," a video composed entirely of youth narration and imagery. It tied together themes of international shooting conflict with local and familial violence, and incorporated multiracial advice on lowering tension through good mediation and assertive nonviolent communication. It dealt with the reality of consequences for violence in the real world, which set it dramatically apart from media fictive portrayals of the crumpled bodies of bad guys and the slow stroll away by the vanquishing good guys. As solid, grimy steel doors clanged shut on jail cells, youth counselors barely out of their teens themselves talked to troubled youth about weighing each situation carefully, and about the inadvisability of violence—and about options. A Native American girl told her story of using traditional dance to combat both the prejudice she encountered in school and her own violent reaction to such ignorance. The video—all about transformation out of seemingly scripted violence into a brighter lifestyle—is making its way around the state, often accompanied by presenters and nonviolent trainers from OPI. If we stop some fights, save some folks who would have been victims, prevent a few potential perpetrators from ruining their own lives and other lives too, we will be well satisfied in our efforts. This kind of work is inspired by other projects and, we hope, will prompt others in turn.

Violent conflict in our neighborhoods needs to be met in a number of ways, including:

- training in interpersonal nonviolent response to attack or threat (see appendix to chapter seven) and conflict resolution, peer mediation and related skills
- neighborhood coöperation and socialization
- family and community responsibility for education
- other creative projects—kidzmedia, toy gun tradebacks, art-for-peace, multiculti powwows, etc.

Clearly, some preparation is individual and some is group. It all tends to make the neighborhood a safer place, not by the introduction of more armed police but by the changing norms and skills of the neighbors. It begins with education and education begins in the home.

Individuals who convince their neighborhoods and small towns to adapt the language, the symbology and the gestures of nonviolence, of human rights, and of friendship across racial and political lines will go some distance toward creating a peaceful neighborhood. Communities that create leadership environments that involve all children, all youth, older people and are not mainstream culturally hegemonic stand a better chance of helping to create peace in the valley.

neighborhood coöperation

Some political scientists believe that a cohort of people with a certain value, if persistent and boldly clear about its superiority to prevailing norms, can seed a much larger group with that value and, over time, change a social more. (Brophy) Those social scientists ought to observe the Catholic Worker communities as a part of their research; some of the CWs do that exceedingly well.

In Minneapolis, Minnesota, two nuns founded St. Joseph's Catholic Worker community in the 1970s. Sister Rita Foster and Sister Char Madigan began offering hospitality to homeless in a neighborhood then linked to alcohol, drugs, theft, beatings and one of the largest concentrations of urban Native Americans in the world, just a block off the intersection of Franklin Avenue and Portland Avenue.

Over the years, more volunteers have joined the community, including many non-Catholics. These volunteers sometimes live in the homes of what is now called Hope Community, but most often simply come to help offer the basic living services and good home order needed to provide stability and an atmosphere of lovingkindness to the residents. Hope Community has grown in size and in influence; when they moved a few blocks from the original St. Joseph House it was to a larger home on a crack street.

Sister Char decided that, instead of adapting to the drugs and violence on the block, Hope Community's role was to help make sure that the block would be a safe zone for community residents, for the children and women. She took to approaching each lingering person anywhere in sight and initiating a conversation about Hope Community, about the neighborhood, about the children and about neighborhood safety. It took some time, but with that bold yet non-judgmental approach by Char and others, the neighborhood became a zone of safety. No drug deals went down on the block that anyone saw any longer, nobody intimidated passersby or made illicit offers. Guests who were in crisis had a haven and were better able to begin to piece together their lives.

And when she wasn't offering hospitality, Sister Char was helping lead the direct action peace movement in Minneapolis in the 1980s and beyond. She and Sister Rita joined Marv Davidov in reinvigorating the Honeywell Project, a peace group that confronted the Honeywell Corporation for its manufacture of nuclear missile guidance components and its notorious cluster bombs, used with such deadly and indiscriminate effect in Vietnam and then elsewhere. World corporate headquarters were only blocks from Hope Community, an oasis of opulence in a desert of deprivation and an object lesson in the opportunity costs of the huge military instead of social programs. Char and Rita went to jail numerous times, on trial publicly, and they talked always of Catholic Worker values, misappropriated monies shifted from the people to war profiteering, dire community needs going unmet and the need for nonviolent modeling. At one demonstration of almost 2,000, during which more than 600 of us were arrested, I was a monitor. Police rioted against us; I happened to be one of the first to sustain minor injuries and to get arrested as I attempted to enjoin activists and Honeywell executives in loud heated argument. Sister Char was among those maced in the face as police picked up children as young as nine and hurled them into chain link fences. Witnesses told me of Char sitting beatifically on the ground, in her usual habit, unable to see any longer for the chemicals in her eyes, as police came striding through hitting people with their clubs. When one policeman dropped his billy club near Char, she groped and found it and held it up to the policeman, saying, "Officer, I expect you dropped this." That particular policeman didn't hit anyone else—at least during the remainder of that particular demonstration. Within a few years, Honeywell divested itself of all military contracts, refusing, of course, to credit the peace movement organization Honeywell Project—begun by two Catholic nuns and a Jewish communist—with having any part in that decision.

Sister Char and Sister Rita cleaned up their block, their town, and continue to change their neighborhood. They use nonviolence without exception and expect nonviolence in return without exception. This is part of the core of the Catholic Worker beliefs and practices, and marks that community wherever it is found in the US or around the world. Indeed, says sociologist Gordon Zahn, the Catholic Worker movement, begun by Dorothy Day in 1933 and now more than 100 homes strong from the US to Australia, was the beginning of the US Catholic peace movement, now expressed not just in Catholic Worker communities but in Pax Christi and other organizations. (O'Gorman: 239) These homes offer one of the best seeds of nonviolence any rough neighborhood can have. Their only drawback is that there aren't enough of them because there aren't enough volunteers to live in the poverty required while doing the intense hospitality offered. As a CW volunteer, I was expected to handle the belligerent drunken man who had found out that "his" woman was in the house. I was expected to do that nonviolently, and did. If police came, they were told that they must not come in the house carrying a gun. This was negotiated successfully in every case in the community I was involved with, thus strengthening the model presented to the neighborhood. In the home I volunteered at, there was zero tolerance for violence or substance use and it was strictly enforced, nonviolently. I watched a 105-lb. woman evict a 200-lb. staggering, drunken man with assertive nonviolence, just a routine evening for her.

The police and others could do worse than to become off-duty volunteers at such facilities; they might learn what others of us learned: it is possible to use nonviolence to deal with violence in tough neighborhoods.

conflict theory and practice in the neighborhood

The idea behind modern conflict resolution is that we ought to be able to find ways to resolve our conflicts without resorting to the use or generally to the threatened use of violence.

How does this goal differ from that of nonviolence? Only in the word "generally" before the proscription on threatened use of violence. In other words, a nonviolent actionist might offer to sit in front of a bulldozer until it stopped threatening to destroy her home. She wouldn't move until that stated imperative had been agreed to. Her home is an unalterable, inviolable right in her mind. She wouldn't call in the armed police to resolve the conflict, nor would she ask a radical guerrilla to bomb the bulldozer. She might get arrested. She might get run over and killed. She might win.

The conflict resolver would not stand in front of the bulldozer. He might call in the armed police if he felt the bulldozer operator were in error. He would ask around for more information and might make some phone calls to see if the home demolition might be forestalled while the conflictual parties tried to make some last-minute deal. He would arrange a meeting, if possible, and listen to all sides, ask everyone to listen to each other, and negotiate an agreement, if possible, amenable to all. If not possible, he would go back to his office and wait for the next call to see if he could do any good somewhere else.

One of our goals in Peace and Conflict Studies is to enable these two people to work together more effectively, even though they have different bottom lines, different perceptual paths and different theories. Those who practice assertive nonviolence are often intentionally ignorant of conflict theory that seems too passive, and those who practice mediation are often dismissive of those who physically place themselves in harms way with no real dialogic approach in mind.

Roger Fisher and William Ury of the Harvard Negotiation Project brought conflict theory forward with their little 1980 book ***Getting to Yes: Negotiating Agreement Without Giving In,*** a study of a four-step program for those trying to create a better model of conflict resolution than the traditional adversarial cops and guns and courts and lawyers and judges and winning and losing. Fisher and Ury gave us these four steps:

    1. separate the people from the problem.

    2. focus on interests, not positions.

    3. invent options for mutual gain.

4. insist on using objective criteria. (Fisher: 15)

When mediators use these methods, neighborhood disagreements over barking dogs, blowing leaves, loud motorcycles, rambunctious children, speeding cars, fighting couples, smelly burning, littering business patrons and other issues (that seem minor to outsiders but can be both major and intractable to those living in the midst of the situation) can be dealt with in ways that usually are acceptable to all. When the nonviolent actionist announces that she is sitting in front of the bulldozer until the mediator is called in, we will have achieved a new synthesis in nonviolent skills. When the mediator refers an out-group without much power to a justice organization that practices responsible nonviolence, the synthesis will be even more complete. *Ben trovato*, say the Italians—ingenious.

Transforming schools

According to an account in The Providence Journal, *Ms. Bowman spent Thanksgiving dinner at the home of her teacher, Ms. Jupin, and again discussed the plan to kill teachers and students with bombs and guns, perhaps on the following Monday. That may be the reason the police acted over the weekend to arrest the three boys.*

Mr. Taylor, the New Bedford police officer assigned to the high school as a school resource officer, had questioned Ms. Bowman about the plot, the newspaper said, quoting court documents, but Ms. Bowman told him she could not say anything. One reason she gave was that she did not want word about the plan to get back to her military recruiter and spoil her chances of joining the military, the newspaper reported.

—Fox Butterfield, *The New York Times* (Butterfield, 28 November 2001)

Guns are one of the primary causes of death of young people your age in the United States; 20 times as many young people die from gunshots in the U.S. as in the next eight countries combined.

—Paul Kivel and Allan Creighton, violence

prevention workshop for youth (Kivel: 131)

One of the best ways to avoid violence is to prevent it. While this seems to indicate a penchant for stating the obvious, it is not unusual to find school administrations rather focused on the mechanics of response to violence. So, for example, the high school in which Oregonian youth Kip Kinkel shot several people has, as of this writing, just completed a comprehensive program of installing locks that will enable a teacher to lock a classroom from the inside during any serious crisis in order to keep a violent actor out. While this is probably a good idea, there are low-cost, no-cost methods of violence prevention that can work to improve the human milieu in the school rather than simply operating in a climate of fear, preparing only for the mid-episodic reactions. Nonviolence trainings, group discussions of methods of social change, tolerance trainings, sensitivity seminars, gender workshops, listening projects and other initiatives will help toward that. In 1993, former president Jimmy Carter advised students to initiate a student mediation team in their schools. (Carter: 175) This relatively simple effort both educates and empowers students who wonder if there is any chance they will fall victim to violence. Indeed, a robust student peer mediation service will serve to give hope to those who feel as though they are destined to either commit or suffer an act of violence.

working with the youngest schoolchildren

Child educator and conflict resolution author Susan Fitzell advances a program that calls for five essential elements in any conflict resolution program for children grades K-12. Modeling, relationship, conditioning, empowerment, and skills are the building blocks, she asserts, toward a viable children's conflict education program.

modeling

It is much harder to teach nonviolent conflict management to a child who is exposed to adult statements such as, "We ought to send the Air Force over there to hunt down Saddam." If, on the other hand, a child watches as we exert power with others—e.g., coming to an understanding of what is fair together and then insisting on it with authoritative but not authoritarian power—that child believes more easily in the power of reasoned, nonviolent methods. (Fitzell: 5) Convincing children that adults are interested in fairness and in nonviolence and in communication will facilitate discussion and sharing of information. Students who are encouraged by such open nonviolence will tend to come forth when they know of dangerous potential. In at least 75 percent of the school shooting cases, another student knew about it beforehand and said nothing. With better outreach, that changed in:

Twentynine Palms, California; New Bedford, Massachusetts and several other communities, where violence has been averted. Bombs, photos of students with guns and letters detailing imminent plans have been found and students apprehended. (Butterfield)

relationship

Teaching basic relationship skills and values will prepare the way for excellent reception of the messages and competencies required for conflict management. So, for example, offering civility and tolerance, courtesy and empathy as proper reactions to other people will make the set-up to conflict resolution much more functional. (Fitzell: 9) Teaching true friendship values is also crucial. If youth feel as though friendship involves using violence to defend a friend, or if friendship includes shielding the behavior and intentions of the friend no matter how abhorrent, or if friendship involves defending a friend right or wrong, or if friendship means ignoring the rights of others in order to advance the position of the friend, then friendship is a deeply flawed and counterproductive institution. If, on the other hand, friendship is defined by defending the good reputation and good intentions and good values of the friend, then friendship can work to improve the environment in school and on the streets.

conditioning

Many environmental elements compose the ecology of a child's life. From the Surgeon General's 1972 report, from the National Institute of Mental Health follow-up in 1982, to the report of the American Psychological Association in 1992, all agree that exposure to violence on television is harmful to a child's development as a nonviolent citizen. (Fitzell: 167) Conditioning toward nonviolence is instead about exposure to discussion of why violence and intolerance and greed and injustice are all wrong—and why intolerance, greed and injustice are best battled with nonviolent means. Children are not only perceptive, but analytical. Talking down to a nine-year-old conceptually is not good conditioning. Use language that can be understood, and explain concepts fully, but don't be condescending; children will reason exceedingly well if they are expected to do so, and will reason with complex but dysfunctional results if they are treated as simple. Awarenesses can help them to achieve a proactive style of logic, which is in turn fostered by talking about the differences between action and reaction.

empowerment

Teaching the bully better means to his ends and teaching the victim the same lesson are empowerment tools. Allowing children to process toward problem-solving is teaching empowerment at several levels, and is preparing the path to good conflict resolution. If children feel as though they are being apprised of the problems, asked to think creatively about them, expected to sift critically through options and offer a considered and listened-to opinion on the best solution, those children are greatly empowered and are far more able—and anxious—to engage in both formal and informal conflict management. They themselves become part of an environment which tends to dampen and mitigate potentially violent situations because they are communicating with confidence and courtesy.

skills

In the end, then, telling kids "Don't fight!" is dysfunctional without also offering the competencies it takes to fight nonviolently. (Fitzell: 15) Fights will happen, period. Conflict is fighting, but fighting with compassion and fair practices is possible, even on a unilateral basis, and when children are trained to employ such skills, they develop them through inevitable opportunity. When they are especially encouraged to use process with each other, to debrief adults on what happened, to vet solutions to interested adults, and to consistently regard conflict as an opportunity to further test theory against practice, they can be the young practitioners destined to take this field large steps beyond where it is now.

nonviolent school systems

> *Any nonviolent intervention program or curriculum may be doomed to failure in schools in which abusive behavior is sanctioned by administrators, including strip searches, verbal abuse, paddling, and other forms of corporal punishment. Although the crime-and-punishment paradigm is the norm in our legal system outside-of-school (witness capital punishment as the ultimate corporal punishment), inside school, programs that purport to teach prosocial behavior cannot work when delivered in an environment laden with fear and permissive of insults to human dignity. In other words, schools must move away from adversarial, crime-and-punishment paradigms before they can successfully model nonviolent ways to resolve conflict.*
>
> —Robert C. DiGiulio, Associate Professor of Education, Johnson College (DiGiulio: 195)

In most schools in the US, the students cannot necessarily look to the authorities for violence prevention instruction or relief. This seems to be because the politicians who issue general national and state mandates join the school districts in an approach that focuses on punishing perpetrators, not on changing cultural and public opinion norms about nonviolence. (Greene: 204)

Indeed, when I offered to teach nonviolent technique to the adjudicated youth at one private institution, the Child Psychology Ph.D. who administered the educational program refused, stating that if the students learned such skills they would lose respect for the manner in which staff and teachers approached conflict.

Bingo.

That frank admission is usually couched in far more subtle terms, but the message is the same: when the discipline of students is retributive-based, it becomes embarrassing to bring in consultants who can show students a better way to manage tension. I told the Board of Education in one city that their rhetoric about the students as future leaders was nice and that in fact the future is here. All too often the students possess more knowledge and skill with regard to conflict management than do many or even most of their teachers and administrators. Naturally, it is easier for the board or for consultants to step outside that box of conflict spiral and offer good advice, harder to stop the culture of vendetta that can establish itself and lead to endless harsh and destructive conflict once an authority—whether the leader of a nation or a teacher—acts even one time in revenge. (Kegley: 236) "Do as I say, not as I do" is a model of inept and ineffectual pedagogy with regard to society, violence, nonviolence and young people.

the humanimals' progress: wu-wei toward peace

> Several young men had to intervene to separate the two hot-blooded boys. ...Such was considered normal behavior among boys.
>
> —Gaspar Pedro Gonzalez, Mayan, professor, Mayan Literature, Universidad Mariano Gálvez (Gonzalez: 132)

From young wolf pups to adolescent human males, physical rough-housing is truly just an animal characteristic and we are human animals—more emphasized in some cultures than others, more acknowledged in some cultures than others, more repressed or more encouraged in some cultures than others. Anthropomorphizing behavior is generally incorrect but being open about our natural and competing tendencies is requisite to honest progress. When Mayan adults allow some physical contest and draw the line at pain infliction, they are adaptively using conflict to bring out issues without drawing blood. When we repress it all, we invite an explosion under pressure. When we shove it under long enough, we create momentum for societal vengeance-taking, beginning at home, on the streets, in the schools and extending internationally to bomb Afghanistan—the poorest nation on Earth—and Iraq, and perhaps Yemen, maybe Somalia, and, while we're at it, Sudan again. We become the bullies we think we are discouraging and we model that kind of retributive thinking for our youth.

Spiritual teachers sometimes stress the necessity for self-honesty as a precursor to advancement, and, in accordance with the Taoist principle of *wu-wei*, an effort to work on ourselves naturally, not against nature. Even those of us who are nonviolent often wish for punishment for the perpetrators when we see suffering innocents—and admitting our wishes might help us convince others it's possible for society to put the retribution aside as mere adolescent fantasizing. "We enjoy a secret pleasure," writes yoga practitioner John McAfee, "when people who have done wrong are punished." (McAfee: 21) Once we have acknowledged that, we can confront intentions and we can sweep aside immaturities and get about the business of preventive effectiveness rather than dysfunctional denial.

Indeed, that obfuscation of motive is impolitic to admit and thus prevents real progress in a vast number of situations. Researcher Matthew W. Greene found that there were stellar exceptions to that sad phenomenon. In one state he studied—Colorado—the more progressive thinking was taking place in pockets around the state, but not at the dispositive upper levels where the general decisions were made. (Greene: 204) As the systemwide model for behavior modification goes further down the path toward the use of expulsion and other punitive measures, they miss the proper focus if they wish to produce citizens who can properly manage conflict. Like trying to present nonviolence as the preferred response to conflict in a nation that threatens the world with nuclear omnicide by its arsenal of mass annihilation, teaching nonviolent practices to students in an environment of negative reinforcement becomes almost heretical and glaringly hypocritical. Add to which the educational baggage of a culture steeped in violence and the problems become even more daunting. "Throughout twenty centuries of Christianity, the Romans and the Hebrews have been admired, read, imitated, both in deed and word; their masterpieces have yielded an appropriate quotation every time anybody had a crime he wanted to justify." (Weil: 36) Our milieu is a medium of violence, from the scholarly reference to the ancients to the modern movies; each act of violence can be rationalized and the received wisdom becomes that the violence of the heroic individual and the nation-state alike is a good thing. 2002 Nobel Peace Laureate Jimmy Carter still felt he needed to bow to the warmakers in his acceptance speech, in which he said that, at times, war is "a necessary evil." With Nobel Laureates making that assertion, who needs war apologists?

Further resistance to teaching nonviolence comes from those who must interface with the law enforcement personnel and infrastructure in the course of operating a school or a school district. Virtually 100 percent of the thinking and practice in the law enforcement community emanates from the fear-based, Old Testament, Mosaic Law model of deterrence through terror. But the terror—however demonstrably effective in many short-term situations and however emotionally attractive to those who are themselves in fear of and angry at violations of the rules—doesn't dissuade those who themselves absorb tremendous amounts of anger and believe it to be properly discharged against those who somehow rob them of their rights. In short, the psychology of the law enforcement system generally reinforces criminal thinking and when that model is also used in schools, someone eventually is hurt, or worse. Film of police inflicting pain on nonviolent demonstrators, from Selma, Alabama in the 1960s to the corporado offices of the timber barons of Humboldt County, California in the 1990s, reveals the crimes and terrorism of the state directed deliberately against those who, by their very methods, are offering an alternative paradigm.

Crucially, teachers bear great responsibility for teaching nonviolence to those students who learn fear and violence at home. Often the teacher is the only person with the opportunity to attempt to impart values and skills to an adolescent who may otherwise be on a path to prison—or the hospital, or worse. The village that we used to need to raise a child has vanished into modern culture; educators are thus often alone when families fail. "Schools can hold the necessary conditions—and perhaps even the sufficient conditions—to disrupt the cycle of violence-to-incarceration-to-recidivism." (DiGiulio: 197) As the quote from Guatemala above reveals, the fistfighting violence between boys is seen as normal for boys in the Mayan culture, but that was the worst that such behavior got; not only did the boys not have access to pistols with which to shoot each other, they would not have been acculturated to believe that shooting each other might be admired behavior by media, which is created and permitted by adults. Our charge in this culture is zero tolerance for violence and yet teaching that by preparing to inflict our own violence teaches the wrong message.

"If every society is a blend of the themes of violence and peaceableness, why is the peaceableness so hard to see?" asks Elise Boulding. "It is there, but not well reported," is her answer. (Boulding: 4) The disservice done to our youth when they are not told the stories of nonviolent success and when they are not taught methods of nonviolent conflict management is that the possibilities remain murky, occluded from their view, and illegitimate even if those possibilities occur to them spontaneously.

Many of us who survived adolescence recall the shifting values and practices that we experienced as a result of experimentation, reflection, more experimentation and more rethinking. It's the way of the world, the tendency of humankind, to use that period of time to formulate a basis for behavior through one bit of personal research after the next. Educators who realize this don't give up on adolescents (though, for dramatic effect, we sometimes offer that as a possibility). The military understands how flexible ethics are for most adolescents; indeed, that is usually the only time humans are available to recruitment into an organization with a mission as insane as waging mortal combat. Those who fervently wish to promote nonviolence are in a battle for the souls and spirits of these young people.

What kind of education produces a war system?

In the most stark case, Katie Sierra, a 15-year-old from Charleston, W.Va., was suspended from school for wanting to start an anarchist club to spread her views against the bombing and for wearing this message on her T-shirt: "When I saw the dead and dying Afghan children on TV, I felt a newly recovered sense of national security. God Bless America."

Sierra and her mother responded to the suspension by filing a lawsuit, arguing that her free speech rights were being violated. A West Virginia judge ruled in favor of the school, saying that the disruption she caused at school overrode her right to free speech. Sierra is appealing.

Sierra's mother pulled her out of school after the girl endured physical threats, taunting and accusations of "treason" from school board members when she went before them to protest her suspension. (Wax)

When a recent survey of some 68 textbooks used in the Syrian school system was undertaken by the Center for Monitoring the Impact of Peace—a peace research and education organization with offices in New York and Jerusalem—the Center reported that Jews were never referred to positively and indeed were always associated with aggression, usurpation, evil and even violative of a basic right to exist. The Holocaust was justified, though the magnitude was exaggerated by the Jews, said the Syrian texts, according this Center, charging that Jews were exterminated because they had engaged in treason against Hitler and because they controlled finance. (Groiss: 23) The state of Israel was always referred to as Palestine and it was even written that Jews smelled and looked sinister. Martyrdom is taught to be a holy act, and armed struggle against Jewish occupation of Palestine is promoted.

Similar studies have revealed that Israel texts treat Arabs in a derogatory manner, excusing violence against them. Is it any wonder that children grow up hating the Other in the Middle East? "Don't let school interfere with your education" might be the motto of the school systems there—and, too often, in the US system as well.

Other war system educational markers would include patriarchal intervention at a certain age with little male involvement beforehand.

> *There are societies where fathers ignore children until they reach the age of six or so, and then suddenly reach in to remove little boys from their all-women's world and put them in an all-men's world, to be raised to be fierce and manly. The attention that fathers give to their sons under these conditions hardly has a gentling effect on either generation.*
>
> —Elise Boulding (Boulding: 102)

Sadly, if you check in on virtually any preschool in our society, you'll find that women are most of the staff and faculty. You'll also find that the vast majority of single parents are women, and that women still comprise the largest segment of stay-at-home mothers to very small children. It is a bit like one of the Indiana Jones movies, when he confronts his father about the dad's lack of nurturance and lack of communication. The father, utterly clueless, answers, "You left just when you were getting interesting." In a war system, in a patriarchal system, men are not interested in helping significantly until it is time to train the boys for manhood, at which point they often assume total control.

What kind of education tends toward a peace system?

> *One significant step toward a gentling society is the creation of social arrangements that provide for both parents to spend more time with infants and small children.*
>
> —Elise Boulding (Boulding: 102)

Boulding goes on to mention that very early training in nonviolent conflict management is another educational marker of a peace system. She notes that the Quakers' Creative Response to Conflict has influenced early education in the US in the last few years, and that some prisoners have access to Alternatives to Violence, another Quaker educational program designed to reëducate those who have never learned proper conflict management tools. It is to be hoped that, someday, former military personnel will take such training and that, subsequent to that, we may eliminate the military altogether, replacing it with a nonviolent disarmy that will require a major educational effort. Another modest proposal...

> *In the 1970s there was a tendency to emphasize social justice and structural violence as issues on the one hand, as against the scourge of physical (direct) violence and the need for an absence of war on the other. Some felt war might be a necessary means to social justice and that poverty and repression were more crucial problems. Right now the field seems again to be bifurcating around the different set of anti-war versus justice-related or liberatory tendencies. Oddly, the roles are somewhat reversed in the 1990s. This time those emphasizing social change and conflict transformation are emphasizing nonviolent means and the role of social movements—we have here an emphasis on peace culture.*

—Nigel Young, peace researcher (Young: 205)

The field of Peace Studies has grown by leaps and bounds since the first directory of all such academic programs was published on two sheets of paper in 1981—the global catalog is now quite thick and comprised hundreds of majors, minors, masters and even doctoral programs. (O'Leary: 1) As these become more accepted interdisciplines and even an academic discipline unto itself, we will naturally see some related preparatory classes offered in high schools. This presents us with a major opportunity for growth and public acceptance and, ultimately, the ability to change basic public policy. We are one the road, potentially, to producing generations with skills that no other youth have had by training in human memory.

> *Most education is aimed at fitting people into existing institutions, but since our institutions have often become obsolete or even pathological, education should not be used to perpetuate them.* (Boyer: 10)

When I advise students, I am usually the first to tell them that they can almost certainly make a living doing work that is good for the Earth, that is peaceful and that has meaning to them. This is not what they've been hearing from parents, teachers, guidance counselors and others who often uncritically prep children to be cogs in a war system. The goal of so many college programs is to find employment out there After Graduation. This means tailoring coursework, and entire programs, for those jobs which already exist—or perhaps jobs that almost exist, and will, in all probability, by the time a students picks up her diploma and hits the streets looking for work that can pay back those student loans.

Education that encourages creativity, thinking in terms of justice and nonviolence and that prepares the student not only for work but for engaged citizenry is rare but becoming more visible. The sheer numbers of peace and conflict studies programs—a handful in the 1980s and more than 600 now—is evidence that education is responding to this need.

identity issues and violence in schools

Most black Americans think that racism is a fact of life in the US; most whites don't. The percentages haven't changed much since the late 1960s. (National)

This is not surprising. Most attitudes changed most significantly with regard to race issues in the early 1960s, when a nonviolent Civil Rights movement was met with violence and yet succeeded in getting major legislation passed in a Congress that had been generally hostile to such change—indeed, many of those in Congress had also been there in the late 1940s, when such measures were routinely defeated, before the Civil Rights movement changed the political equations. Nonviolent action on the part of African Americans built up an image nationally of a positive regard for blacks. The riots that began in the mid-1960s and degenerated into widespread inchoate rebellion after that generally reversed the sympathetic trend in majority public opinion of blacks; simply put, whites began to fear blacks, which precluded sympathy. Thus the advances begun with such sacrifice and bravery were stopped and some of them even reversed.

Black Americans, by the same token, have every right to be fearful of and hateful toward whites in the US. Any population coming from a history of chattel slavery, subsequent disenfranchisement, overwhelming poverty and various discriminations must at last be sensibly afraid and angry. Thus, the identity conflict in the US between African Americans and Euro Americans; we have not resolved much of it yet, and the conflict continues unabated in schools across the nation. And if we think that holding Dr. King up as a national hero in the way we do—which is to completely ignore the true radical message of his mature vision—is going to moderate black youth, think again. Only by truly exploring King's resistance can we continue to make him relevant to new generations of African Americans. In December of 2002, an African American student of mine told me that he never felt King was relevant until I exposed him to King's speeches of the last five years of his life—a truly sad commentary on what we've done by our national Hallmarking of a nonviolent resister's life.

When the black community developed an awareness of being colonized, they never surrendered that identity, which is adaptive in some ways, but builds the sense of victimhood in some cases past the point of adaptability. When, for example, Huey Newton—founder of the Black Panthers—called for both armed self-defense of the black community and the exemption of blacks from the military (Marine: 35), a white progressive could sympathize, but the white majority was totally alienated. Newton's analysis on the basis of nationhood was clearly correct and his public relations were, ultimately, quite poor with the majority, with the decisionmakers in a democracy. When gun battles did ensue in Oakland and other places, the public turned away when police began to murder Panthers with impunity.

How can we reintroduce nonviolence into racial conflict?

There are some interesting group exercises that build awareness. One, developed by two teen-violence-prevention experts, is called People of Color Stand-Up and begins with all participants sitting in a circle. Statements are read aloud and only people of color are asked to stand when the statement applies to them. Included are 25 statements that go to identity conflict, such as: "You were ever ridiculed by a teacher, employer, or supervisor because of your racial heritage." The entire group then processes their feelings about the exercise. (Creighton: 35+)

When such roleplays or facilitated exercises are done with good debriefing, people learn. At one in Chicago recently, many of the white people learned that some of what they were doing and saying was causing hurt and anger in people of color, who in turn learned that white people who have either made sacrifices for the advancement of human rights or have been in danger for their advocacy of human rights (e.g. marching in the Deep South during the 1960s) were hurt that their language was being used to impugn their motives. This collaborative realization was somewhat dampened when the facilitators focused solely on the justifiable pain and anger of peoples of color—thus discounting many of the participants—but was valuable nonetheless. It served to illustrate that identity conflict was alive and "well" in the US, even in communities of those committed to ending such conflict.

Indeed, racism is so crucial to the success of the war system that, in a nation dependent upon violent conflict to keep its economy rich, racism must exist and, at some level, most people of color know it. Some, of course, will attempt to join the elite in the war system by their loyalty to it, but that won't help the average person of color. Much more likely, the war system will develop a new path to create division between peoples who ought to be working on unifying under a peace system. When African Americans are given percs for joining in the general objectification of, say, immigrants from the Mideast, it may be hard to resist the opportunity to at last feel part of the dominant power structure by subscribing to the zero-sum mentality (*put him down and I move up).*

military recruitment and the validity of violence

Washington Post columnist Colman McCarthy wrote of a mother in Erie, Pennsylvania, who decided that her five children and all the rest were being taught little about peace in the schools, and that, in fact, more money was going to provide recruitment literature for the armed forces than on peace education books and periodicals for the library. In 1986, Laura Quiggle proposed to the school board that she be allowed to provide peace literature to the town's four public high schools. Since it would have cost the district nothing, since it was much less quantity than the literature provided by the military, since none of it would be obscene or violate community standards, it seemed an easy request.

No.

Quiggle asked the American Civil Liberties Union for help, they took it to court, and the chief judge in Erie's US district court found that Quiggle was correct. She could do her best to counter the $1.1 billion spent by the Pentagon during the 1980s on recruitment. (McCarthy: 131)

working with gangs—on all sides

> *I belong to the biggest gang in town.*
> —Chicago policeman

Membership in gangs increases likelihood of involvement in criminal activities and also tend to make those crimes more violent. (Shelden: 108)

Saul Alinsky, famous community organizer, gave us the dictum *Organize the organized*; go to unions, to clubs, to federations, to churches and synagogues and ask them to help in whatever community improvement plan or project you may have. Go to gangs; they are more organized than you might think. Getting a preacher to advocate for you from her bully pulpit works much better than standing outside with a petition waiting for church to get out, and even that is better than standing on a street corner, though that is better than nothing. Going to the gangs—of youth or of police—with a more effective method of managing conflict is a great challenge but a great opportunity. Talk to leadership first—or to someone sympathetic who can get the ear of the leadership.

Police violence is increasingly problematic in both reality and perception. And people "in conflict situations respond to one another in terms of their perceptions." (Lulofs: 31) Changing the perceptions is precursor to—indeed, tantamount to—changing the situation on the ground. The range of realities within each of us is wide, often wider than the screen that appears to show us the facts, the picture, the scene. That scene is perceived differently by each observer and thus is acted upon differently, making reality a flexible concept, one malleable to our efforts, to our words, to the picture we are able to paint for the internal vision of each participant. Using 20-20 insight is a faster path to change than is "pushing the river" by telling others that the problem is huge and probably irresolvable. The image of a street tough and a cop picking up litter together—or picking up the wounded together—changes reality for both. If they cannot see it in their mindseyes, it will be less likely to actually happen.

Combining these factors, why not approach gangs and ask them to host a nonviolence training? Then go ask the sheriff or police chief. Go amongst them, pay it forward, change social norms.

Rapists and robbers: more evidence

> Merely being distressed about the extent of gendered violence will not lessen it. We must ask how we can be agents of change who resist violence and who compel revisions in cultural attitudes toward it....The most basic personal choice is to decide that you will not engage in or tolerate violence in your relationships.
>
> —Julia T. Wood (Wood: 333)

> We are born female and male, biological sexes, but we are created woman and man, socially recognized genders.
>
> —Heidi Hartmann (Hartmann: 674)

The *his-story* of humankind has been the history of violence and domination, much of it male over female. From the fundamentalist Christian dystopia of Margaret Atwood's ***A Handmaid's Tale*** to the fatwa death decree placed upon the heads of women who dare to claim liberation from certain practices of some sects of Islam, one identity of humanity—religion, in these cases—has been used to justify another identity oppression—gender. In some cultures, rape is regarded as a minor offense, unless the rape happens to a woman already taken—and then is viewed more as a property crime against another man. Thus, the man is viewed as the primary victim and retribution is severe.

Feminists went through a period of cataloging male violence without offering much alternative, a point at which some are still stuck. (Eschle: 97) For those who reject violence with as much ethical vehemence as we reject any oppression, a violent mode of self-defense is not best. It is not up to any man—and this author is one—to judge any woman's reaction to rape, attempted rape, or domestic violence of any kind. Nevertheless, in our study of violence and nonviolence, it is incumbent upon us to attempt to understand as much of it as we can and, from there, point toward possible nonviolent alternatives.

The catalog is ugly. From rape committed by a stranger to battering committed by a husband, victims are usually women. Overall, victims of family violence are overwhelmingly female; 94 percent in one study, 95 percent in another. (Browne: 8) Women are smaller, physically, in most cases, and violent self-defense is certainly used at times, but is often, obviously, not effective. Not only are most men bigger than most women, the men are trained to use physical force. Even that training for a woman, however, doesn't guarantee that she will use violent self-defense, even when society would likely approve.

One battered woman with whom I had several conversations while she stayed at a shelter at which I volunteered told me that she was an Army veteran and, though she was small, she was comfortable with weapons and, at one point, "My face looked like hamburger and he was sleeping and I had a .357 pointed at his face, but I knew that I would be stuck living with myself after." She fled across several states and we gave her and her three teens shelter for most of a year while she built a new life. Some women are acquitted when they kill in self-defense and most go to prison. (Browne: 188+) Other methods of self-defense, sometimes including flight, are more adaptive, certainly. But women usually have to know about them to use them with anything other than minimal success.

As we learn from conflict resolution researchers, a face issue doesn't need to involve physical face battering; face is another word for prestige, for dignity, for self-image, self-esteem. Preserving everyone's face is in everyone's interest. Even though different cultures seem to value it differently—one study showed that, in the US, southern white males are our quickest demographic group to resort to physical violence in response to perceived insult—the concept is important to virtually every human being. What differs most widely are the items likely to injure face and the responses.

In China, loss of mientzu—face—is related to prestige, to embarrassment before a group. Flattery is employed, even transparently, in order to help the other maintain face. (Lulofs: 45) In the US, such unmerited praise or deference is usually rejected. We seem to expect either honesty or better acting.

It is hardly a complex notion that, for those who feel a loss of face, they are drawn to literally hurting someone's face in return. It may literally be a face—the woman who "fell down the stairs" again and is wearing sunglasses at all times—or it may be an attack on what is most crucial to a person's sense of dignity. Rape is a crime that is more about taking away dignity by brute force than it is about gaining sexual access, though a man's idea of sexual conquest may draw him to attack the forbidden beauty, thus complicating his face issues with the victim's. The person under attack will do better with a nonviolent response if she keeps her face and his in sight and in consideration. She needs to know how he is regarding her loss of face as his gain and turn that loss into his loss as well. She may begin to do that not so much by humanizing herself—especially if she is known to the perpetrator—but by humanizing him to himself. His self-image is what is at stake and her reconstruction of that, insofar as she can maintain composure and do so under extreme duress and in a rapid fashion, is what will help save her from her own loss of face.

Rape researchers Pauline B. Bart and Patricia H. O'Brien conducted interviews and survey instruments with women who had been attacked with rape as an element of that attack. They examined their sample population for outcomes if the women did any of five resistance strategies: flight or attempted flight; screaming; physical resistance or "force": cognitive verbal techniques—reasoning, attempts to con him, self-humanizing attempts, pleading; environmental intervention (e.g., passerby, appearance of police) or no strategy.

The worst strategy involving an attempt to do something was pleading. That only reinforced the power differential and legitimated the relative power of the rapist.

Interestingly, researcher Bart began to believe in a parallel between the unsuccessfully pleading women and the European Jews who were used to negotiating or accommodating oppressors for centuries, failing to understand with the nazis that the Final Solution meant the ultimate oppression, genocide. Acting like a victim—begging, whining, cajoling, flattering—works in situations where the oppressor needs something from the victim that cannot be obtained by raw force, but it most emphatically will not work at a high rate of success when the dominant aggressor is fed by such behavior.

The most successful rape-avoidance strategy was the one least tried by the interviewed group: flight. To complicate the findings, those women who avoided rape usually used multiple strategies, such as screaming, physical resistance and flight. Raped women tended to stick with one losing strategy: pleading. The very least adaptive reaction was to freeze and offer no resistance; all of those women were raped.

The conclusion the researchers arrived at was that it is best to physically resist. "Each woman has to make her own decision about what risk she is willing to take. We will close this section with a quote from the mother of an avoider: 'He broke her arm, but she won.'" (Bart: 110+)

However, as is natural for any researcher, it is hard to tell the results of a strategy if you haven't considered it. Thus, there was nothing in these researchers' model that accounted for the possibility of a trained nonviolent resister's reaction under such circumstances. If those who have been trained to stand up to violence calmly but with conviction and confrontation had been a part of the study, perhaps the results would show that population able to resist rape most effectively. After all, some of the women studied had almost certainly been beaten worse once they began to physically resist, though the statistics still showed this to be more adaptive than pleading and certainly more successful than doing nothing.

Additionally, just as an untrained violent resister can manage to avoid rape by screaming, making attempts to physically fight back, and then fleeing, so too could an untrained woman invent a successful nonviolent defense on the spot. In fact, it is quite likely that some did, since a relatively strong percentage of those women who attempted negotiation were never raped. Perhaps some negotiated from a standpoint of fear, flattery and acquiescence while others negotiated from a position of determined righteous but not self-righteous nonviolent assertion. There is a huge difference, though it may not have been measured differently. Nonviolent training is often so counterintuitive that it is never considered by those who believe they are controlling for all possible variables. The Bart and O'Brien study is valuable indeed, but we await the research from someone who understands nonviolent strategies and can measure their results.

But we are progressing.

The feminist movements that have come in waves for millennia have very slowly changed social norms; in most societies nowadays, women are closer to full citizenship by both legal guarantee and societal regard. Rape is slowly becoming a crime that directly offends a real human, a fellow citizen, and is thus more thwartable by methods of nonviolent psychology because those methods are only possible once a mutual humanity has been recognized and mutually accepted.

Key in preventing rape, then, is the quick and certain shift from any regard of a woman as a dehumanized object to the status of a real person. This is at the center of all violence prevention and all nonviolence and the question is, "how?"

Unlike the situation, for example, in which a mass of humanity faces a phalanx of police, there is no need to reassure the potential attacker that he is not in physical danger. In contrast with a robbery of a strong young man by another, for example, a woman in a threatened rape situation needs to change the game by changing the perception of who she might be. She is perceived as weak, whiny, compliant, passive and bothersome but dominable. She needs to alter that perception.

Loud, strident assertions of her individual rights may knock aside the attacker's concentration on ignoring consequence. Hesitation can open the door to further nonviolent surprise strategies. Soft, compassionate questions may then elicit gratitude and regard from the attacker.

Cold logic won't work, generally. Pleading only fuels the predator-prey relationship. These games have been considered and rejected as powerful by the perpetrator. But he can be approached and moved from angles for which he has not prepared.

Gendered violence—and nonviolence

Violence is most easily committed by bullies against vulnerable victims. Nonviolence, in an apparent paradox, is often most effectively practiced by those we think of as vulnerable. Women—tiny, young, old, single and married, perhaps widowed by war or other violence, often mothers—are most frequently found on the front lines of the battlefield. If the most effective front line armed troops are young males, the most effective front line nonviolent troops are often mothers whose children have been hurt or are in danger.

Indeed, when the military marched through the streets of Guatemala City in the time of the overtly military governments, the only ones with the courage and ability to confront the mass swagger and beweaponed arrogance of the seemingly invincible army were the mothers who had begun to act in nonviolent resistance. As the army marched past, the Mothers of the Disappeared swung into the parade from their alley staging area, uninvited and illegal. The people lined up to watch began to buzz, *¡Son los Madres! ¡Son los Madres!* ("It's the Mothers!") The Mothers held up banners of soldiers with blood dripping from their bayonets, and photos of disappeared loved ones. They walked in the parade until they were confronted by the military, at which point the Mothers stood their ground and the military left without arresting or otherwise harming any of the mothers. This is the kind of story that we hear from all over the world—Argentina, Bosnia, Chile, and many more places. Once women stand up to the bullies, the bullies often shrivel. In Argentina, for example, the Madres de Plaza de Mayo—beginning with just 14 grieving mothers in 1977—grew to an active membership of 3,000 or more and became the shock troops for a nonviolent rejection of the military junta. (McManus: 80)

This is true domestically as well. Women—the primary victims of domestic violence—are standing up for themselves and each other. That mere act is saving lives, stopping beatings and giving back dignity to former victim and perpetrator alike. The Thelma and Louise model of violent retribution may be emotionally satisfying to some angry women but for those who prefer to survive—unlike Thelma and Louise—nonviolent resistance offers a different hope.

retribution or rehabilitation?

> *When Pilate saw that he could prevail nothing, but that rather a tumult was made, he took water, and washed his hands before the multitude, saying, I am innocent of the blood of this just person: see ye to it.*

—Matthew 27:24

When I was in prison in Wisconsin for an act of nonviolent direct disarmament of a nuclear command and control facility, the overwhelmingly dispiriting truth that prisoners were being dehumanized much as one objectifies any enemy was painfully obvious. It felt like boot camp. It was meant to; the prison guards were a self-selected population of people who were drawn to that kind of work. They were sometimes sadistic. They were generally authoritarian. Many seemed to thrive on the kind of bullying that establishes a pecking order based on physical might, on the ability to inflict pain and loss of privilege.

Society is vastly in error in thinking that this method is solving our crime problem; it is in fact exacerbating it. The simple understanding that virtually all these prisoners are going to be getting out amongst us again ought to rattle our cages. As we damage these criminals instead of rehabilitate them, we act in a self-defeating, self-harming fashion essentially guaranteed to redound poorly again and again on the most vulnerable, on the targets naturally selected by a former inmate now loose and itching for vengeance. The cycle we set up with a retributive model of justice is not just and not smart.

In Britain, the Prison Act of 1952 required that prisoners have access to reasonable materials and personnel in order to be able to practice their faith. A Buddhist minister, the Venerable Ajahn Khemadhammo, founded Angulimala, which has become an organization of visiting Buddhist ministers. Khemadhammo teaches mindfulness and helpfulness, two rehabilitative practices that will tend to turn raging criminals into good citizens once they are free. Zazen in prison—sitting meditation that promotes an attitude of love for all beings—is preparation for a mindful and helpful life "on the outs," as prisoners call life out of prison. (Parkum: 355)

On the job

In my 20s I was a member of the International Brotherhood of Carpenters and Joiners. Violence was a part of the legends passed along on the job. "Ron grabbed Daryl one day and held him by the shirt, dangling out in the elevator shaft on the thirtieth floor." "Mel threw Jerry the foreman straight through the sheetrock wall and then jumped through after him. It took five of us to get him completely off Jerry." "The foreman for the general [contractor] came up to Denny at about 10:30 one morning and told him not to do something. Denny was on stilts and he just stared at him and said, 'OK for you,' and kept on working. At noon, Denny gets down off his stilts, puts down his tools, and goes looking for the general's foreman, finds him and decks him without a word."

Those were real quotes from actual stories I heard in the gang rooms on construction sites, sometimes with either the victim or perpetrator sitting in one corner of the room eating his lunch, nodding. The stories impressed me as generally true. My fellow construction workers just seemed to be from a culture that valued being able to intimidate others physically or being able to exact revenge with violence. Still, I cannot imagine any of those men pulling an automatic weapon and slaughtering co-workers. But that was then and this is now; going literally ballistic on the job seems entirely possible in our modern free-fire work zone.

According to the National Institute for Occupational Safety and Health (NIOSH), nearly 7,000 workers were victims of homicide in the workplace during the period of 1980 to 1989. Among female employees homicide was the number one cause of death. In 1992, five states and the District of Columbia reported that homicide was the leading cause of occupational deaths for all employees, men or women. (Jurg: 1)

Whether we work in a huge mail-sorting room in a major postal station, on a production line, or in a cubicle in an endless office, we know that violence is a possibility as frustrations mount and solutions seem non-existent. What kinds of workplace skills and institutions can we help to develop that might mitigate the chance of bloody noses or bloody pools by fallen co-workers?

Listen to each other

When you are approached by an angry co-worker, listen. Attend to both the content and the emotion of the message. Suspend your judgment and analysis. Convey understanding of both explicit and implicit messages. Remain sensitive and responsive to signs of resistance and defensiveness. (Van Slyke:

120)

❂❂

<u>sources:</u>
Bart, Pauline B., and Patricia H. O'Brien, *Stopping Rape: Successful Survival Strategies*. NYC: Teachers College Press, 1993.
Boulding, Elise, *Cultures of Peace: The Hidden Side of History*. Syracuse NY: Syracuse University Press, 2000.
Boyer, William H., *Education for the Twenty-first Century*. San Francisco: Caddo Gap Press, 2002.
Brophy, Bryan, panel presentation, Wisconsin Institute for Peace and Conflict Studies, September 1998.
Browne, Angela, *When Battered Women Kill*. NYC: The Free Press, 1987.
Butterfield, Fox, and Robert D. McFadden, "3 teenagers held in plot in Massachusetts school" *The New York Times*, 26 November 2001. http://www.nytimes.com/2001/11/26/national/26PLOT.html?todaysheadlines
Butterfield, Fox, "Student charged in plot she warned about," *The New York Times*, 28 November 2001. http://www.nytimes.com/2001/11/28/education/28SCHO.html
Carter, Jimmy, *Talking Peace: A Vision for the Next Generation*. NYC: Dutton Children's Books, 1993.
Creighton, Allan, and Paul Kivel, *Helping Teens Stop Violence*. Alameda CA: Hunter House, 1992.
DiGiulio, Robert C., "Nonviolent interventions in secondary schools: administrative perspectives," in: Forcey, Linda Rennie, and Ian Murray Harris, *Peacebuilding for Adolescents: Strategies for Educators and Community Leaders*. NYC: Peter Lang, 1999.
Eschle, Catherine, *Global Democracy, Social Movements, and Feminism*. Boulder CO: Westview Press, 2001.
Fisher, Roger and William Ury, *Getting to Yes: Negotiating Agreement Without Giving In*. NYC: Penguin Books 1981, 2nd edition, 1991.
Fitzell, Susan Gingras, *Free the Children! Conflict Education for Strong & Peaceful Minds*. Gabriola Island BC: New Society Publishers, 1997.
Gonzalez, Gaspar Pedro, *A Mayan Life*. Rancho Palos Verdes CA: Yax Te' Press, 1995.
Greene, Matthew W., *Learning about School Violence: lessons for educators, parents, students, & communities*. Binghamton NY: Peter Lang, 2001.
Groiss, Dr. Arnon, *Jews, Zionism and Israel in Syrian School Textbooks*. NYC: Center for Monitoring the Impact of Peace, 2001.
Hartman, Heidi, "The Unhappy Marriage of Marxism and Feminism: Towards a More Progressive Union," in: Grusky, David B., *Social Stratification: Class, Race, & Gender in Sociological Perspective*. 2nd ed Boulder CO: Westview Press, 2001.
Kegley, Jr., Charles W. and Gregory A. Raymond, *How Nations Make Peace*. NYC: St. Martin's/Worth, 1999.
Kivel, Paul, and Allan Creighton, *Making the Peace: A 15-Session Violence Prevention Curriculum for Young People*. Alameda CA: Hunter House Inc., Publishers, 1997.
Lulofs, Roxane S. and Dudley D. Cahn, *Conflict: From Theory to Action*. Boston MA: Allyn and Bacon, 2000.
Marine, Gene, *The Black Panthers: Eldridge Cleaver, Huey Newton, Bobby Seale*. NYC: Signet Books, 1969.

Mather, Melissa, "Hartland, Vermont: a town for peace," in: Farren, Pat, ed., *Peacework: 20 Years of Nonviolent Social Change*. Baltimore MD: Fortkamp Publishing Company, 1991.

McAfee, John, *The Secret of the Yamas*. Woodland Park CO: Woodland Publications, 2001.

McCarthy, Colman, *All of One Peace: Essays on Nonviolence*. New Brunswick NJ: Rutgers University Press, 1994.

McManus, Philip, and Gerald Schlabach, editors, *Relentless Persistence: Nonviolent Action in Latin America*. Philadelphia PA: New Society Publishers, 1991.

National Public Radio, "All Things Considered, "10 July 2001.

O'Gorman, Angie and Pat Coy, "Houses of hospitality: A pilgrimage into nonviolence," in: Coy, Patrick G., ed., *A Revolution of the Heart: Essays on the Catholic Worker*. Philadelphia PA: New Society Publishers, 1988.

O'Leary, Daniel E., *Global Directory of Peace Studies and Conflict Resolution Programs*. Fairfax VA: Consortium on Peace Research, Education and Development, 2000.

Parkum, Virginia Cohn, and J. Anthony Stultz, "The Angulimala Lineage: Buddhist Prison Ministries," in: Queen, Christopher S., *Engaged Buddhism in the West*. Boston: Wisdom Publications, 2000.

Shelden, Randall G., et al., *Youth Gangs in American Society*. 2nd ed. Belmont CA: Wadsworth, 2001.

Van Slyke, Erik J., *Listening to Conflict: Finding Constructive Solutions to Workplace Disputes*. NYC: AMACOM, 1999.

Wax, Emily, "The consequences of objection: students who speak out against the war find themselves battling to be heard," Washington Post, 9 December 2002. http://www.washingtonpost.com/wp-dyn/articles/A14157-2001Dec8.html

Weil, Simone, *The Iliad or The Poem of Force*. Wallingford PA: Pendle Hill, 1956.

Wood, Julia T., *Gendered Lives: Communication, Gender, and Culture*. 2nd ed. Belmont CA: Wadsworth Publishing Company, 2001.

Young, Nigel, "Peace Studies at the millennium," in: Fisk, Larry & John Schellenberg, editors, *Patterns of Conflict: Paths to Peace*, Peterborough, Ontario: Broadview Press, 2000.

CHAPTER THREE

Identity violence

> *The master says it's a glorious thing to die for the Faith and Dad says it's a glorious thing to die for Ireland and I wonder if there's anyone in the world who would like us to live.*
>
> —Frank McCourt, **Angela's Ashes** (McCourt: 113)

Psychologist Abraham Maslow places identity very high in his hierarchy of human needs. Indeed, he says, "the greatest attainment of identity, autonomy, or selfhood is itself simultaneously a transcending of itself, a going beyond and above selfhood." In this way, ego drops away and the sense of fusion with others is heightened. (Maslow: 105) This produces a cycle of search for peak experiences that are associated with that all-powerful, all-knowing, utterly justified and totally validating group with whom one identifies. From that, we can begin to see both the suicide bomber in Jerusalem and the endlessly generous nun in Calcutta. Both are seeking that ultimate sense of identity, though one is focused on exclusion and one on inclusion in the end. One is violent and one is nonviolent. One has hatred all around the center of love and one seems free from hatred. Identity with life, then, seems to be our mission if we believe in promoting nonviolence. Identity with a certain group is a bit more risky.

> *...I am the child in Uganda, all skin and bones,*
> *my legs as thin as bamboo sticks,*
> *and I am the arms merchant, selling deadly weapons to Uganda.*
> *I am the 12-year-old girl, refugee*
> *on a small boat,*
> *who throws herself into the ocean after*
> *being raped by a sea pirate,*
> *and I am the pirate, my heart not yet capable*
> *of seeing and loving....*

—Thich Nhat Hanh, from *"Please Call Me by My True Names"* (Hanh: 63-64)

Each of us, says Thich Nhat Hanh, could be anyone else, and therefore we ought to have compassion for all. Indeed, identification with the other is the beginning of compassion on an individual level and compassion for the other on an individual level is the beginning of compassion group-to-group. With identity conflict, which is as elemental as it can be, there are dangers and setbacks at every stage. This is why, for example, progress of some type is virtually required at both the micro and macro level for nonviolence to have a chance.

Consider Northern Ireland. Conflict resolution practitioner Loreene O'Neill lived there with her husband and worked at the grassroots level. She described the reaction of members of the Catholic community in which she lived when they discovered she was married to a Lutheran. While they tolerated him because they were US Americans, they marveled at the complexity of working through what they assumed were major marital obstacles—indeed, there is a predominance in Northern Ireland of religion over political affiliation or even nation-state identification. Catholics identify with the Irish nation and most Protestants identify with the British nation, although Protestant identification is weaker, since the Queen may be Protestant but she doesn't control Parliament. (Carter: 52) Religion is thus experienced as core identity and as a virtually impermeable barrier to intimate friendship, much less marriage. Loreene and her husband were actually asked to lead workshops on how to learn to live in a "mixed marriage."

During her time in Northern Ireland, O'Neill noted that the community-level grassroots mediation and intercultural outreach was prevalent, but that there was little concomitant institutional relief for poor Catholics, which kept the tensions reasserting themselves. While progress can be made when only one level of change is occurring, it is attenuated and incomplete unless change is happening at both levels, says O'Neill. (O'Neill) And in fact, the hope of the 1994 peace accords is not manifesting itself in the streets; those Belfast streets are instead becoming even more—not less—segregated. Fewer Catholics work in Protestant neighborhoods, fewer Protestants work in Catholic neighborhoods, and those neighborhoods themselves are becoming progressively more sectarian. Before the peace accord, 63 percent of the people lived in neighborhoods that were 90 percent Catholic or 90 percent Protestant. Now, some eight years after the accords, 66 percent live in communities with at least a 90 percent concentration of one religion. (Henderson, Mark: 8) Clearly, the peace process has failed at some levels to be the panacea some were hoping it would be. Work remains to be done in the communities to bring peace, justice and harmony to a state of hate. Signing a piece of paper wasn't enough in Northern Ireland—it never, ever, is.

How is it, though, that the efforts to change the old patterns of violence ever began at the local level? Who helped bring this about?

Two ordinary women in Northern Ireland, Mairead Corrigan and Betty Williams, decided that hatred and constant low-level warfare wasn't acceptable any longer. They began serious community organizing that helped push the possibility of a peace accord from the people's level. The world affirmed their efforts when it awarded the two women the Nobel Peace Prize in 1976. It could be that, had the women and their methods been used instead of the IRA terror versus the Protestant state terror, Northern Irish society would not be so segregated—and the peace process in such constant backsliding and sluggishness. When violence is used to bring the parties to the table out of raw fear the results are not going to look like those gained through nonviolence. When nonviolence incorporates elements of social psychology and group-to-group mediation, its effectiveness can grow significantly.

Empathy is the key to developing a path to break through identity conflict, which naturally tends to foster negative attribution to the other. The belief, when one is a member of a conflicting identity group, is that "everything bad they do against us is innate and characteristic; everything we do against them is reactive and situational." (Rothman: 44)

How do we develop, elicit, engender and help create empathy and compassion for members of a conflicting identity group? Peace Studies and Conflict Resolution professor Jay Rothman, who has worked with identity conflict groups from Palestine and Israel to post-uprising Cincinnati, says that the best method is "analytic empathy." We understand our actions, as Thich Nhat Hanh noted, but we have a harder time separating the character of the actor from the circumstances that produce the action when the actor is doing something negative to us or to our loved ones. Understanding the complexity and layers of dimensions involved in the decisions to commit an act of theft, violence, betrayal or other injustice is a challenge, especially when we believe we've done all we could reasonably. But that is the work of the conflict resolver much more than coming up with "solutions."

Rothman says that a free opportunity to present the facts in the presence of the other party—or the other party's representatives—can pave the path to analytic empathy, which is not the same as emotional empathy. Emotional empathy is what happens when two parties come to feel just like each other. Analytic empathy, on the other hand, slowly reveals similarities that can help the parties to account for the other's actions reasonably rather than as a failure of ethical or civil or just behavior. (Rothman: 45)

In a mediation, then, a session begins with a hearing of the stories, of the problems, from the standpoint of the conflictual parties. Reaction is relegated to the time allotted for each side rather than immediately. There needs to be a sense, verbally agreed upon by all parties, that the milieu is safe in the sense that very tough issues can surface—and in fact must come to light—without recourse to name-calling, to walkout, to threat or to physical attack or any other interruption. This becomes a venting process that is crucial, says Rothman, to freeing up the two sides to begin to develop empathy for each other by feeling safe to express what, to them, is the truth without fear of reprisal or ridicule. Hearing the other side's major complaints without the possibility of instant rebuttal eventually develops an analysis that allows for the reactions of the other. Those reactions begin to seem reasonable if considered without condemnation, which is the purpose and hope of the venting session.

> *It was hot and tense. And these were two very large, loud men. I think they were standing on chairs at this point. ... Finally they stopped shouting and sort of looked at me. ... I was able to say, 'OK, here's where we've come in the discussion so far. You've raised some points on this side and some points on that side.' ... After that, things were much calmer.*
>
> —white graduate student instructor on a racial outbreak in class (Fox: 53-54)

The graduate student instructor did a nice job after the altercation began. How could she have avoided it in the first place? or did it work out best to have that temporary discord? Rothman would say that it did, since she paraphrased the grievances so that each side could hear the reasonable sense of injury coming from the other.

The first item of business in a mediation is to assess our situation. If we are teachers, we need to assess our classes for conflictual possibilities. What are the identity issues?

On the first day of class, I hand out a sheet for all students to complete and hand to me before they leave that session. It's titled, "Stuff about me," and it is a pedagogical instrument for both the students and me, as well as a logistical helper for me. It always asks a few identity questions phrased in a casual manner, such as, "One of my favorite religions or spiritual beliefs." These questions are interspersed with email addresses, expected graduation date, a few multiple choice or T/F questions that go to perspectives on the topic (e.g., "True or false: The military won the right to vote for my mother.") When identity is a part of this little opener questionnaire, I can begin to shape my class around this information. If I have a student from Bangladesh, I will

Identity violence 49

be searching for topics to allow that student to perform the expert's role some days. To borrow a military concept, it's a bit like softening the target. The more I know about a member of a group I'm facilitating, the more I can level the playing field in order to achieve mutual respect, which is a requirement before we can combat identity conflict and violence.

Alarmingly normal:

identity conflict pervasive, natural, destructive

> *"Lord of the forest, lord of the mountain, you who know everything, keep us from danger, deliver us from the evil intentions of the Ladino."...They went to consult the diviner once more, and he kept seeing the same thing.*
>
> —Gaspar Pedro Gonzalez (Gonzalez: 137)

> *The identity of the state with any particular group or groups residing inside a single dominion makes the deprived groups (groups outside the purview of such inclusion) perceive that they are being dominated by others, which makes assimilation difficult. In this complexity of nation building, minority groups often feel marginalized, which further strengthens the feeling of alienation. This, if not taken care of in time, might lead to a situation where the very foundation of the state security is jeopardized.*
>
> —Smruti S. Pattanaik, Researcher, IDSA (Pattanaik: 1)

From the interpersonal to the international, identity conflict is finally recognized as fundamental, normal, and utterly human—but not exclusively human. We are like chimpanzees who divide themselves into troops and who kill any other chimp—no matter how pleasant that chimp may be—unlucky enough to cross an invisible line into our territory. There is, in all of us, some measure of that territoriality, that need to identify with our group and to defend that which we perceive is ours.

Like conflict, identity is inevitable. Like conflict, identity can be very negative or exceedingly positive. For some, conflict and identity alike have a permanently bad image; that leads to conflict avoidance and unrealistic identity aversion.

Experts have disagreed on the question of identity for centuries. Karl Marx clearly sought to efface national and religious identity in an effort to equalize all in a system of sustainable conflict-free global governance. Max Weber decidedly disagreed with Marx on the question of religion as an opiate (Eitzen: 486), and we find, in fact, leadership of social change and national liberation movements often motivated by and constantly evoking religious, ethnic and nationalistic identity as both an organizing tool and as a descriptor of social norm definitions. Identity rights are human rights—until the rights of one group occlude the rights of another group, at which point the assertion of identity rights by the oppressed group becomes an issue of justice and self-determination. Embracing and transforming identity can be key in embracing and transforming conflict.

> *Well, we were a chosen people*
> *once more chosen! The gears ground fine*
> *the fires were stoked. Our children*
> *included*
> *in the vast 'definitive solution,'*
> *swept along, a minor debris—shoes, scraps of clothing,*
> *a scrawled diary—in the universal tide,*
> *crying like caged birds*
> *at the railroad sidings,*
> *shoved like matzoth trays*
> *into the ovens.*
> —Daniel Berrigan, S.J., "Prayer of the Vindicated"
> (Berrigan, 1968: 85)

When Mohandas Gandhi was asked about his religion, one of his replies was that he was a Hindu, a Muslim, a Christian, a Buddhist and so forth. He was indicating the commonality of all religions when compared to each other. He also wrote, in 1922, that "Nonviolence is the first article of my faith. It is also the last article of my creed." (Straus: 5)

The best of virtually any religion can be employed in the attenuation of violence—just as the worst of any major religion can exacerbate violence. The Islamic practices of peoples at peace usually include a special mandate to mind the needs of the poor, of the starving, of the weary wanderer. This practice has historically helped initiate relationships of peace and tolerance. On the reverse side, looking at Islam in our modern Western culture is all too often an exercise in trying to understand the concept of jihad and suicide bombing. Why would believers kill civilians in a pizza restaurant, in a trade

Identity violence

center building, or on a city bus? In this case, we are generally aghast at the use of faith to make conflict management a cruel and deadly practice—it was a poor day for Christianity when Harry Truman announced that God gave the bomb to a Christian nation. Indeed the US was a self-referential Christian nation until very recently and the victims of US policy, beginning with the Arawaks Chris Columbus "discovered," have learned to associate US violence with Christianity. Osama bin Laden usually refers to the "Zionist-Crusader Alliance" in reference to the US and Israel, taking the oldest and most fraught language that will "sell" to his audience. It sells because we use violence and it smacks to those Muslims on the receiving end as tantamount to yet another crusade, a time of great waves of Christian violence that resulted in a loss of overland trade routes to Asia and, ironically—because Turks controlled the Silk Road—sent Europeans off to sea in pathetically small boats to search for a water trade route. That water route brought Europeans the "New World," and European monarchies were thus enriched enough to wage war against each other, and the entire rest of the world—almost constantly after that. War against other Europeans was couched in intraChristian terms (Catholics v Protestants) and in flat out Christian conversion need-based rhetoric when invading other lands heretofore not a part of Europe's long reach. Usually those wars were waged in the name of Christianizing natives.

In the case of Islam, the turn toward violence is a shift to a warped view of that faith—bent by oppression and perduring humiliation. The spread of so-called fundamentalist Islam has had more to do with the spread of conquering cultures—whether those cultures are capitalist or communist—and the indignities heaped upon Islam as a result.

> *We used to be a moderate Muslim society. In 1978, when there were moves in Afghanistan toward land reform, literacy campaigns, the emancipation of women, some of the Pashtun here in Peshawar, in the intelligentsia, thought it a good thing.*
>
> –Sarfraz Khan, Pashtun professor of Central Asian history (Hilton: 66)

But those reforms were Soviet-initiated and, in the end, severely rejected—and funding for the fundamentalists came from the US by the hundreds of millions of dollars annually during the 1980s. Sarfraz Khan told journalist Isabel Hilton that "People like me—who criticized the jihad, hundreds, thousands of us—were persecuted. You had to go into hiding. Our state was doing it, and you, the West, were pumping money in." (Hilton: 66) The same has been true when the US dictated terms to Muslims. In Iran, for example, the US installed a world-class tyrant, the Shah, in 1954, who brutally suppressed opposition, breeding an Islamic uprising. When the Soviet Union attempted to change the Islamic culture of Afghanistan it fostered the twisted, predictable, reactive result: an Islamic fundamentalism so intolerant that the rulers of independent Afghanistan decided to force women to wear the burqa, to stay at home unless accompanied by a male relative—and thus to give up education, careers, commerce and community. The Taliban—which seized power in 1996 from other, less rigid fundamentalists—also used religious identity—so long abused by European invaders—to justify a myriad of brutal, intolerant, practices. Christians were arrested as infidels if they merely made their religion known. The Taliban ordered and effected destruction of all statuary of the Buddha. Women who disappointed the Taliban by their failure to observe what the Taliban had decreed were correct Muslim practices—such as listening to a music video, dancing or failing to pray five times daily,—were taken to the Kabul stadium and subjected to amputation and even execution following Friday prayers. Clearly, women as an identity group were severely oppressed by this quasi-religious reactionary product of war and occupation, making the competing identities of religion and gender a source of profound conflict. And, as in most civil conflicts, men are the fighters and must eat, while women and children get the leftovers, if there are any. To be sure, Islam in its most fundamental form has been what has welded Afghanistan into a fighting, unified nation capable of resisting invaders for the past 250 years; the tribes were otherwise usually in conflict with each other and Islam was not an issue. Only when the British, the Russians, or the US makes war on that poor country is Islam used in such a tragically cynical yet unifying manner. The twisted political Islam—sometimes referred to as Islamism—is essentially a 20th century phenomenon and blends the most fundamentalist aspects of Sunni Islam with powerful reactionary anti-Western culturally focused political discriminations. (Goodson: 18) It is simply a manifestation of all that is harmful about identity conflict along with the useful unifying elements in the face of existential danger. In the end, the women suffer the most at the bottom of the identity pecking order—that doesn't change from oppression to war.

Indeed, the vast majority of that poor nation's estimated 2.5 million refugees—and, with the US attack, the number grows rapidly—are women, children, the elderly and the sick. As of 2000 there were more than 50,000 war widows just in Kabul; we know that number is much larger since the revenge bombings began 7 October 2001. (Mertus: 53) Mixed in with these religious and gender identity conflicts are the usual xenophobic identity stereotypes. "The Pakistanis, you know, will sell their own mothers for four thousand rupees," says one spokesperson for the Northern Alliance, the contenders and pretenders to power in Afghanistan. (Anderson: 68)

Islam in the Far East, however, spread in a different era, and did so via trade and teachers, with no military component. (Harris: 95) Indeed, comments Rabia Harris, founder of the Muslim Peace Fellowship, jihad is mistranslated and misunderstood by many. It means ceaseless activity and, she asserts, the "work of nonviolence is the ultimate root of jihad." (Harris: 96) While the Prophet Himself undertook violent means, the question of when that is permissible under Islamic beliefs is crucial. Harris notes that Muhammad only used violent means after 12 years of nonviolent resistance to religious persecution in his home town of Mecca and eight years of further nonviolent work to convert Mecca from the Prophet's new home in Medina. (Harris: 98) Only in the end, as Muhammad attempted to spread a Pax Islamica, did the sword spread the Muslim message—thus arguably offering another example of man creating God in his own image, backward from the usual assertion.

The clearest example of a truly nonviolent Islamic warrior was Abdul-Ghaffar Khan—who became known by the honorific Badshah Khan—leader of the notoriously warlike Pathans, who converted to nonviolence during his association with Gandhi, continuing that path for the rest of his long life. At one point, during the campaign for independence from British rule, the Khan's Servants of God—who had taken a pledge of absolute nonviolence and total resistance—numbered in excess of 100,000 and helped convince the British of the futility of their colonial Raj. (Harris: 103)

The line separating Pakistan from Afghanistan—the so-called Durand Line, created by Europeans—cuts directly through the natural, historical, recognized territory of the Pashtuns, a typical maneuver often used to separate natural indigenous bases of power into smaller parts. The identity of those who live in the Northwest Frontier of Pakistan and those who live in the southeastern half of Afghanistan are much closer to each other than to their respective nation-states even though the Pashtuns control Afghanistan. The nation of Afghanistan is weak at best, with Uzbeks, Tajiks and other nationalities located in other regions with scant identification as Afghans and more as their original nation. (Goodson) The real dividing lines in the tribal territories are the natural ones that led to divisions of peoples; half of Afghanistan is above 6,000 feet above sea level, the mountains splitting the Pashtuns from the northern ethnic groups are pungently called Hindu Kush—Hindu Killers—and the Pamir Knot in the northeast is home to more than 100 peaks higher than 20,000 feet above sea level. Afghanistan is the size of Texas with hardships and suffering much greater than those of the entire US combined, with their 2.5 million refugees and starvation of approximately half the population. The GNP per capita is less than $1 per day. While the Soviets lost approximately 15,000 in the war of the 1980s, the Afghans' figures are impossible to tally, ranging in estimate wildly between 100,000 and 1 million, both figures far in excess of the losers, of the Soviets. (Brogan: 117) The Afghans are used to paying any price for their ultimate independence.

Like any great religious tradition, the possibilities for either violence or nonviolence exist in the hearts and minds of the earnest observers. Appealing to the best—salaam, after all, means peace—is the path to eliciting the most dedicated nonviolent practices from followers of Islam. This is true of literally every one of the world's great religions, each of which has been used to justify unspeakable horrors and heroic compassion for all. Christian minister A. J. Muste named the call to faith and resistance "Holy Disobedience," and engaged in it with all his heart, head and faith. "It may well be that more harm has come into the world by virtue of obedience than disobedience," writes peace scholar David Barash about Muste. (Barash: 214) Like a powerful drug, fully engaged religion amplifies the extant emotions amongst true believers. Turning those emotions toward peace and nonviolence is our constant task.

domestic US identity conflict

Jews & Blacks: Let the Healing Begin

> The Jewish quest for identity presupposes a European background, an experience that had been ugly and by the 1940s had become incredible in terms of the depths of evil. This, and the huge numbers of Jewish immigrants coming to the States between 1880 and 1920, made it trans-American in a fundamental way. In contrast, the quest for Black identity has rarely been trans-American in a substantive sense. Yes, there has been a lot of rhetoric about Africa. But when you look at the content and substance of it, even in the Garvey movement—the largest Black mass movement—it's very difficult to give that trans-American identity any sort of concrete palpability.

—Cornel West (Lerner: 62)

Why is it that so many Blacks and Jews seem to hate each other? What happened to their alliance that at one time was the darling of liberal politics and the bedrock of radical human rights activity in the US?

Both populations come out of persecution, including their experience in the US; that helped cement their relationship as fellow victims of a society that had little tolerance for non-WASPs. Jews substantially funded Negro colleges and radical Jews were leaders in human rights battles that included

Identity violence

civil rights for Blacks in the US. It was no accident that, for example, my friend Dean Zimmerman, a Jew from northern Minnesota, found his way to the Deep South as a young college kid in 1964 to help Robert Moses and others with the Freedom Schools. Indeed, the famous assassination of three young Civil Rights workers in Mississippi that summer was also no accident; two Jewish college kids from the north were beaten and shot and buried along with their Black co-worker, a young man from Mississippi, James Chaney.

Part of what happened is that Malcolm X converted to the Nation of Islam and he was so charismatic that he presided over a huge growth in that religion. The conflict between Israel and the surrounding Arab world became one of religious identity in the aftermath of the founding of the state of Israel, which became a parallel to how black nationalists like Malcolm X and others viewed the Jewish relationship to the Black community in the US. The actual phenomenon was radically different than the Black nationalists portrayed it but the rhetoric was inflammatory and the target was an easy one.

Housing laws and natural identity clusters turned some parts of northern US cities into Jewish ghettos, even as they also turned the worst sections of northern US cities into African-American ghettos. The demographic phenomenon that developed was typically that the less desirable areas for the WASPs gradually converted to Jewish neighborhoods, which in turn became Black neighborhoods as Jews were able to flee to the suburbs. Part of the difficulty was that many African Americans were too poor to buy, many Jews were from a European culture that put a premium on rental income and other methods of making a living that didn't rely on crafts from which Jews had been excluded for centuries. Thus, Jews rented to Blacks and the landlord-tenant relationship is never ideal. It was made much more difficult when Blacks were so persecuted and so poor that just getting meager rent was often a struggle for the relatively poor landlords who were regarded as relatively rich by Black standards. The dynamic of real life relationships in the teeth of general oppression of both ethnic groups in the greater US culture made it easy for the enemy to become the "Zionist" landlord. This transition happened just as Israel was in existential conflict itself. The epitome of this entire phenomenon in my personal experience was when, in 1969, in the neighborhood in Minneapolis, Minnesota that had gradually changed composition from Jews to Blacks, I answered our apartment door one Sunday as my African-American wife and our children looked on. It was our Jewish landlord come for the rent on a place that was falling apart, with cockroaches scurrying to the baseboards every time you turned on the light at night. I looked at him and went for the hard-earned money, handed over in exchange for living in this dump, and he was wearing a pin that said, "Israel must live." This was, of course, just two years after the 1967 war, when Jewish-Americans were being tapped to support Israel financially and politically, which they did to a huge extent, since Israel was founded as a direct result of the Holocaust and American Jews often had not only some discretionary income but better access to American lawmakers than did the Israelis. I knew at some level that the rent money I handed over to my Jewish landlord might be in some way on its way to Israel, which was fine with me, but I could understand why many African Americans might resent the entire setup.

Cornel West is a professor of Afro-American Studies and Religion at Harvard University. Michael Lerner is editor of *Tikkun: A Bimonthly Jewish Critique of Politics, Culture and Society.* They collaborated on a book called **Jews & Blacks: Let the Healing Begin,** in which they dialoged at length on many of these questions.

West, an African-American, points out, for example, that of the "1,800 physical attacks on Jews" in the year preceding the conversation—which might have been any of the six years of their talks between 1988 and 1994—"very few of them were by Blacks." And yet, as West points out, a great deal of the Anti Defamation League outreach addressed the threat of Black anti-Semitism even more than, for example, the neo-Nazi or skinhead threat, which was presumably greater. Lerner replied that the ADL needed to raise funds by exaggerating the threats to Jews, but also points out to West that Jews are shocked by anti-Semitism from the Black community. West responds that the factors explaining that are numerous, from the Jews-as-Christ-killers for Christian Blacks to the economic relationships to the Jewish achievements that have left Blacks envious, while at the same time left Jews with a preoccupation with the id at the same time Blacks have a preoccupation with the ego. That is, Jews are attracted to and jealous of the physicality of Blacks and Blacks are attracted to and jealous of the intellects of Jews. (Lerner: 135+)

Of course, this all becomes lost in the heat of rhetoric when Louis Farrakhan describes Judaism as a "gutter religion," or when Jesse Jackson talks of New York as "Hymietown," two low moments indeed for Jewish-Black relations in the US. It is identity conflict at its most typical when such gasoline-on-the-fire hate language is used by leaders of the Black community, so it is little wonder that the ADL exaggerates successfully. The conversations between West and Lerner range across the spectrum of Jewish-Black relations to each other, to the dominant mainstream culture, to American foreign policy and to other, analogous identity struggles, such as the identification some Blacks feel with Palestinians. The talks generate plenty of heat, but mostly light, and they turn the problem so that light can shine into places often underexplored in discussions of identity conflict.

fear of bloody identity conflict, embracing other identities

Identity violence

> Religion played its part, a large one. That boundary, closely drawn, those rituals, their memories enshrined and recalled. That banquet; its approved or forbidden foods; then its approved or forbidden guest!
>
> It came to the perhaps: the first and last question hammered home, in the liturgy, in the lessons taught children, in the wisdom of the elders passed. What is the price of survival? Then the answer: we must pay it, and others as well, bitter though the payment.
>
> —Daniel Berrigan, S.J., ***Whereon to Stand: The Acts of the Apostles and Ourselves*** (Berrigan, 1991: 136)

Naturally, we fear identity conflict; it has produced more wars and state-sponsored murders than any other phenomenon. Some seem to regard discussion of identity conflict as bad form, as though it will stay at bay if ignored, and some nurse victimhood like a blunt weapon with which to attack all others perceived as threatening. Like a beam of burning energy, identity conflict caroms off situations, societies and otherwise innocent people to produce guilt, hatred, murderous intent and shame.

- Jews justify oppressing Palestinians because of Hitler. Palestinians use IDF attack to justify suicide bombing Jewish teens.
- Irish Catholics rationalize bombing pubs full of young revelers because Protestant or British soldiers may be enjoying a pint in there. The RUC justifies all its brutality by noting well that only with unblinking force can they rule over such troublesome Catholics.
- In the former Yugoslavia, Serb soldiers felt duty bound to rape Muslim women. Muslim KLA fighters then ethnically cleansed Serbs.
- Whites fear to *drive* through black neighborhoods in large US cities, let alone walk those streets. Blacks fear to be caught in some white neighborhoods.

The list is endless, of course, but the questions remain; how can we as individuals deal with identity conflict nonviolently and promote nonviolence as a method of dealing with such issues?

In one prison, I was asked by a student to extend my position as tutor to include some evening assistance. He was a young African American gang member who was interested in writing to a young Native woman, a relative of another inmate. Inmates often used names and addresses of young women as a kind of currency; the Native fellow had given up the contact information for this young woman as a part of some deal.

We sat down in a little-used basement room in the main bunkhouse of the prison camp one night and my young African American charge began to write, laboriously, with some phrasing help from me. Another African American man from the same nearby city sat first at the adjoining table and then moved to ours as the letter proceeded. We were the only three people in the room.

My young student, a man who had been assigned to me because he was virtually illiterate and had behavioral problems in the group studying for their GED (high school equivalency) examinations, became stuck after a couple of generally friendly introductory sentences. The other fellow looked over his shoulder and suggested the next sentence, a statement that made a claim about my student that was utterly false and that might increase the chances that the young Native woman would be interested enough to write back or to accept a collect phone call.

"Yeah," said my student, "let's write that."

"But it's false," I said.

The other fellow looked at me as though I were clearly mentally inadequate. "It's a black thing," he said.

"I don't think so," I responded. "It's a lying thing and I can't help any more if these kinds of things are going to be in the letter."

My student was angry with me, clearly growing more so as I stood to leave the room. I went upstairs and headed back to my bunk. Within minutes, he was at my open door, telling me to meet him in the bathroom. The bathroom had no cameras and guards didn't usually go there. It was where any inmates could go and so it was where conflicts or other business between inmates from different cells might happen. I knew the request to meet him in the bathroom was dangerous but I also knew that, like any other prison situation, backing down was asking for misery. I trusted my nonviolence to help me through this conflict, one that involved face and at least three overarching identity issues; race, gender, relative education. There was my undereducated African American man, the undereducated Native woman, the coalition of two African American males incarcerated by white society, and a white educated man.

In the bathroom, he walked to the back shower room and I followed. He turned on me, towered over me and glared down at me. I stood very close to him, virtually nose to nose.

"What the fuck," he growled through clenched teeth. "What's wrong with you? You said you'd help me and then you fuckin' walk away."

My only hope was to defend the woman, an honorable position that might engage his rage and send it off with a thought. But I knew couldn't do it in a way that he would feel accused of being a dishonorable person. An acceptable explanation, delivered with respect, was my only hope in the moment.

"She's young and Native and from the reservation," I said. "She doesn't understand city men. I don't see how telling her something about yourself that isn't true is going to help you get to know her better."

He asserted himself again, but the moment of potential violence had passed. Any illogic he might proffer at this point was simply to save face. I needed to help him do that, but he also needed to know that his image would be improved in my eyes and in the eyes of any woman he might approach if he used the truth. I gave him a qualified apology for walking away, saying that I was stumped and couldn't think of a way to go on. That apology helped us manage the conflict in the moment and we were able to continue the letter—honestly.

We managed our identity issues nonviolently—he retained his dignity and felt he honored both his own identity and hers by his decision to tell her only truthful things. He was able to push through a conflict without giving in but without using either violence or the threat of violence (he made the attempt, it was ignored, and he was able to safely ignore it too, thus making the use of the threat essentially nonexistent). I was able to hang onto my dignity and identity as a nonviolent practitioner and we were able to continue the relationship. As a result of not balking at heading into the bathroom when challenged to do so, I even maintained my relationship with the other fellow who had originally suggested the dishonesty. Nonviolence is a dead letter if it is perceived as weakness and, in this particular episode in prison, nonviolence worked and made a reasonable impression in a conflict fraught at several levels with identity issues.

context

> *The context of a conflict gives it meaning and creates expectations for behavior.*
>
> —Roxane S. Lulofs and Dudley D. Cahn (Lulofs: 32)

When those who study conflict attempt to understand what the conflict is about—and those who study conflict might be policy analysts, mediators, diplomats, journalists, academics, politicians, military officers, each with a different agenda—those students of conflict will do better when they account for the context.

For example, how can identity conflict in the Persian Gulf be understood without grasping the influence that the discovery of oil has had in that region in the last century since oil was found in southwest Iran in 1908? Indeed, the "story of the Persian Gulf in the twentieth century is the story of oil—the exploration, discover and export of petroleum—and the effect this has had on traditional societies," according to one analyst. Into any consideration of any conflict in that region must go the factors that helped create, exacerbate or mitigate whichever conflict we examine. Thus, the more we know about traditional societies, economic structures, cultures, external influences, politics and so forth, the more we can grasp the true nature of the conflict. Further, when associated conflicts are involved, how are they affecting the conflict in question? Nixon took full advantage of this in the early 1970s, when he parlayed disintegrating Sino-Soviet relations into US recognition of China at the same time he fostered some Soviet rapprochement timed to piggyback on newly elected West German Social Democrat thawing of relations with the SU. All these acts of comity were fostered in order to reduce Soviet and Chinese support for Vietnam, presumably in the vain hope of winning that war. (Kriesberg: 197) Those who wish to move conflict in different directions will need just as firm a grasp on context.

Killing the spirit in the name of religion: oil and identity in the Mideast

The success rate of religious extremism leaves much to be desired. Neither the riots and random hate crimes fostered by the extremist movements nor the assassinations, bombings, hijackings, and kidnappings undertaken by their underground terrorist organizations have brought justice to the people they profess to represent.

—R. Scott Appleby, professor of history, University of Notre Dame (Appleby: 121)

Continuing with the example of the Mideast, we can look to history to understand some of the layers of conflict? and looking to history, especially involving conflict, is how identity conflict is kept as alive as a peat bog fire that smolders underground for decades, eventually erupting into open flames when conditions are ripe.

Looking at the past five hundred years of human history, we find that religion has been a growing source of human conflict—and, as with so many kinds of genuine human conflict, it has been cynically manipulated by demagogues seeking their power and wealth through the age-old strategy of divide and conquer.

In the sixteenth century, empires emanating from various European nations began to expand across the globe, often times using religious

Identity violence

conversion as the excuse needed to colonize and subdue indigenous peoples. Christianity became a religion of conquest and empire—exactly what it was founded to resist and avoid. Priests came peacefully, for the most part, and, as one Native American said, "When they came, they had the Bible and we had the land. Now we've gotten the Bible and they have the land." Indeed, the preachments of the Church about nonviolence, followed by the violent takeover of indigenous territories has been perhaps the primary root of bitter rejection of both Christianity and nonviolence in many quarters of communities of color.

At that time, in the sixteenth century, the world of Islam also burst forth into expansion that rivaled, clashed with and at times exceeded the Christian explosion. Although it didn't achieve the same global numbers as Christian conversion, Islamic proselytizing won it a great deal of territory. The Ottoman Empire advanced westward while the Safavid dynasty in Persia enjoyed a period of great prosperity. Muslim khanates controlled the Silk Road to China, West Africa became largely Muslim, the Hindus were overthrown by Muslims in Java and Babur established the first Mogul Empire in 1526, controlling northern India from Kabul, Afghanistan. (Kennedy: 9) Islam may have been the more sold, ultimately, though not as fleet and flexible as Christian cultures in Europe at that time. While Christianity remains the world's largest religion, Islam is still the most rapidly expanding with more than one billion followers, and where it is a majority, it generally eliminates the separation of religion and state. The only Islamic nation with a secular government is Turkey, specifically and intentionally secular since its founding in the 1920s by Ataturk.

Thus, we find that there are identity tensions between religious groups in the Mideast that begin on the macro level—Christians, Jews, Muslims—and cascade into more finely divided identities. Islam is the overarching religion for Sunnis, Shi'a and Sufis, all of whom have been persecuted by fellow Muslims through the centuries, all in the name of true Islam. Similarly, various tribes of Jews and sects of Christianity have battled each other in identity conflict.

When, for example, the sultans of Turkey—Sunnis—contended with the shahs of Persia—Shi'ites—over hegemony in the Mideast in the sixteenth century, the Shi'ites in Turkey and the Sunnis in Persia were considered potentially disloyal and thus were both logically and illogically persecuted. Like the split in the Christian church between Protestant and Catholic, the Sunni-Shi'ite split is at times at the center of conflict. Unlike the Christian division, the origins of the Islamic divide were more political than doctrinal in nature. Eventually, the concentration of Shi'ites in Iran under a Shi'ite ruler identified Shi'ism as Persian, tripling the identity by combining making a racial and religious identity with a nationalistic identity. Practicing tolerance—relaxing identity differentiation negative consequence—has been understood as a necessary compromise in Eurocentric culture since the conclusion of the great Wars of Religion in Europe. In the Mideast, however, tolerance was the rule all along. There has never been the Mideast equivalent to an Inquisition. (Lewis: 128+) This makes the question of terrorism-as-Islam a serious question for the pundits and proclaimers who claim to understand that religion as an irrational, violently intolerant belief system.

Understanding how World War I loomed over Europe—and thus the colonial powers that had invaded the Gulf—helps us see how Brits and Persians and Arabs might see the conflicts nowadays. For example, the creation of the Anglo-Persian Oil Company in 1914 was a force in that conflict and how control over the Mideast became crucial during and after the Great War. When oil was found in the Kurdish region of Iraq in 1927 it became an influence on conflict there ever since, even though the conflict has been considered an identity issue. (Potter: 20) Bringing a systemic analysis—or at the least an understanding of as many of the contextuals as we can—to any conflict will help toward the nonviolent management of that conflict. Conflict resolution practitioners call this scoping or assessment and practicing nonviolence is much more effective when it's practiced thoroughly.

revenge, retaliation, relief of reconciliation

> *Gordon's forgiveness allowed him to come to terms with his daughter's sudden death, and its effect reached far beyond his own person. At least temporarily, his words broke the cycle of killing and revenge: the local Protestant paramilitary leadership felt so convicted by his courage that they did not retaliate.*
>
> —Johann Christoph Arnold (Arnold: 23)

When the Protestant father refused to seek revenge for the slaying of his daughter by Catholic terrorists, the father's manifest grief and concomitant strength satisfied the collective emotional need for community revenge; his forgiveness probably saved a life, or two, or ten, or a hundred. Because he short-circuited the cycle of vengeance, he used forgiveness as a weapon. Religiously required or individually inspired, forgiveness in a world of bloody conflict is political, conflict-oriented, and nonviolent. The personal is the political, and "nonviolence requires the politics of forgiveness." (Satha-Anand: 69)

As psychologist Eric Berne told us in 1964, games are handed down from generation to generation and the only possible way to stop playing them is to simply decide to stop. We inherit our genes and we inherit our interpretation

Identity violence 63

of events. We receive instructions on how to react to any situation; are we then powerless to alter our patterns of interaction? Is temper loss as inevitable as hair loss?

Berne said no and a growing number of conflict analysts say that we can learn new ways to respond to insult, injury, betrayal, attack and loss. Just as nursing a grudge can take on a life of its own, so too can forgiveness; when Gordon Wilson forgave the terrorists who bombed his daughter to death in Enniskillen, Northern Ireland, his words were recorded by the BBC just hours after he and his daughter were dug out of the pile of rubble that had crushed her and injured him. Having said those freeing words, he worked hard to live up to them as he faced scorn from those who regard vengeance as the only honorable reaction to such a situation. "It wasn't easy, but they were something to hang on to, something to keep him afloat in the dark hours." (Arnold: 22) Thus, we can set standards for ourselves that prove our mettle, that show our willingness to sacrifice for our principles without using principles as an excuse—a mandate in most cases—for yet another round of violence.

Revenge and retaliation are watchwords in identity issues, when any group considers what kind of attitude they will present to another group. Increasingly, dispute resolution analysts are regarding forgiveness as a crucial step in moving toward resolution or even sustainable management of conflict. (Yarn: 189)

Issues of identity were never more starkly apparent than between the Japanese and US during World War II. Japanese-Americans—citizens, sometimes several generations removed from Japan—were interred in work camps, simply because they were Japanese. The enemy was not a nation-state so much as an entire people. The US was actually able to overcome what any decent person would regard as bare minimal moral norms and we dropped two atomic bombs on two cities full of civilians, including thousands of utterly innocent schoolchildren. We had dehumanized the Japanese as completely as they had objectified Chinese in the 1930s, when the Imperial Army raped and ransacked Nanking and other Chinese cities and regions. Indeed, there are those who nurse a lifelong grudge against Japanese people—against anything Japanese.

"You have no idea how much lots of folks around here hate the Japs," a prison guard told me during one of my occasions of incarceration for the crime of dismantling a portion of a nuclear submarine command facility. "There are old ladies hereabouts who won't even plant a Japanese Elm, they hate the Japs so much."

This pathetic example of blind hatred was offered to me in 1997, some 52 years after the end of World War II. While the enmity of a minority of backwoods US Americans isn't much of an issue for the people of Japan in the 21st century, those hatreds, unless properly addressed, will fester down through the generations in some form. The cultural chasm between Euro-centered nations and all others is at times immense; Samuel P. Huntington has declared that the important conflicts in the near future will not be ideological or economic, but will be cultural, identity-based conflict on a scaled so grand he calls it a "clash of civilizations." To the degree that he is correct, a culture of forgiveness may be key to ending or at least attenuating such conflict. The ideological differences between communists and workers in a capitalist system are actually minimal in contrast to the cultural differences between an Asian and a Eurocentric culture.

> *Of a hundred and fifty doctors in the city, sixty-five were already dead and most of the rest were wounded. Of 1,780 nurses, 1,654 were dead or too badly hurt to work.*
>
> —John Hersey, **Hiroshima** (Hersey: 32)

Hiroshima was not a military target; it was a civilian target. Ground zero was set over a hospital, not over the military base some three or more miles away. It was a baldface terror attack on a civilian population, annihilating schoolsfull of children, convents of nuns, clinics full of medical personnel and neighborhoods of uninvolved and "protected" citizens—something the Japanese never did to the US, heinous as Pearl Harbor was.

Early post-World War II attempts to repair the American-Japanese relationship helped pave the way for initial and helpful steps at some levels. While an official Japanese apology for Pearl Harbor and all war wrongs finally came in 1993, two members of an unofficial delegation of 64 Japanese addressed the US Congress in July of 1950 and offered sincere apologies that caused the US press (e.g. the New York Times and the Saturday Evening Post) to wonder if the hatred could be transformed someday. (Henderson, Michael: 106) Further apologies have not been forthcoming from either side, and the failure of apology for the atomic attacks on Hiroshima and Nagasaki indicate to the world that the US is still capable of such atrocities—indeed, that need on the part of the nuclear establishment to maintain a credible threat of willingness to use irrational weaponry will block any apology for those two atrocities.

An apology is not necessary for forgiveness, of course; it only facilitates it. And the point of forgiveness is not the feel-good glow that the self-indulgent can bestow upon themselves in a wash of noblesse oblige—though certainly there is no harm in that. The value to those who wish to practice nonviolence is that forgiveness clears a line of sight to uncontaminated action that cannot be easily derailed, emotionally or psychologically. Certainly for

Identity violence

some us who are unevolved, a focus on forgiveness as we prepare to engage in any nonviolent confrontation with those who practice or protect violence is crucial. Forgiveness is what separates those who are calm and centered from the shrill, shrieking harpies in black ski masks who so successfully alienate the public. Forgiveness thus dramatically enhances the effectiveness of nonviolent action by helping to attenuate natural desires for revenge and retaliation, those endless tape loops that keep the Irish at each other for centuries, that keep kids hating cops, that keep the Palestinians and Israeli Jews in constant readiness to shoot and that simply look, to the rest of the world, like madness. Forgiveness, it might be claimed, is the first step toward sanity in any situation that has deteriorated into the emotionally sick regions necessary to permit violence against another human.

Forgiveness, unfortunately, is often portrayed as the province of the saintly, of the spiritual virtuosi, from Jesus to Gandhi, from St. Francis to Martin Luther King, and thus unattainable and unrealistic for mere mortals. The challenge, then, to those who wish to make nonviolence and tolerance public policy is to begin the shift in consciousness toward the apprehension of forgiveness as normal, as mature, as representative of a people evolved past a Stone Age, Industrial Age, backward consciousness. Thus, in the end, there is no substitute for personal work expressed publicly.

This presents a dilemma. Is it a good thing that we focus on Mother Teresa, on Martin Luther King, on Dorothy Day, on Gandhi, on Aung San Suu Kyi, on the moral and ethical giants? After all, they are sheroes and heroes, they inspire, and they are a model to those of us wishing to evolve. Or are they simply cardboard cutouts of the unreachable heights of spiritual perfection set "up there" to worship, even as we seek absolution for our multitudinous sins committed as normal humans? Diane Nash told me that she felt the sum total of Martin King's life was a good thing, but just barely at times, because not only was his behavior in reality far short of the image sold to the public, but his loss helped to ruin the movement. She talked of his persona as a cultish, almost guru-like weakness in a movement that, in reality, was composed of many leaders, none of whom received the credit necessary to enable them to continue the work following MLK's assassination. "Perhaps the most familiar discursive strategy labels the religious militant a 'saint,' thereby lifting him or her out of what is considered the ordinary realm of religious behavior." (Appleby: 122) Thus, it could be argued—and Nash did argue—the idealization of a leader, however charismatic, makes that leader a less sustainable item. King was in danger from the moment he became a leader in 1955; it took just twelve and one-half years for the assassin's bullet to catch up with him. Both the movement and the saintly leader are in serious danger when one has been vaulted into that position, but the question remains, then, whether the movement could have grown and accomplished what it did without such saints?

Dorothy Day wished people would not propose to "reduce" her to sainthood for that very reason. Gandhi was quite pained at his honorific title Mahatma. When I delivered a eulogy for Walter Bresette to my students, I assured them that this charismatic hero—a man who had recruited many of them to accompany him as he struggled to reaffirm Anishinabe treaty rights, defeat the Ku Klux Klan, stop giant transnational mining companies and other social struggles in the Upper Great Lakes region—this man was just a man. I acknowledged that he gambled, that he was unfaithful to his wife, that he had a terrible temper at times, and I could see my students begin to wonder if he was really a good man. I then assured them that Walter would be remembered as a hero, as a man who defended the vulnerable ones, as a generous heart who could rally people to do good work, but that Walter would also want them to be leaders. Walter risked his life several times in service to his community and would expect much of each of them in turn. Walter would want them to understand that anyone with a good heart and commitment could do the same good works he did, and perhaps do those works even better. Walter's faults made him accessible; to the extent that we forgive our leaders their sins and recognize that they can fall short of our behavior and still be correct about the issues they lead us to address, we emulate the very forgiveness we so admire in the best of them. It is a dicey line, admittedly, with no clear path to an easy model, but to be aware of the complexities, at least, is a beginning.

Accepting the warty humanity of our visionaries, then, enables the rest of us flawed humans to do our part, to be one of the thousands—millions—needed to reify those visions. We understand that Gandhi was in error often and we feel more free to experiment with nonviolence, as he urged us to do. We can launch a campaign to outreach to the poorest in Afghanistan, we can call for experiments in reconciliation with the people of Iraq, we can sign up for a committee in school, in church, in our mosque, to do the work of tolerance. Unless and until we are unafraid to volunteer to do our part, our part remains undone, intolerance and violence can again take the day, and our dreams remain misty fantasies instead of resolved realities.

> *I look forward to some point in history, whether it comes in my lifetime or later, when people will no longer think of people who live on the other side of a boundary as strangers and often as enemies.*
>
> —Howard Zinn (Zinn: 153)

If you live in the northern arc of Italy, you may be in French-speaking country, German-speaking areas, or there may be a concentration of those who speak one of the Balkan tongues. From west to east, the Italian border starts at the Mediterranean boundary with France, goes north to Switzerland,

Identity violence 67

zigzags east to Austria and across to Slovenia, then south to the Adriatic. From time immemorial, wars have pushed people back and forth, cultures have been shifting north and south, languages have interpenetrated, and hate has mixed with love. Identity and intentions have been mixed and suspicious, with external factors riding high in the atmosphere, depending on conditions between and amongst governments. The mix of loyalties and animosities historically often leaves the visitor puzzled. German influence through Austria and behind Slovenia in Croatia collides with Francophone leanings from both Swiss and French regions. Geopolitics bred a mix of deep fear and shoulder shrugs in northern Italy as potential invaders travel through a society more based on tourism than anything.

In 1991, Slovenia left the Yugoslavia federation, as did Croatia, and it was momentous when, in December of that year, Germany announced that it would recognize both as independent nations on 15 January 1992. (Glenny: 163) The overwhelming tendency of nation-states, of which there are fewer than 200 in the world, is to refuse to countenance liberation movements that have independence as a goal. The obvious reason is that, in a world of hundreds—some anthropologists say thousands—of ethnic groups, each one has a history of complete independence at some point. To allow for one to achieve nation-state status is to open the floodgates for all, or at least to establish a precedent that most nations would find uncomfortable at best.

Germany's historical ties to Croatia, including ferocious alliance during the rise of Hitler, made many cringe, but the US joined Germany in helping Croatia develop an armed fighting force, thus once again throwing the US self-anointed role as peace broker into disrepute. While identity conflict flared into flame, many pointed to the influx of US arms—justified as necessary to counter Slobodan Milošević's Serbian seizure of most of Yugoslavia's weaponry—as tossing gasoline on the ethnic fires. Indeed, it was the war system at its most tragic; the solution to all presenting problems became more of the same.

While many of Marshal Tito's armaments pointed at NATO bases in Italy during the Cold War, he was unaligned with the Warsaw Pact and thus referred to Yugoslavia's forces as strictly protective of that nation's sovereign independence. That "defensive" arsenal was quickly seized and used by the Serbs against other Balkan peoples upon the confluence of Tito's death and the end of the Cold War. Identity suddenly went from quaint and folksy—in a land of inter-religious and inter-identity marriages and neighborhoods since Tito's rule began—to survival questions.

"I can hardly start calling myself a Moslem or a Serb after all these years," a former law professor at Sarajevo University told journalist Misha Glenny. (Glenny: 161) But for many, the question of identity hatred was like a latent disease in remission, only awaiting a demagogue like Milošević to facilitate a resurgence, a fatal attack. It wasn't long at all in the Balkans before paramilitaries joined the fray, underground war economies became the norm, and the war system asserted itself in full force, sweeping aside 40 years of tolerance and defensive posturing.

During the NATO air attack of the spring of 1999, I spoke at a teach-in at a Catholic college in Minnesota. The other speaker was a Serbian priest from the local community. After I talked about the partially completed and now-derailed Kosovar nonviolent revolution, the Serbian priest talked of the generations of conflict in his country. Even though Tito had succeeded in suppressing ethnic conflict in the Balkans during his rule in Yugoslavia, this Serb priest recounted a childhood during which his mother and aunt sung songs of Serb history, including a long account of the battles during the 14th century for Serb independence—battles the Serbs lost, thus solidifying their role, their identity, their place within the system, as downtrodden victim. That is serious grudge-nursing with zero forgiveness factor. This priest had come to the US in part to escape this sick pattern of retaliation in favor of reconciliation. His disclosures taught all of us about the need for a simple but profound posture of reconciliation if we are to avoid war.

These kinds of identity-based collective repositories of trauma that generate hate are found around the world and throughout history. Modern struggles include the Tamil-Sinhalese conflict in Sri Lanka, the Catholic-Protestant battles in Northern Ireland, the Hindu-Muslim clashes in India and the Islam-West struggle that erupts at various points. (Satha-Anand: 70) The megatonnage of resentment and desire for revenge outweighs intelligence until some path to reconciliation can be developed by some courageous party.

sources:
Appleby, R. Scott, *The Ambivalence of the Sacred: Religion, Violence, and Reconciliation*. Lanham MD: Rowman & Littlefield Publishers, 2000.
Anderson, Jon Lee, "In the Court of the Pretender," *The New Yorker*, 5 November 2001 (62-71).
Arnold, Johann Christoph, *The Lost Art of Forgiving: Stories of Healing from the Cancer of Bitterness*. Farmington PA: The Plough Publishing House, 1998.
Barash, David, *Approaches to Peace: A Reader in Peace Studies*. New York: Oxford University Press, 2000.
Berrigan, Daniel, S.J., *Love, Love at the End: Parables, Prayers and Meditations*. NYC: The Macmillan Company, 1968.
———, *Whereon to Stand: The Acts of the Apostles and Ourselves*. Baltimore MD: Fortkamp Publishing Company, 1991.
Brogan, Patrick, *The Fighting Never Stopped: A Comprehensive Guide to World Conflict Since 1945*. NYC: Vintage Books Edition, 1990.

Carter, Neal, and Sean Byrne, "The dynamics of Social Cubism: a view from Northern Ireland and Québec," in: Byrne, Sean and Cynthia L. Irvin, *Reconcilable Differences: Turning Points in Ethnopolitical Conflict*. West Hartford CT: Kumarian Press, 2000.

Eitzen, D. Stanley and Maxine Baca Zinn, *In Conflict and Order: Understanding Society*. Eighth edition. Boston: Allyn and Bacon, 1998

Fox, Helen, "When Race Breaks Out": Conversations About Race and Racism in College Classrooms. NYC: Peter Lang, 2001.

Glenny, Misha, *The Fall of Yugoslavia: The Third Balkan War*. Third ed. NYC: Penguin Books, 1996.

Goodson, Larry P., *Afghanistan's Endless Wars: State Failure, Regional Politics, and the Rise of the Taliban*. Seattle: University of Washington Press, 2001.

Goodson, Larry B., lecture, 19 October 2001.

Gonzalez, Gaspar Pedro, *A Mayan Life*. Rancho Palos Verdes CA: Yax Te' Press, 1995.

Hanh, Thich Nhat, *Being Peace*. Berkeley CA: Parallax Press, 1987.

Harris, Rabia Terri, "Nonviolence in Islam: the alternative community tradition," in: Smith-Christopher, Daniel L., ed., *Subverting Hatred: The Challenge on Nonviolence in Religious Traditions*. Maryknoll NY: Orbis Books, 1998.

Henderson, Mark, "Belfast more divided in 'peace' than strife," The Times, 4 January 2002 (8).

Henderson, Michael, *All Her Paths are Peace: Women Pioneers in Peacemaking*. West Hartford CT: Kumarian Press, 1994.

Hersey, John, *Hiroshima*. NYC: Bantam Pathfinder, 1966. (original 1946)

Hilton, Isabel, "The Pashtun Code," *The New Yorker*. 3 December 2001. (58-71)

Kennedy, Paul, *The Rise and Fall of the Great Powers: Economic Change and Military Conflict from 1500 to 2000*. NYC: Random House, 1987.

Kriesberg, Louis, *Constructive Conflicts: From Escalation to Resolution*. Lanham MD: Rowman & Littlefield, 1998.

Lerner, Michael, and Cornel West, *Jews & Blacks: Let the Healing Begin*. NYC: G. P. Putnam's Sons, 1995.

Lewis, Bernard, *The Multiple Identities of the Middle East*. London: Weidenfeld & Nicolson, 1998.

Lulofs, Roxane S. and Dudley D. Cahn, *Conflict: From Theory to Action*. Boston MA: Allyn and Bacon, 2000.

Maslow, Abraham H., *Toward a Psychology of Being*. 2nd ed. NYC: Van Nostrand Reinhold Company, 1968.

McCourt, Frank, *Angela's Ashes*. NYC: Simon & Schuster, 1996.

Mertus, Julie A., *War's Offensive on Women: The Humanitarian Challenge in Bosnia, Kosovo, and Afghanistan*. Bloomfield CT: Kumarian Press, 2000.

O'Neill, Loreene, interview, 11 June 2001.

Pattanaik, Smruti S., "Ethnic Identity, Conflict and Nation Building in Bhutan," http://www.idsa-india.org/an-jul8-10.html

Potter, Lawrence G., "Oil profits have created conflict," in: Williams, Mary, ed., *Why Is the Middle East a Conflict Area?*, San Diego CA: Greenhaven Press, 2000.

Rothman, Jay, *Resolving Identity-Based Conflict in Nations, Organizations, and Communities*. San Francisco: Jossey-Bass Inc., 1997.

Satha-Anand, Chaiwat, "The Politics of Forgiveness," in: Herr, Robert and Judy Zimmerman Herr, eds., *Transforming Violence: Linking Local and Global Peacemaking*. Scottsdale PA: Herald Press, 1998.

Straus, Virginia, "Preface," in: Smith-Christopher, Daniel L., ed., *Subverting Hatred: The Challenge on Nonviolence in Religious Traditions*. Maryknoll NY: Orbis Books, 1998.

Yarn, Douglas H., *Dictionary of Conflict Resolution*. San Francisco: Jossey-Bass, 1999.

Zinn, Howard, *The Future of History: Interviews with David Barsamian*. Monroe ME: Common Courage Press, 1999.

CHAPTER FOUR

Civil strife

> Although people differ a great deal in their values across cultures, everyone everywhere is concerned about their children, and when children are sick and dying, people are always deeply upset. Infant mortality is therefore a reasonable surrogate measure of the level of grievance and frustration in a society, which is, in turn, a key precursor to civil violence.
>
> —Thomas Homer-Dixon, peace researcher, Director of Peace and Conflict Studies, University of Toronto (Homer-Dixon, 2000: 300)

> Our faces thrust between the bars of the prison gate, we wait, clinging to the cold iron, a silent crowd of women, wondering if we will see our husbands, sons, brothers, again. My son is inside the stone walls with his father. ...Outside the walls, we wait and wail and hope and a woman screams from behind her veil, seeing that her son's name, and her husband's too, are there among the executed. ...We know that there are no more men left in her family or she would not be here alone. ...These words are useless. I will be dead when you read them. ...I, a woman who dared to dream of love... when I see my husband's beloved name, my son's among the executed of the prison, I will tear my veil from my face.
>
> —Anonymous Afghan woman, "Testimony," translated by Daniela Gioseffi (Anonymous: 80)

We in the field of Peace Studies and Conflict Resolution examine the notions of positive peace and negative peace and come away with this distinction: negative peace involves keeping the peace irrespective of the means used and without regard for the presence of justice. Negative peace is the peace that comes after we've won the war; the *Pax Romana, Pax Britannica, Pax Americana*. (Shifferd) Negative peace ignores structural violence, which is why it is a flawed state of peace, and perhaps not even a precursor to positive peace, which may be defined as the rule of nonviolence and the presence of justice. Peace, said de Chardin, is more than the absence of war, "more than bovine placidity." Conflict Resolution expert Kenneth Boulding devised an analytical tool measuring peace on a continuum from stable peace through stable war, with unstable peace and unstable war along that line. Peace researcher Jo Vellacott has added an element by her descriptor, dynamic peace, which implies the use of active nonviolent methods to resolve conflict. (Vellacott: 203) How we use the methods of dynamic peace to address violence takes calculation, evaluation and dedication.

What is civil strife? It comes in many forms with many causes and correlates. Some examples:

- *ethnic rebellion*

One ethnic group opposes another or opposes the dominant pluralist culture.

- *religious conflict*

One religion opposes another or opposes usurpation or violation by dominant religion.

- *resource battles*

One group—or coalition of groups—battles with another group, or with the state, for resource capture or allocation.

- *proxy or surrogate wars*

An external power provides arms, funds, training, propaganda, ideology for a civil war, possibly different external powers to different warring sides.

- *indigenous lifeway struggle*

An indigenous nation struggles for its ability to live the way it traditionally has, or did, which is often mutually exclusive with dominant culture's use of land and people. (LaDuke: 129) This may involve a struggle for political, legal and cultural autonomy.

- *economic desperation*

In a society with relative opulence for some and abject poverty for others, civil strife is ultimately inevitable whether undertaken by the actual poor or by their self-appointed protectors who are relatively well off.

Civil strife 73

- *famine-driven conflict*

Humans have been driven to seek food for their families and villages whenever they have none. Some cultures seem to suffer from more of this in a violent form, especially those societies that have been taught that violence is appropriate in many cases.

- *class war*

Dialectical materialism dictates ultimate class war and it has appeared to have occurred in some societies.

- *racial oppression*

When any group is clearly treated differently than another, the seeds of inevitable civil strife are planted and watered.

- *environmental defense*

It has been shown that destruction of the environment is the functional equivalent to theft of resources, and thus, increasingly, environmental defense is rising (or descending) to the level of civil strife.

> *Blessed is he who masters nature's laws,*
> *Tramples on fear and unrelenting fate,*
> *Not for him the "mandate of the people,"*
> *The royal cloak of kings, not dissonance*
> *Creating civil wars, the swift onslaught*
> *From Balkan coalitions; not for him*
> *The Roman State or Empire doomed to die.*
> —Virgil, first century B.C. (Chatfield: 14)

Violence at the level of civil strife has many drivers and many correlates. Can we ever begin to attenuate conflict that, for example, has led to a collapse of a nation-state, such as Sierra Leone, where children bear arms and fight with various factions at ages as young as eight? And if we live, for example, in the US, at a remove of thousands of miles from such conflict, how can our behavior affect the amount of violence inflicted on citizens—certainly the children—who live in such wartorn regions?

> *Child soldiers are not unique to modern warfare. Children fought during the Crusades, on the battlefields of World War I, and during the Iran-Iraq war of the 1980s. But in recent decades, the problem has grown worse. During the 1990s alone, more than 2 million children were killed as a direct result of armed conflict. More than six million were seriously injured or left permanently disabled. In addition, experts estimate that*

> at least 300,000 children currently serve as soldiers in conflict around the world. The saturation of weapons in some areas of the developing world, as well as the extent to which violence envelops entire societies, contributes to the exploitation of children in growing numbers and ever younger ages.
>
> —Denise Groves, Center for Defense Information (Groves: 1)

In the case of Sierra Leone, which is cited by many as the worst case of intractable, random, pervasive and inexplicable violent civil conflict extant, we can do at least three things.

First, we can work to insist that our own government signs and ratifies the Optional Protocol to the Convention on the Rights of the Child, thus raising the legal world conscription and combat participation age from 15 to 18. Incredibly, the current international law keeps it at the younger age as "a concession to the United States and Great Britain," but only for nation-states. Guerrilla forces must adhere to the age 18 minimum. (Groves: 5) This astonishing hypocrisy at the highest levels of the societies that claim to be setting an example of decent behavior recalls the famous answer Gandhi gave when asked by a reporter what he thought of Western Civilization. "It would be a wonderful idea," he responded.

The second individual behavior that can help reduce the violence in such regions is to pay attention to consumer choices. So-called "conflict diamonds," for example, are directly driving the ongoing slaughter in Sierra Leone, which has created what the UN calls the worst refugee crisis on Earth. "These refugees are not, ultimately, victims of ethnic hatred or of ideological war, but rather of rampant thievery in a mineral-rich region that has been consumed by organized crime." (Berkeley: 60) There are weapons dealers and diamond smugglers who fuel this intensely sad situation for sheer profit, much like slave traders did in the past. International nongovernmental organizations research and publicize information on who sells such "conflict diamonds," or other consumer items that drive violent conflict. Individual education, coupled with educational activities—from word-of-mouth news-sharing to letters to the editor—helps. And when a person signals willingness to join others in a nonviolent presence protesting the unfair economic practices that undergird violence, it can help lead to change. When, for example, organizers told Starbucks Coffee executives that they ought to either begin to offer coffee that was obtained from countries that allowed collective bargaining or be prepared for massive demonstrations at their retail locations, Starbucks immediately switched their corporate position on purchasing such fair trade coffee.

Third, we can monitor and resist any arms aid or sales to the region in question. West Africa, for example, has its own moratorium on such imports and exports, but most of the world does not. To the extent we can act to influence our congress—the body which must act on such proposed aid or sales—we can potentially influence a diminution of the arsenals available for use in civil conflict.

What of other conflicts and injustices around the world? We can help, in many ways, at various levels, no matter what our station in life. As ever, we have much more power and influence than we know. When the guidon of nonviolent resistance is displayed and it changes the dynamics of a conflict toward justice, we see its power in subtle yet powerful ways.

identity conflict within nation-states

The lesson of racism and the war system needed to be learned once more in Vietnam by the mighty US, who retreated in defeat from a nation we were "defending" against communism by referring to the natives as gooks, by sexually exploiting their women, by bombing and napalming their children. The bottom of that conflict was wide and deep, but one point of note was certainly the explanation by a US major that the village of Ben Tre had to be destroyed in order to save it. (Barash: 192) The clarity of corruption and profundity of confusion couldn't have been greater at that moment. Identity conflict will bring down the mightiest empires at long last because people will be free, people will get their identities satisfied somehow.

> *I have been a Pashtun for six thousand years, a Muslim for thirteen hundred years, and a Pakistani for twenty-five.*
>
> —Wali Khan (Hilton: 64)

The US learned many lessons from that war in Vietnam. One was about identity; identity is a great basis for the necessary dehumanizing of the enemy but it can backfire if used too bluntly. It was during the Korean War that the US armed services finally desegregated officially; during the Vietnam War the African American soldiers were aghast at the level of raw racism toward the Vietnamese. Although African Americans fought hard for their lives, for their country, for each other and for the Vietnamese, many became disenchanted with what more and more Black leaders called a war fought by the Black Man against the Yellow Man for the benefit of the White Man. This not only added to dissension at home, but within the armed services. Domestic identity conflict in the US thus contributed to the difficulty with which the US could commit troops to fight elsewhere, especially after the UN peacekeeping mission became prevention of genocide. The difficulties were complex, but the inability to objectify an enemy, to demonize the Other, when ethnic conflict was all about the horrific results of that, fostered tremendous tension and confusion in troops. The Pentagon does not like such missions and is frequently blunt about it, though they never say that it makes their job harder because it's not quite cricket to train their fighting forces to hate the enemy if the mission is peacekeeping.

Saving lives and avoiding battle are not military values, nor is elimination of racism, historically. This is very challenging to their entire training program. To the extent that we can institute nonviolent methods of conflict management, we make identity struggle a positive endeavor. Otherwise, it is fraught with the dangers that lead to the slaughter at Ben Tre, Auschwitz, Hiroshima and every other locale that has been a symbol of killing the Other. Teaching tolerance is a counter, however slowly, to the violence that is promoted by and in turn supportive of the war system.

Interposition in intrastate conflict

> *Shanti Sainiks have two jobs to do. In normal times, they contact people, render them whatever service they can and thereby spread the thought and ideals of Shanti Sena. In emergency, when peace is disrupted, they concentrate on restoring peace and normalcy.*
>
> —Narayan Desai, *Guidelines for Shanti Sainiks in times of emergency* (Weber: 212)

There is a grand vision forming of a massive international peace force that would replace armed force in managing conflict. Gandhi called it *Shanti Sena* and it was the last project he was working on when he was assassinated in January 1948; indeed the first major conference to discuss how to form this disarmy was scheduled for February of that year. One current iteration is simply called the Nonviolent Peaceforce. This is an extrapolative notion, based on smaller successes using interpositional nonviolence to effect social change. Can it be carried to a mass, international level?

Nonviolent interposition is happening on a small experimental level in some situations of intrastate—civil—conflict.

Since 1986, for example, Christian Peacemaking Teams have been traveling to interpose between belligerents in various locales of intense conflict. The first two delegations were sent out to do what they could in conflicts that were vastly different in scale and in superpower interest: one, the gathering of war forces in Iraq in late 1990 and two, the conflict between the Mohawks and Quebec provincial police on the Oka reserve in Quebec.

I've had the opportunity to offer nonviolence training to many CPT trainees and am impressed with the simple determination to work with small groups to change the dynamics of a situation enough to save some lives. Composed of regular folks—college students on a semester leave, young folks between jobs, middle-aged people who each arranged a leave of absence from a job, retirees with new purpose—these teams become a cohesive unit. The camaraderie and care for each other grows even as they prepare to bring a nonviolent presence into a situation that needs extraordinary compassion. I have seen the model work and it is so clearly a replacement for the tightly organized military unit.

Indeed, CPT has also acted in Haiti, Hebron, Bosnia, Washington DC, Chechnya and Chiapas. (Kern: 168) They only go where invited and where they can hope to be involved for the duration. They concentrate on training in culture, conflict and language and can have a unit prepared to send in about as quickly as a military unit can be trained. The set of skills is simply very different but part of the objective is the same, to provide security for the citizenry. In many ways, excellent preparation for such international work can come by volunteering at a Catholic Worker house working with domestic civil strife. You do not have to be Catholic or even Christian to become involved in this movement. It offers experiential education in nonviolent conflict management to anyone who chooses to participate.

When I've worked with various Catholic Worker communities a common source of friction between some donors and the community is the attempt by givers to dictate the activities of the members of the group. "This is for beans, not pamphlets," is the refrain from a few who recognize the incredibly efficient nature of CW hospitality—essentially, there is no overhead; every dollar goes straight to relieving the crush of poverty and homelessness—and yet disagree with the politics developed by the visionaries Dorothy Day and Peter Maurin.

Indeed, the work of the CW communities makes them at once a thorn in the side of the political powers and their adherents, even as the CW work on behalf of—and directly for—poor people makes it virtually impossible to outright condemn them. In fact, the only people who severely criticize either Dorothy Day or the Catholic Worker movement are usually forced to lie about them. "I believe Dorothy Day was a millionaire—twice over," said one Catholic who had been lied to. "She accepted killing babies," another said to me.

Most CW communities are blessed with at least one, and often more than one, really fine community organizer—someone who can meet for morning coffee with a city council member to discuss the city's support for additional women's transitional housing, who can leave the coffeeshop and stop at a supermarket to pull some discarded produce out of the dumpster or off the back loading dock where it has been left by arrangement, and who can then return to the community to do an afternoon of house duty and help prepare dinner for ten or more before an evening meeting to plan nonviolent civil resistance at a local military base.

It is the clear care for the children that makes the CW communities accepted, however grudgingly, by the power elites—some of whom even send donations—and by the most radically explosive political activist groups as well. This enables the CW organizers to make inroads in two directions, toward the establishment and enhancement of a positive peace system and toward the dismantlement of the war system.

Similarly, the Christian Peacemaker Teams can go into the most politically volatile and dangerous regions on Earth and work in both of those directions because everyone is convinced by their obvious commitment to both the children and to nonviolence. No one gains by hurting the CPT; indeed, anyone attacking them loses face toward all sides. It becomes clear in time that CPT is an intentional community intent on bringing serenity and humanity to some of the world's most chaotic and brutal corners, demonstrating by acts of extreme altruism that it is possible to live differently in the world we've created—a functional "microlevel utopia," (Boulding: 49) in the midst of a dedicated dystopia.

Of course, those who profit from the war system—the weaponry sales, the extraction of irreplaceable and valuable natural resources, the use of cheap human labor—realize that opposition must be eliminated, but they need to do so without serious losses to themselves. This is exactly why, for example, Peace Brigades International can operate in dangerous environments explicitly in opposition to the violence of an oppressive regime, can do so nonviolently, and can achieve thus far almost inevitable success. PBI has done so in Guatemala, Sri Lanka, Mexico, El Salvador and Colombia and they protect the very people who are working to dismantle the tyrannical governments of those nations. The key is assertive nonviolence, the kind that doesn't threaten the face—the image—of the militaristic rulers as long as the rulers leave the local organizers and human rights workers alone. In other words, PBI doesn't come into a country and demand that the government step down, but they do make it much harder for that government to quash democratic opposition. "We create political space," says Andrew Miller, co-director of PBI. (Miller)

This is not to claim that all the experiments have been successes. Far from it, and the best researchers learn more from errors than from apparent successes. When, for example, 3,000 would-be peacemakers from a variety of

Civil strife

North American-European nations decided to go together to try to stop the 1993 war in the former Yugoslavia, they utterly failed to make a single advance. Their collective effort, dubbed *Mir Sada*—Peace Now—degenerated from an action of dedicated internationals to a two-week discussion about mission and methods and ended with most participants alienated from the very notion of an international nonviolent PeaceForce.

The first doubts flared into dissension when the fighting—low-flying warplanes, visible grenade launching—caused a reaction amongst some of the contingents. "Hey, this really is a war," is the sardonic if hyperbolic attribution to some of the participants by some of the others. The bickering between the French—who wanted to abandon the operation—and the US Americans—who didn't—was bitter for some time. Other groups had opinions as groups, usually based on their training and the philosophy of the movements and organizations with which they affiliated. (Coy)

Equilibre left first, taking most of the French, calling those who chose to stay both suicidal and murderers, an interestingly peaceful set of charges. They also took almost all the logistical equipment, leaving the rest of the participants camping in a field with little communication or medical infrastructure. Other groups split into smaller units that acted here and there on their journeys generally out of the country. Participants say they failed primarily because of lack of precise goals, divided opinions about the war itself, widely variable levels of participant training and preparation, and no real decision-making apparatus. Lessons learned.

From the successes, from the failures, come these lessons, which are written, which are discussed, which are being codified into a growing body of knowledge about what works and what doesn't. The Nonviolent Peaceforce has attempted to bring it all together and has an initial project in the civil war in Sri Lanka, a nation both beleaguered by ethnic conflict and one which is somewhat exposed to the positive methods of at least something of a *Shanti Sena*. The mission of the Nonviolent Peaceforce:

> *The mission of the Nonviolent Peaceforce is to build a trained, international civilian peaceforce committed to third-party nonviolent intervention.*
> (Nonviolent: online)

The decision to proceed with the pilot project was not made lightly; lives are on the line when any force of people interposes between armed camps or between an armed force and citizens. Some of the criteria included:

- invitation by local group
- scope small enough to be doable

- great need
- hope for success

The methods envisioned by this organization are tried and tested.

> *At the invitation of local groups, NP will deploy hundreds of peaceworkers to protect human rights, prevent violence, and enable peaceful resolution of conflict using proven methodologies such as international presence, protective accompaniment, witnessing, and interpositioning.* (Nonviolent: online)

The needs of the Sri Lankans who invited the Nonviolent Peaceforce to come to their country were two: land reform and the peace process. The peace process in Sri Lanka has been subjected to efforts to spoil it, as are most peace processes anywhere on Earth. There are those who are too far into hate to countenance peace, there are vested interests in war and there are individuals who are simply warped by the trauma of violence and injustice and will do anything—even to the point of suicide—to wreck a peace process. A nonviolent interposition force can help stabilize the peace process in many ways, and that is the hope for Sri Lanka.

An interesting aspect of this initiative is that regular citizens started it and ordinary people will comprise the teams and mass forces. The leader of the initial evaluation team, for example, has a BA in English and no government service (other than prison time for an act of direct disarmament at a nuclear command facility). She is a middle-aged Catholic Worker with nothing but an adult life of service, advocacy and nonviolent activism to offer. This is the kind of citizen initiative that is changing the world and it is accessible to anyone who can craft a life open to such service. Civil strife is amenable to civil intervention by people armed with nonviolence training and commitment.

☙ ☙ ☙

In the field of Conflict Resolution, we are trained to make an attempt to determine what people's interests are—the needs and often-unspoken or assumed true wants—behind their stated and often apparently irreconcilable positions. Indeed, as those who wish to promote nonviolence in all conflict learn more about the real factors affecting the interests of the parties in a particular conflict, they can assist more effectively in dampening the drive toward the use of armed force.

When, for example, a rebellious indigenous group shoots at the national army, the likelihood that the national government will thank them for pointing out injustice and then proceed to correct the situation is nil. Armies

Civil strife

react violently to any threat; when the government and the military are essentially the same group of decisionmakers, that reaction is even more assured. Those who are trying to attenuate and ultimately eliminate violence, then, are charged with at least two tasks in those circumstances. One, we ought to be able to offer persuasive evidence to the uprising people why nonviolence works and violence usually entails higher costs. Two, we should be able to help initiate and open discussion between and amongst the parties.

When weapons merchants talk with indigenous leadership, they offer apparent hope for change; if we don't understand that we are handicapped. "If the group perceives that the structure of power relations surrounding it has changed in its favor, then it will perceive greater opportunities to address its grievances." (Homer-Dixon, 1999: 143) That change can be accomplished with violence or nonviolence. There are two opportunities for those who favor nonviolence to influence the choice of methods.

One, we can indeed point to success by others in achieving maximal social advance with minimal cost to innocent group members. These precedents may not offer the superficial quick fix that the armaments do, but it is our job then to point out the long-term costs in choosing the violent path.

Two, we can learn to intervene much earlier in any particular conflict, before a people has made a clear and less-alterable choice about the methods to be used.

In order to be able to do that, we could hearken back to the idea put forth by Elise and Kenneth Boulding in the 1950s, when they proposed a kind of conflict radar system worldwide, by which those who wished to anticipate conflict could read the signs much earlier and take positive measures to help the parties correct, manage and even resolve incipient conflict.

This is not an easy proposition, but it could be compared to the relative difficulty of waging armed conflict and all its attendant costs. Then the monitoring costs might be more appealing.

Tracking at least some of the contributory factors in various societies is already happening; some are watching environmental scarcity indices and other social benchmarks to begin to understand how to predict potential outbreaks of violence. (Homer-Dixon, 1999: 106)

Naturally, it is much harder for nonviolent interposition forces to operate in an atmosphere of distrust and unclear affiliations. When practices are allowed to slide, when lines of allowable behavior are fuzzy and not bright, everyone is in greater danger. It is always good to gain the trust of everyone, so that, for example, the brutal parties frankly understand that the issue is promoting nonviolence, not a particular religion, ideology, leadership or economic system. When nonviolence becomes the issue, trust grows and doors to justice begin to open. When the Zapatistas announced their rebellion on 1 January 1994—the same day the North American Free Trade Agreement took effect—they did so with a display of clandestine power. The obviously armed leadership wore face masks. Their initial act was to occupy four towns in Chiapas, brandishing guns, machetes and clubs. It was inordinately stupid of them to do so, if they wished to promote peace and justice, since all they did was to alarm the Mexican national government and induce fear and thus militarization. Chiapas was a more-or-less forgotten provincial area that, following this armed uprising, became the most militarized province in the nation. Is this what the people really wanted or did they stand a better chance with no mixture of tactics, with only robust nonviolence? They say they gave nonviolence a chance. Perhaps they did. Maybe it needed another one.

One self-proclaimed "intellectual" makes the claim that the Zapatistas are practicing Gandhian nonviolence and even quotes Gandhi in one of the Mahatma's odder moments to "prove" his case. (Estava: 20) Lucifer delights in quoting the Bible, for that matter. Gandhi wanted us to keep experimenting with nonviolence, not rush to his writings every time we needed to make ourselves feel better about some violent behavior. His hoary old letters to a strange assortment of friends—written at the pace of up to 60 in a single day—are the motherlode of contradictory and downright out-of-context foolish quotes mixed with brilliant analysis, revelatory introspection and myth-busting information. To use Gandhi to call the Zapatistas nonviolent is as facile as calling Hitler a Gandhian because Gandhi actually said, about Hitler, that he wasn't so bad and could probably be worked with. The Great Soul wasn't always a totally keen observer of other cultures or leaders halfway around the world. Mixing nonviolence with violence in a civil struggle or in any other battle is a costly gamble that can carry a dear tag indeed.

The 70,000 Mexican soldiers stationed in Chiapas—some one-third of the entire Mexican army—have managed to make the situation infinitely worse, and would never have come there if the only opposition had been nonviolent. The Zapatistas have thus inadvertently contributed to conditions that have resulted in a movement of at least 20,000 in the state of Chiapas who have become internally displaced—fleeing in mortal fear from their own homes since 1994. Unlike the puffed-up and yet fearful Zapatistas, who almost never appear live and in person in public, the nonviolent *Abejas*, a village of Mayans devoted to their own brand of nonviolence, are quite open and public in their opposition to the policies and arsenals of the government. These "Bees" suffered the worst massacre in the region—some 40 of them slaughtered by the *parras*—thanks, no doubt, to their open vulnerability right after the Zapatista declaration. And yet they remain nonviolent. 400 of them converged on the nearest military base for the Lenten season of 2000, fasting and celebrating, bringing gifts and messages of peace to the soldiers. They and seven CPT volunteers converted the military helipad with peace signs, flags, a choir and a large message on the pad itself: *PAZ*—peace. (Kerr: 4) They wore no ski masks, and carried only art supplies, no guns or machetes. They didn't hide; they approached. They didn't issue communiqués; they engaged in face-to-face dialog. They made friends. They converted the helipad and not a single one of them was arrested by a military who would probably shoot a Zapatista if one would actually do something.

🕊 🕊 🕊 🕊

civil war, conflict management and peace

> *Non-violence has been identified with creative altruism, tolerance and social pluralism, methods of conflict resolution and minimization of frustration, and finally as a way of life.*
>
> —T.K.N. Unnithan, professor of sociology, University of Rajasthan, Jaipur, India (Unnithan: 279)

> *During the ninety-five years from 1900 to 1995, the number of human deaths from war amounted to 109,745,500.* —Ronald L. Glossop (Glossop: 7)

When anyone rightfully claims to have a foolproof method for eliminating conflict short of the peace of the graveyard, that person will have achieved more than anyone in history. Conflict is human, is a part of our creative process, helps us evolve and keeps us problem-solving. Conflict is progress. "Conflict is a fact of life." (Oregon: 3)

Conflict is a fact of death as well. Or, more accurately, the methods of managing conflict cause death—in excess of 100 million war dead in the 20th century alone. When conflict is acknowledged and solutions are sought early enough, a process of dialog or multilog can substitute for an arms buildup and an eventual shooting war.

Without resolving a single conflict, without even searching for stories, causes or correlatives, it is possible for a handful of ordinary people to help save lives that would otherwise be lost in lethal conflict. This was recently demonstrated in the process that led to the historic moratorium on the importation, exportation, and manufacture of light weapons for a period of three years, involving 16 nations who belong to the Economic Community of West African States. This is the first time in recorded history that a sovereign nation has voluntarily forsworn these "rights." A few individuals were instrumental in proposing and negotiating this document. Initially, the tone was set by a professor of history who jumped into Mali politics, Alpha Oumar Konaré, and who, in 1992, was elected president of that West African nation—a country suffering from the effects of a six-year civil war. Konaré asked the UN to send in good negotiators, and this led to a process involving both UN personnel and INGOs. As significant as the instrument itself is the demythologizing of the light weapons—automatic guns that have shed so much blood in Africa and other conflict hotspots. Of equal value is that the UN process actually led back to an ancient indigenous African negotiating style of meeting with a certain protocol "under the Palaver Tree." Thus, the agreement was not simply the result of outsiders conducting a foreign-style series of talks, but rather a respected and traditional application that therefore may hold longer. (Murray: 265+) Juniata College professor of Peace Studies Andrew Murray was one of those outsiders who helped facilitate the agreement.

What causes conflict? "Actual or perceived limitations in resources, divergent or competing goals, ineffective communication, missing or erroneous information and differences in personal style are potent seeds of conflict." (Oregon: 3)

When a party—a person, a nation, a race, a gender, a group of common-interest identity-related people—believes that a resource is scarce and unequally distributed, or merely thinks that it has conflicting goals, or is convinced that it has been wronged, perception becomes reality. A conflict exists. The fact is that when a party believes a conflict exists, it does. When two or more parties believe a conflict exists, it does and it's resolution will not be simple. When there is a true basis for the conflict, the resolution may be exceedingly difficult.

The ease with which that conflict is managed depends not nearly so much on a facile solution as upon the maintenance or repair of the dignity of all parties. Some analysts call face issues—dignity, pride, sense of worth, acknowledgement of rights, respect, validation of humanity—core to all conflict and its resolution. Certainly, those issues have historically caused more bar brawls, mob violence, divorce and shooting wars than, for example, a shortfall in national access to ferrous ore. Managing communication in a manner that preserves and enhances everyone's sense of esteem is a stronger skill than any in a conflict manager's entire toolkit. This is true for the nonviolent activist or the mediator alike.

It may appear to the observer that some conflict is intractable and that all parties are committed to violence. This may be the case at times, or it may be that better communication could fix the perception of loss of face. When a party is committed to violence, the goal of the nonviolent practitioner may be to change the equation that provides a sense of self-worth.

For example, in American labor history, a rash of violence followed an anarchist convention in Berne, Switzerland in 1876, where the dominant ideology became the promulgation of "propaganda by deed." The use of violence by labor didn't help them gain rights. (Taft: 175) Was it simply an unsophisticated cry for dignity? After all, the US didn't even recognize the basic rights of collective bargaining, which clearly dismissed the workers as a group. They felt utterly devoid of corporate power while corporations were afforded every power by the willingness of the state to use violence to defend private property. Arguably, labor violence was much more about face issues than real bread and butter issues, especially when it was obvious that the violence undertaken by labor was ineffective. The crying need was for better communicators, not more armed revolutionaries.

౪ ౪ ౪ ౪ ౪

civil resistance: generating civil strife

Be realistic: demand the impossible!—movement slogan

> *She pressed on and managed to reach the lunch counter where her colleagues, also trained in nonviolent civil disobedience, were enduring the swarming crowd of whites around them. She sat down at the counter, thinking that if this gripping fear did not leave her she would have to call off the sit-in and return to the church from which the group had started out. "I gave myself a short period, ten or fifteen minutes, to make a decision. Either I would resign as chairperson, because I could not be effective if I was paralyzed with fear, or I would overcome the fear and get my mind back on my work." At the end of the allotted period, Diane Nash, twenty-one years old at the time, had found calm.*
>
> —Catherine Ingram (Ingram: 201)

It is the role of the nonviolent actionist not to end civil strife—which, after all, is almost always due to a shortage of justice for some people in some way—but rather to bring to bear the kind of creative tension to which Dr. King referred when he wrote in favor of producing more civil strife out in the open. He wished to expose the strife denied so long by the oppressors—the combination of structural violence enforced by the occasional act of state-sponsored violence that kept African Americans in their low status in the

Deep South. Thus, when injustice is so rampant that it is an integral part of the society, that society *needs* some overt civil strife in order to bring to light the actual deeply harmful civil strife that results in oppression of entire classes, races, faiths, genders or ethnicities.

Keeping a nonviolent campaign from eliciting a violent reaction is one of the key elements in preserving the nonviolent nature of the campaign. It is simply much easier to convince those involved to remain nonviolent when they aren't getting beaten to a pulp. And it is much easier to avoid the predator-prey dynamic when the nonviolent leadership doesn't act like victims. When Diane Nash helped lead the 1960 lunchcounter sit-in movement in Nashville, Tennessee in 1960, she knew from her nonviolence training that remaining calm—or regaining calm—was crucial to the success of the events of the day. She knew that any other very human reaction—paralysis, hysteria, rage, cowering—would contribute toward a downward spiral of reaction into the potential for mob violence. Mortal danger was omnipresent throughout the various campaigns for human rights in the Deep South in the 1950s and '60s; Nash struggled to find her center and her reflection on that necessity ought to be an instructive to us today.

I sat on a panel with Diane Nash some years later at a university in the northern US. Our topic was "Nonviolence and Public Policy," and her observations after decades of reflection and further analysis were noteworthy. (Nash) Her calm in the face of angry mobs or television cameras and hostile politicians was key; she point-blank asked the mayor of Nashville if he felt that keeping some citizens out of public facilities because of the color of their skin was fair. Mayor Ben West, not threatened but rather asked a question about fair standards in public, with cameras rolling, had to answer much differently than if he had been called a name, or if the leadership had threatened him or his city in some way. He had to look at the nice-looking young African-American woman—clearly of mixed-race herself—who stood next to him, and he had to answer a very personal question posed in a very personal manner, asking him about his very specific opinion on a described aspect of principled human justice. Later, he commented on her question and his answer, noting that she forced him to "answer as a man, not as a politician." When we can get to the humanity of the others in a campaign that pits one portion of the citizenry against the government, we can transform civil strife into a positive evolution of social norms and public policy.

When, as it was in the case of the Civil Rights movement or the movement to stop the war in Vietnam, the struggle is literally life and death, nonviolence is literally a lifesaver. And only when it becomes assertive and persistent does it qualify as resistance to injustice; anything less is merely registering an opinion from a distance, a safe and ineffectual response. Lifelong human rights and peace activist and nonviolent resister David Dellinger recalls the moment in history when the increasing objections to US deadly policies in Vietnam moved, finally, in October, 1967, "from protest to resistance. On October 21 and 22, over 150,000 people rallied in Washington at the Lincoln Memorial and then marched to the Pentagon, where tens of thousands trespassed on forbidden territory, confronting the war-makers eyeball-to-eyeball on the steps and grounds of the Pentagon. Over 700 were arrested and perhaps double that number were beaten or gassed. There was no mistaking that this was determined resistance, not passive dissent or petitioning." (Dellinger: 53)

Years later, I spent some time with Dave Dellinger at various events from Georgia to Minnesota to Wisconsin. He reached out to me when I was in prison and we eventually collaborated on a writing project for a national peace group. His originality, his indefatigable commitment to the rights of all and his ability to searingly confront and defeat his own internal demons and fears all hallmark his remarkable life of dedicated devotion to nonviolence and justice. For me, Dave Dellinger is a model of the notion that we always look beyond the current situation to our long-term impact. In his mid-80s as of this writing, he is losing his physical and mental acuities yet his training is so powerfully embedded that he remains active and effective as well as inspiring. One of his natural talents is his validation of everyone else—his default setting is total acceptance of the worthy humanity of each and every one of us. This is crucial to his success as a nonviolent organizer and activist.

Movement for a New Society did nonviolence trainings for years, as do the various groups that spun off MNS. They taught others to do nonviolence trainings, offering many reasons for such skills, including but not limited to:

- exposing students to an overall analysis of social conflict and the ways in which many are connected to other issues
- instilling a rationale for and skills to develop positive visioning of the desired society
- teaching lifelong skills applicable from the interpersonal to the international
- training for nonviolence within the context of a campaign builds community and group cohesion (Coover: 181)

Added to that list might be one of the most important of all outcomes of engaging in nonviolent training, the internalization of the perspective of making means and ends indistinguishable. This one element does possibly more than any other to profoundly challenge and fundamentally alter those who learn nonviolence. If forces them to make their vision even more likely by living it in the present and being willing to suffer the consequences for embracing that vision.

For example, if our issue is diversity and equality, we cannot get there by a white-directed movement; we must confront the question of leadership first.

And if we are desirous of a society in which all feel both safe and free, there is no alternative to nonviolence in the end, so that undertaking to live the nonviolent revolution is to live in the vision now and to accept the training for nonviolent methods.

Nonviolence training

If you or a group with which you are working is likely to face either arrest or hostility, you will handle it more effectively with nonviolence trainings. Contact activists in your area, sympathetic lawyers, and, if you cannot find a trainer, contact the War Resisters League. They keep a directory. If all else fails, you can train yourselves. (Butler: 31)

There are numerous techniques you can use in your nonviolence trainings, but the primary lesson to remember is that the military is training to commit violence every day. One training is not enough. A group serious about promoting nonviolence will train before and after each event, in order to incorporate learnings and ideas into action scenarios. This style of action-reflection-training-action is how the nonviolent forces learn to achieve greater results with fewer casualties.

When I train, I do a brief recount of the history of nonviolence in order to establish possibilities and honor those who have sacrificed. I try to tailor this presentation to the group. So, for example, if I am asked to provide training in a Unitarian church, I will remind them that one of their ministers, James Reeb, from Boston, was one of the heroes and martyrs of the 1965 voting rights campaign in Selma, Alabama. Reeb was slain by a racist mob for his nonviolent courage on behalf of southern blacks simply trying to be full American citizens. (Halberstam: 515) Or, if I am training Catholic Workers, I talk about Dorothy Day, Ammon Hennacy and the long tradition of nonviolent resistance to injustice engendered by that movement. If Native Americans are present, I talk about the Anishinabe treaty struggles, Whitefeather of the Ojibway and other nonviolent heroes. There are always historical examples. See later chapters for more on techniques and simulations.

🕊 🕊 🕊 🕊 🕊

civil conflict bleeds into the international:

here come the terrorists

> *Do not be led astray be a false sense of honor—a thing which often brings men to ruin when they are faced with an obvious danger than somehow affects their pride.*

Civil strife 89

> —Athenian negotiators to men of Melos, calling upon them to submit to rule by Athens or to suffer certain conquest and death, as recorded by Thucydides in his history of the Peloponnesian War. (Thucydides: 114)

Conflicts brew, grow, morph and refocus when they proceed without good management—that is, with violence. One strikingly tragic example of that has been the Osama bin Laden-led group of terrorists who began operations out of frustration with tyrannical regimes in the Mideast—or regimes installed by foreigners. Bin Laden is a Saudi. He grew to resent his despotic homeland's ruling family, which controls Saudi Arabia with an iron fist.

That resentment became violent after bin Laden was trained with US funds to use US weapons to fight with the *mujahadeen* in their struggle to evict one invader—the Soviet Union—from a Muslim country, Afghanistan. That violence worked and bin Laden and/or others (his fellow terrorist freedom fighters) have turned it on the US, though initially focusing mostly on the US in Saudi Arabia. Indeed, their first attack was on the security force that oppresses Saudis in particular, the Saudi Arabian National Guard in a 13 November 1995 attack in Riyadh that also killed five US armed forces personnel attached to the SANG. (Klare: online) From that point, when the Saudi government didn't fall or change (hardly a surprise), the terrorists escalated in June of the following year to the bombing of the Khobar Towers in Dhahran, which killed 19 U.S. military personnel on 25 June 1996. At last the conflict spilled over the border when the terrorist network bombed US embassies in east Africa—in Dar es Salaam, Tanzania and Nairobi, Kenya on 7 August 1996, killing 234 people, including 12 US Americans. The most recent before 9.11.01 was the 12 October 2000 suicide bombing of the USS Cole, a warship docked at Aden harbor in Yemen, killing 17 US sailors. (Alexander: viii) Thus, his conflict with his homeland's government has become international as he takes it to his homeland's senior military partner and sponsor, the US. Clearly, resolving a matter in earlier stages is preferable to ignoring it until it is a global issue with casualties in various locales.

We don't negotiate with terrorists (until we do)

The Vietnamese war dragged on and on while the conflictual partners attempted to determine who could sit at the bargaining table in Paris. Eventually all the terrorists from all sides were represented and progress was made. Since civilians were targeted by all sides, since atrocities were committed by everyone with the possible exception of the Buddhist monks and nuns, everyone in that war practiced terrorism. Indeed, the US military made films showing the massive bombing of general civilian areas and the chemical denudation of the forests, as well as the general use of indiscriminate landmines by all sides. Civilians are still being killed by those on all sides who committed their terrorist actions decades ago, for that matter. And, when everyone finally came to the table and began to talk about what it would take to find peace, they found it.

Years, later, the Reagan regime loudly pronounced, repeatedly, that, "We don't negotiate with terrorists." Turns out that they certainly negotiated with the government of Iran—selling them boatloads of weapons during the bizarre Iranamok Contra lawbreaking, wordbreaking debacle. And that regime funded bin Laden and the other *mujahadeen* through the 1980s, reaching its high-water mark in 1986, when the Reaganistas funneled $600 million to the forces that drove the Soviets out of Afghanistan—and helped initiate the fall of the Warsaw Pact. The Taliban, al-Qaeda and the Northern Alliance all grew from that funding and all were proxy troops for the US in its superpower struggle, and all were nonplussed when the US showed no gratitude for their bleeding and dying later. Indeed, when journalist Isabel Hilton visited Afghan general and Taliban supporter Hamid Gul, he showed her a piece of the Berlin Wall, given to him by the West German foreign-intelligence service, which was engraved: *With deepest respect to Lt. General Hamid Gul who helped deliver the first blow.* (Hilton: 67) We didn't just negotiate with those terrorists, we created them and called them the equivalent of our founding fathers.

On another continent, the Irish Republican Army and the Ulster Volunteer Force have been blowing up pubs and blowing off kneecaps for decades, certainly labeled as terrorism by most of the world, and they—in one form or another, as themselves or as "the political wing" of themselves—negotiated, with the governments of Northern Ireland and England, and reached the Good Friday Peace Accord. Until the 1997-1998 "All-Party Talks" the violence looked endless. (Starkey: 72) Now, even though violence simmers and various parties balk and violate portions of the Accord, the situation has vastly improved. The IRA has even apologized to all civilians who were ever hurt directly or indirectly by their bombing campaign.

In El Salvador, the FMLN guerrillas were clearly terrorists, with a human rights violation record second only to the government of their nation in the entire region, according to Americas Watch. They certainly sat at the table when peace was finally negotiated in that nation. The same general phenomenon was true in Guatemala as it came down to its December 1996 peace agreement ending its 35-year civil war.

Simply, governments don't negotiate with terrorists until they actually want peace. As long as we aren't talking, we almost guarantee the

Civil strife

continuation of violence and usually contribute to the worsening situation. And more often than we'd care to know, the governments in question are talking secretly with representatives of terrorists long before it's a public matter.

This is why nonviolence works when violent parties are stuck in such scenarios. The conflict doesn't have to end, the very struggle and the exertion of coercion doesn't have to end just because everyone is talking. Staging a demonstration against an unjust practice is not going to derail peace talks designed to negotiate some of those unjust practices, but a bombing of troops enforcing such injustices usually will knock the entire peace process into disarray or even end it. Here is a core matter for many power-down or underdog conflictual parties; how can we stop the struggle when the talks may simply be a way to mask the preservation of the status quo? It cannot be resolved for a struggle that is violent without alienating some or virtually all of the natural constituency, but it can happen relatively easily if the nonviolent resistance continues, giving the campaign the flavor of a multitrack campaign rather than a co-opting, *de facto* capitulation tone of suspending street activities while the important people talk. When having negotiators at the table is seen as a partial victory rather than as submitting to the power of the state—which is much more likely in the case of nonviolent campaigns—progress is much more possible.

At times private parties initiate negotiations and proceed without the nominal authorities. If negotiations are happening and changes are underway in a parallel process or in a process that can serve as a model and challenge to the government, the public can be drawn in and can force the government to the table. When, in the late 1960s, delegations of US Americans went to Vietnam to meet with the government of North Vietnam and declare peace between the people of the US and the people of Vietnam, many regarded that as a propaganda victory for the communists, who, after all, continued their violent opposition to the US occupation even as they were joining in such declarations. But, in the end, it was mostly a challenge to the government of the US to respond to the wishes—stated more and more often, in more and more creative ways, by more and more people from all sides—for peace. As long as the citizens didn't appear to favor the communist government, and as long as they were clear to make their declarations on a people-to-people basis, they made the day of a peace agreement draw closer. Nongovernmental initiatives, undertaken by groups of ordinary citizens, can be quite effective in bringing more parties who are engaged in the conflict to the table, where the end of the shooting will be negotiated. There or nowhere. Shooting never just ends (though it can spontaneously lull); talking stops it if anything will.

Similarly, outreach by ordinary citizens, especially with the help of professional negotiators willing to become involved, could possibly draw terrorists—even those responsible for gross misdeeds, such as the 9.11.01 disaster—to the table to talk, and could help in getting the belligerent US government to that table too.

tolerance, terrorism, profiling, imaging

"I think I was an alcoholic in Saudi Arabia," says my friend Khalid. He described his early life in the highly patriarchal and stultifyingly oppressive society, including the underground access to alcohol. When I asked him how that was possible in a Muslim state, he smiled and talked about the allure of the forbidden, available to those with some discretionary income, at some risk. Indeed, when they could get a bottle of liquor, he said, they drank it all in one evening, both to destroy the evidence and to make sure none of it would not be consumed. (Alafif) Now Khalid possesses something else not permitted in Saudi Arabia; his education is in nonviolent conflict management and he brings it into the streets and into the negotiating rooms with equal grace.

At 29, Khalid came to the US to study—not piloting, not microbiology, nor structural engineering, but conflict resolution. He holds exactly the same analysis about the US influence on his homeland that Osama bin Laden does, except Khalid believes fervently in nonviolent methods of conflict resolution. He is heading back to Saudi Arabia "because there are more peacemakers over here and we have so few back home." He is called, he says, to be a seed of peace in a climate of brutal oppression that breeds such civil strife, eventually washing across borders. In a way, our small nonviolent network is going global just as the small terror network has gone global. Ours is comparatively low profile. We will see which set of social norms prevails in the end. Like Khalid, like Osama, we are all individuals, and our levels of commitment are what greatly determine our effect. Will Khalid use his nonviolent beliefs and skills to oppose Osama bin Laden or to oppose the ruling Saud family or to oppose the US, which is a large presence in his homeland?

Yes. Yes to all.

He opposes violence and all those organizations practice it. If Khalid has the courage to do the work in Saudi Arabia, surely we can grow nonviolent power in our communities. His road will be particularly tricky, since he is Muslim and most of the Arabs in the Mideast who have initiated nonviolent campaigns have been Arab Christians, with a community to support them. (Zunes: 41) As Khalid and—we hope—others offer nonviolence in places like Saudi Arabia, we can take inspiration and challenge.

Our US leadership—such as it is—calls on us to believe that the terrorists attacked the World Trade Center towers and the Pentagon on 9.11.01 because we are free and they are not, because we are tolerant and they are not, because we are democratic and they are not, because we love sports and babies and apple pie, presumably, and—if we hear and believe Christian fundamentalist Jerry Falwell on our targetability for our tolerance of homosexuality and feminism. In reality, as CNN terrorism analyst Peter Bergen notes, "If we may judge his silence, bin Laden cares little about such cultural issues. What he condemns the United States for is simple: its policies in the Middle East." (Bergen: 222) Naturally, it has been feminists worldwide who have registered dismay, disbelief, and disapproval of the Taliban since its rise to power in 1996—and those same feminists, who stood alone in that opposition while the mighty US did nothing whatsoever about women's rights at home or abroad—were amongst the first to oppose US bombing. It is typical that the US media is now crowing about the US military freeing the women of Afghanistan—as though there weren't literally hundreds of nonviolent measures that could have been initiated before resorting to war, a war which never had as its announced objective to free the women of Afghanistan. When, in the spring of 2000, the Revolutionary Association of Women of Afghanistan was finally awarded a human rights award, where were the media analysts who now pretend concern about those women? (Ippy: 5)

Whatever the civil strife in question, nonviolence holds the key to the best answer.

❂ ❂ ❂ ❂

sources:
Alafif, Khalid, personal conversation, 18 September 2001.
Alexander, Yonah, and Michael S. Swetnam, *Usama bin Laden's* **al-Qaeda** *: Profile of a Terrorist Network*. Ardsley NY: Transnational Publishers, Inc., 2001.
Anonymous Afghan woman, "Testimony," in: Gioseffi, Daniela, ed., ***Women on War: Essential Voices for the Nuclear Age from a Brilliant International Assembly***. NYC: Touchstone, 1988.
Barash, David P., ***Approaches to Peace: A Reader in Peace Studies***. New York: Oxford University Press, 2000.
Bergen, Peter L., ***Holy War, Inc., Inside the Secret World of Osama bin Laden***. NYC: The Free Press, 2001.
Berkeley, Bill, "The Method and the Madness," *Mother Jones*: July-August 2001 (58-63).
Boulding, Elise, ***Cultures of Peace: The Hidden Side of History***. Syracuse NY: Syracuse University Press, 2000.
Butler, C.T., and Keith McHenry, ***Food not Bombs***. 2nd ed. Tucson AZ: See Sharp Press, 2000. (original 1992)
Chatfield, Charles, and Ruzanna Ilukhina, ***Peace/Mir: An Anthology of Historic***

Alternatives to War. Syracuse NY: Syracuse University Press, 1994.
Coover, Virginia, et al., *Resource Manual for a Living Revolution: A Handbook of Skills & Tools for Social Change Activists*. Philadelphia PA: New Society Publishers, 1977.
Coy, Patrick, conversation, Albany NY peace education conference, 1999.
Dellinger, David, *More Power Than We Know: The People's Movement Toward Democracy*. Garden City, NY: Anchor Press/Doubleday, 1975.
Estava, Gustavo, "People power and coalitions of discontent," Peace News, June-August 2000. (19-21)
Glossop, Ronald L. *Confronting War: An Examination of Humanity's Most Pressing Problem*. 4th ed. Jefferson NC: McFarland & Company, 2001.
Groves, Denise, *Rebuilding the Future: Child Soldiers and Sustainable Disarmament*. Washington DC: Center for Defense Information, 2000.
Halberstam, David, *The Children*. NYC: Random House, 1998.
New Yorker, 8 October 2001 (34-40)
Hilton, Isabel, "The Pashtun Code," *The New Yorker*. 3 December 2001. (58-71)
Homer-Dixon, Thomas, *The Ingenuity Gap*. NYC: Alfred A. Knopf, 2000.
———, *Environment, Scarcity, and Violence*. Princeton NJ: Princeton University Press, 1999.
Ingram, Catherine, *In the Footsteps of Gandhi: Conversations with Spiritual Social Activists*. Berkeley CA: Parallax Press, 1990.
Ippy, "Stoned to death," *Peace News*, June-August 2000. (5)
Kern, Kathleen, "Applying civilian peace teams," in: Herr, Robert and Judy Zimmerman Herr, eds., *Transforming Violence: Linking Local and Global Peacemaking*. Scottsdale PA: Herald Press, 1998.
Kerr, Scott, "Chiapas: for the eyes of heaven to see," *Signs of the Times*, Spring 2000. (4)
Klare, Michael, email, 18 September 2001.
LaDuke, Winona, *All Our Relations: Native Struggles for Land and Life*. Cambridge MA: South End Press, 1999.
Miller, Andrew, meeting, Portland State University, 1 August 2002.
Murray, Andrew, "Under the palaver tree: a moratorium on the importation, exportation, and manufacture of light weapons," *Peace & Change*, 25:2. April 2000 (265-281).
Nash, Diane, public panel and private conversation, March 1998.
Nonviolent Peaceforce website: http://www.nonviolentpeaceforce.org/
Oregon Public Policy Dispute Resolution Program, *Collaborative Approaches: A Handbook for Public Policy Decision-Making and Conflict Resolution*. Salem OR: Oregon Dispute Resolution Commission, 2000.
Shifferd, Kent, film interview, "Bellringer," Beth Austin, director. 2002.
Starkey, Brigid, et alia, *Negotiating a Complex World: An Introduction to International Negotiation*. Boston: Rowman & Littlefield, 1999.
Taft, Philip and Philip Ross, "American labor violence: its causes, character, and outcome," in: Weiner, Neil Alan, Margaret A. Zahn, and Rita J. Sagi, *Violence: Patterns, Causes, Public Policy*. Orlando FL: Harcourt Brace Jovanovich, Publishers, 1990.

Thucydides, "The Melian Dialogue," in: Ringler, Dick, ed., ***Dilemmas of War and Peace***. Madison WI: University of Wisconsin-Extension, 1993.

Unnithan, T.K.N., "Towards a sociology of non-violence," in: Boulding, Kenneth, et alia, ***Proceedings of the International Peace Research Association Inaugural Conference***. The Netherlands: Van Gorcum & Comp., 1966.

Vellacott, Jo, "Dynamic peace and the practicality of pacifism," in: Fisk, Larry & John Schellenberg, editors, *Patterns of Conflict: Paths to Peace*, Peterborough, Ontario: Broadview Press, 2000.

Weber, Thomas, ***Gandhi's Peace Army: The Shanti Sena and Unarmed Peacekeeping***. Syracuse NY: Syracuse University Press, 1996.

Zunes, Stephen, Lester R. Kurtz and Sarah Beth Asher, ***Nonviolent Social Movements: A Geographical Perspective***. Malden MA: Blackwell Publishers, 1999.

CHAPTER FIVE

International conflict

Were you in the war?

yes
What was it like?
like nothing you can imagine
Did you kill anyone?
yes
how did you feel?
I felt like a murderer, a
savior, a cog in a machine
Did any of your friends get
killed?
yes
How did that feel?
Get the fuck out of my face!

—Jim Northrup, Jr., Native American poet, "War Talk" (Northrup: 9)

We are all cogs in a machine; we gradually learn that we have choices in our lives that can help us be a part of a different machine, one that feels better to us than being a murderer—while still making it possible to feel like a savior. The hardest part is in fact not the possibility that we ourselves will be burned out in the function of the machine, but that our loved ones will be. Indeed, that is a serious factor in choosing which machine to be a part of. On the one hand, we must consider the effects of our actions on the other actors who are choosing to join our effort; for a military person, that means killing the enemy before he can kill our fighting comrades. For a nonviolent actionist, that means being careful not to trigger violence in whatever conflicting party we confront. On the other hand, we need to think of the effect of our actions on those who are helpless, vulnerable, noncombatants. Will our actions tend to help or hurt them? Will what we do tend to elicit revenge exacted upon visible vulnerable villagers rather than invisible armed guerrillas, if that's who we are? Or will our actions tend to draw the response—whatever it may be—to us, the actionists? If we act nonviolently, we can usually depend upon being the recipient of the response of the conflicting party, which makes nonviolence more risky in some ways to those acting, but less risky to the innocent. A machinery comprising nonviolent forces is often a tactically, strategically and philosophically superior machinery, especially if it has a similar number of moving parts (human participants).

Organized nonviolent forces are not a random response to a highly abnormal situation. When the forces of violence accommodate—and even turn back in defeat from—organized nonviolent resistance, that makes perfect sense. It is a modality that satisfies logical requirements. It simply fails to engage the analytical minds of those who are steeped and trained in considering violent war the last option for freedom-loving patriots. It seems the best way to the minds of the analysts is through their stomachs; nonviolence has little of the visceral appeal of a series of bloody campaigns that kill and demolish the enemy and his infrastructure. Rather, the enemy is destroyed by making him a friend—or at least a coöperating neutral. This destruction may not make headlines, but if the journalistic rule is *If it bleeds, it leads*, perhaps we can live without headlines. Journalist Bertha von Suttner urged us in her acceptance of the 1905 Nobel Peace Prize to realize that history doesn't condemn humanity to periodic war; she pointed to the then-recent theories of evolution and challenged us to be better, to change, to evolve past war because we can and because it is the right thing to do. (von Sutter: 213) Others continue to note the possibility:

> *Like slavery and cannibalism, war too can be eliminated from humanity's arsenal of horrors.*
>
> —John H. Stoessinger, war scholar, University of San Diego (Stoessinger: 252)

War is not a biological necessity; humans can live without it and have done so in some cultures. What kinds of tools do we possess to prevent and transform war and other acts of violence between and among nation-states? We could name many: media, education, community-building, nonviolent resistance, political organizing, economic measures, religion, independent scientists, other independent experts, the law, nongovernmental organizations, the United Nations and withdrawal of coöperation.

The media is a tool of the military. It makes capitalistic sense to all parties: "In April 1991, CNN's audience was 17 percent higher than it was in April 1990." (Smith: 179) The Gulf War was a gift to the news purveyor's 24-7 star network. But we who promote nonviolence can use the media too. Working with the media is all about strategy and relationships. The strategy that works

International conflict 99

best employs the understanding of what makes a good news story, and thus a usable media release. It involves building relationships with reporters, editors, and editorial boards. Understanding that everyone needs individual approach, media experts advise us to "woo the gatekeepers," very personally and very professionally at once. If we respect what they must do, we will be able to mutually enjoy the published fruits of our mutual labors. In some ways, it is bringing the elements of conflict resolution to the public storytellers, allowing them to pass along the tales of justice, of the suffering and possible solutions. (Ryan: 215)

Peace Studies and Conflict Resolution education is in a growth phase; from the handful of programs in 1980 the field has grown to more than 600 degree and certificate programs worldwide, including Ph.D. programs that are helping define the interdiscipline. Each class taught sends out seeds of informed students who will change society.

When peace communities—not communes where people actually live together, but the more general sense of community where like-minded people begin to organize many activities together—begin to grow they empower themselves and each other. The social norms of an area change as the public discourse over issues changes due to a strong community presence. This can alter the make-up of the larger community, sometimes significantly.

Undertaking nonviolent resistance to injustice, militarism and violent foreign policy can start small and help to change the policy in the end. As the campaigns grow the politicians must take the views of the resistance community into account, especially if what they are insisting on is demonstrably just. Keeping the resistance nonviolent deprives the war system of an excuse to use violence on the movement. Keeping the resistance robust keeps the struggle in the eye of the public and, if there is truth to it, policy will change.

Policy will change more quickly as organizers move to develop political skills, which will involve good facilitation and negotiation competencies.

- From Montgomery, Alabama in 1955-'56 to South Africa in the 1980s, economic measures are vitally important. Boycotts, sanctions, tax resistance, lawsuits and budget hawks can all affect public policy. Congress funds all wars; they are elected or they can be replaced.

- When key religious figures support or condemn a war, it is commensurately more or less likely to occur or continue or stop.

- Independent scientists and other experts can blow the whistle on warmakers and dampen plans. When former weapons inspector Scott Ritter denounced the idea of bombing Iraq again, his voice carried weight. When former weapons designer Robert Aldridge quit Lockheed at the peak of his career, lawmakers and others tended to regard his analysis as credible.

- Lawyers can alter the law. They can stop a weapon from shipment—as in the case of the BAe war helicopters denied to Indonesia because of their brutality toward East Timorese, precipitated by the actions of four women hammering on those helicopters and taking their case to court. Civil suits can also halt militarism in some of its forms.

- Nongovernmental organizations can interpose and halt wars, or help the warring parties negotiate, or help bring hostilities to a halt by affecting large external forces.

- When the UN is doing its mandated peace and human rights work, and when they are careful to offer first rate mediators and design truly smart sanctions, they can influence the end of a war or prevent it altogether.

- Finally, when war is "inevitable," it takes massive people power and complete strike or noncoöperation to stop it in its tracks, which was done in the Philippines in 1986 and has been done elsewhere.

War is always worth stopping. There is no such thing as "honoring those who have fallen" by compounding the mistake. Each death is not to counterbalance another, said Arundhati Roy, it must be **added** to the grisly, immoral total.

> *the last error shall be worse than the first*
> —Matthew 27: 64

Can two or more violently conflictual nation-states suddenly gain their senses and decide to backpedal and review the dysfunctional path they seem to have chosen? Is leadership which approved an act of state violence—or even years of shooting—likely to grasp how maladaptive that method really is?

Of course. That is almost invariably what happens, in fact, between and amongst nation-states who have chosen to use violence on each other. One or more of them comes to their senses. The problem with coming to one's senses, whether that is in the personal or global arena is that such a change is usually associated with losing. *First one to go sane loses* seems to be the dictum subscribed to by barroom poseurs, tort attorneys and international brinkspeople alike, and that directive seems to govern the thinking of back alley brawlers and commanders-in-chief as well. Indeed, from the time of Tacitus it has been noted that leaders who are extreme may gain some cache in the beginning, but the people usually lose the taste for such robust, ongoing power over others—which invariably translates backward into a paranoid power over the citizens who are benefiting from the aggressive leadership. Most of humanity tends to revert most of the time toward more moderate, less frenzied, leadership that will tend less to oppress foreigners and domestic alike. (Walter: 38) Of course, in that process, some practice and many are affected by periodic terrorism directed inward and outward. Humanity seeks homeostasis on the one hand and progress on the other, with terror at the nexus all too often.

Vom Krieg: why?

The many factors that drive war operate in a connected web of negative energy that ultimately needs a triggering event—real or manufactured—to actually give justification to launch the armed attack. Whether a terrorist action shielded by a state—like Osama bin Laden's 9.11.01 attack on NYC/DC while hosted by Afghanistan—or perhaps an outright surprise attack—such as the Japanese on Pearl Harbor in December 1941—or, if necessary, by artifice—such as when German soldiers dressed as Polish soldiers and attacked a German border post in order to precipitate the blitzkrieg (Andregg: 131), some threshold must be crossed. People will not otherwise kill people, even group-to-group. We would rather help.

nongovernmental organizations and nation-state violence

What, indeed, can one woman do?

- She can convince others to care, one at a time.
- She can form a group to seek peace between nations.
- She can form a coalition of groups to promote protection of civilians.
- She can use electronic organizing to inform innumerable activists worldwide.

These are the kinds of steps taken by Jody Williams, a US-American nurse who served for years in Southeast Asia and who saw the horrific consequences of landmines. She and other nurses helped convince Doctors Without Borders to become involved in the attempt to ban landmines. She appealed to her own government with the group Women's Commission for Children and Women Refugees in January 1991. Joined by Asia Watch and Physicians for Human Rights in that year, they helped convince Prince Sihanouk of Cambodia to call for a ban on antipersonnel devices. Jody Williams was hired to lead Vietnam Veterans of America Foundation, who joined the growing list of international nongovernmental organizations in coalition over this issue by the end of 1991.

It was hard work. There were innumerable defeats, cowardly retreats, and other political arena disappointments. There were many small victories, such as the 1,400 signatures on a petition brought to the Australian government in February 1992, calling for the total ban on manufacture or possession of landmines.

By 2 October 1992 the international coalition of groups formally published an international call for the total ban of antipersonnel landmines and did so in formal coalition, calling themselves the International Coalition to Ban Landmines.

The countries of the world all waffled and made excuses to the ICBL, saying that the way that they use landmines ought to be excepted from any discussion of a ban, although they all liked the idea, they claimed. Throughout this bleak period, the nurses and doctors who dealt directly with the victims of landmines took to the editorial pages, the airwaves of public radio and other public outreach venues. They were everywhere, changing public consciousness about the permissibility of such indiscriminate killers. Landmine victims were given opportunities to talk; photos of beautiful children learning to walk with artificial legs pierced the hearts of people everywhere and the people began to contact their governments.

Finally, on 2 March 1995, Belgium followed the NGOs and led the world of nation-states by being the first to pass a law domestically that bans landmine use, production, procurements, parts and technology. The campaign to make such a ban international law was given a shot in the arm and a historic conference of many NGOs plus 50 nations met in Ottawa in October 1996; they challenged the world to ban landmines by December of the following year. (Handicap: 42)

The world did—at least enough nations to trigger a new international law based on the treaty. The campaign continues, seeking the signatory and ratification status of every nation-state on Earth. Jody Williams was recognized for her unique role in the campaign when she was named co-recipient of the 1997 Nobel Peace Prize and she later made the startling analogy and assertion that the people of the Earth, when acting in coalition of NGOs, are "the new superpower." No statement about the power of the people—beginning from the bottom, involving working women, acting without the initial imprimatur of any government—has ever captured the global potential for people power more dramatically or effectively. What, indeed, can one woman do about slowing the violence committed by nation-states?

This ban on landmines would be a great victory if it saved human lives directly, which is clearly does, as nations quit planting more landmines. But it does much more. It takes away the hardware of curse, the silent but deadly evidence of enduring national hatred for the other. It removes one of the seeds of war—literally planted in the Earth—it takes away one driver to war even as it bans one weapon of war, because landmines commit fresh and provocative atrocities long after the formal end of a war—thus making another war more likely.

These are the kinds of initiatives that are changing the world, that are promoting a new peace coming from the people. The first woman to be awarded the Nobel Peace Prize—the person who convinced Alfred Nobel to found the award when they met in Berne in 1892—was an Austrian who, in her acceptance speech in Oslo, noted well the inertia of a European system committed to war and who then spoke especially of the hope she had that the fresher ideas and younger energy of America. Bertha von Suttner hoped that American idealism and practicality would help its people evolve past war, past killing as a solution. In a way, she anticipated Jody Williams, the can-do idealist who came almost a century later. Bertha von Suttner said that the peace system would come to us "a step at a time," (von Suttner: 216) and Williams took her personal step from the US to the world, leaving her nation behind but challenging us all to catch up.

NGO-initiated mediation

When an organization of citizens becomes involved in advocating for peace between conflictual nation-states, it actually has some advantages over the official diplomats. A covey of Quakers isn't going to be excoriated by Muslim fundamentalists as enemies of the true faith, but an Islamic ruler who negotiates openly with the Jews from Israel will be attacked as a traitor to both state and religion—which, for virtually all Muslim-majority countries is the same. Thus, a backchannel approach, conducted quietly and with zero public knowledge—let alone fanfare—can achieve results few diplomats can accomplish.

Part of the idea behind NGO-facilitated discussions is to remove "face" from the set of factors. During a crisis between nation-states, communication and information become increasingly distorted, tunnel vision sets in, and facts become malleable under the heat and pressure. "Compromise is then difficult because the original contest is replaced by one over prestige." (Ziegler: 288) This is when we "send in the Mennonites" so that neither side sends in the Marines.

At times, nation-states will seek the good offices of neutral nations, or of the UN. This has helped preserve the peace in specific crises; when Algeria suddenly found itself involuntarily hosting a PLO-hijacked Israeli airliner in 1968, both Israel and Algeria approached U Thant, then Secretary General of the UN, who settled the issue with skillful mediation.

Other times, a neutral nation will calm a crisis by simply providing a neutral meeting venue, such as the Austrian-Italian dispute over Tyrol, which was settled in Denmark meetings. (Ziegler: 289)

Citizens and citizen groups who see that these solutions are possible can quietly clamor for them. When some Norwegians decided that peace in the Mideast was enough of a good idea to pursue, they approached the PLO and Israel with absolutely no publicity. Indeed, Israeli officials who agreed to talk to the PLO in this Norwegian-citizen-initiated setting lied to their coworkers about where they were going and what they were doing. The Oslo process was entirely off-screen to the media and even to the diplomatic community beyond a very tight circle indeed. Two Norwegians—Mona Juul and Terje Larsen—were the initiators of a process that probably saved thousands of lives during the tumultuous mid-late 1990s. Because that process ultimately broke down in September of 2000 doesn't mean that the effort was not worthy; it most decidedly succeeded where other approaches failed. No one ever elected or appointed the couple from Norway to open a path to peace in the Mideast; they unilaterally decided to Just Do It and it was remarkably successful for several years, saving how many innocent lives?

Against war, for nonviolence

National defense is now the greatest enemy of national security.

—Kenneth Boulding (Mitchell: 117)

Exploitation of one nation by another cannot go on for all time. Industrialism depends entirely on your capacity to exploit, on foreign markets' being open to you and on the absence of competition. ...I have no quarrel with steamships and telegraphs. They may stay, if they can, without the support of industrialism and all it connotes. They are not an end. We must not suffer exploitation for the sake of steamships and telegraphs.

—M.K. Gandhi (Gandhi: 287)

We live in a war system. The face of that war system is imperialism and globalization, two names for an economic engine that generates great wealth for a few and dire poverty for the many. In the early 1980s, when a former weapons designer for Lockheed was researching how the nuclear arsenal affected the global economy, *Fortune* magazine was advertising blatantly to its readers that the poorest nations were where the opportunities for riches lay. *Build your facility in the Philippines and pay workers less than $1.50 per day. Further, there aren't any of those expensive environmental laws.* (Aldridge: 276)

Robert C. Aldridge was a combat grunt in World War II in the South Pacific. He came home, got an engineering degree and went to work for Lockheed eventually. His assignment—which became his specialty—was submarine-launched ballistic missiles. He worked on the design of five generations of SLBMs. His brilliance earned him the position, finally, of design team leader for what would become the missile now on board the Trident submarines, the D5.

But the Catholic Aldridge, father of eight children, finally fell to the moral, religious and humanitarian blandishments of his daughter, who challenged him to really think about what he was doing. It took years, but he eventually made the major personal decision to leave a lucrative life and devote himself to researching the war system and offering his findings to those who might be able to use them.

I was one of many who read his second book, ***First Strike! The Pentagon's Strategy for Nuclear War***, and was moved to action by its cold logic and hot message of urgency. I corresponded with Aldridge and participated more and more in nonviolent acts of witness against the weaponry and against components of the nuclear arsenal that both backed the system of gross inequality and threatened all of life on Earth. It was extreme peace and justice and this independent former insider convinced me to make my stand. Eventually, Aldridge visited to testify at one of my trials and we became closer friends. I remain indebted to Bob Aldridge and hold him in my mind as an individual who answered the challenge of conscience and offered something to us that no one else has.

Being against the war system is a fine activity; creating a peace system is the logical solution.

Handily for those who subscribe to nonviolent antiwar activity, their method of struggle not only has a chance for victory in any particular campaign, but it actively models an alternative conflict management style to the military.

Of course, there is more. Nonviolence cannot provide for international power projection, upon which our globalized economy is built. This means that, for those who believe in nonviolence, there is no getting around the fact that nonviolence won't work well for those who wish to maintain economic disparity between the people of the US and the people of Indonesia—or Guatemala, or Uganda. Nonviolence thus demands examination of how we may also model lifestyles that are sustainable by nonviolent defense.

The worldwide movement in opposition to globalization—a neutral word that has come to mean an illimitable bounty to a few and unfair rapacious plundering to more and more—didn't, in fact, start in the streets of Seattle in November of 1999. Many smaller, barely connected, locally reported nonviolent witnesses had been taking place around the world leading up to a mass nonviolent action that shut down the World Trade Organization at its meeting in Seattle. Many more actions have taken place since.

For example, hundreds of Adivasis, indigenous Indians from Madya Pradesh, blockaded the World Bank building in New Delhi as a reaction to WB policies that were ruining the lifeways and lands in that region. Such Indian actions were not uncommon in the land of Gandhi and in the land of Vandana Shiva, an Indian scientist and activist who has been championing indigenous and environmental rights for years. Her research and outreach has called attention to the destructive policies that lead to ravaging practices in the wake of economic and environmental decisions made by WB, WTO and the International Monetary Fund. (Tabb: 10)

blood thicker than water:

resource war and peace

> *Two of Gandhi's key campaigns were about concrete, basic staples of life: cloth and salt.*
>
> —Michael Nagler, scholar of nonviolence, University of California-Berkeley (Nagler: 2001)

The Jordan River basin is one of the smallest major riparian basins on Earth—and through it flows some of the most contested water. Indeed, it could be argued, if someone would enable the peoples of the region to enjoy access to enough clean water, a great deal of the "ethnic" and "religious" conflict might deëscalate.

Israel began to warn its neighbors against altering the flow of the Jordan early. Major tributaries flow from Lebanon and Syria and, sure enough, one of the military objectives that precipitated the June 1967 Six Day War was the destruction of the partially completed Mukhaiba Dam, Jordan's East Ghor Canal, and riparian regions of the Jordan above Lake Tiberias in the Golan Heights, then in Syria. "Some analysts have hypothesized or asserted that Israel's occupation strategy was driven by the fact that by 1964 Israel was reported to be already making full use of all the surface and underground water resources within its territory as well as 540 million cubic meters of water from the Jordan River." (Elhance: 108)

Water flowed straight through the center of the channel of the river of regional conflict before 1967; at the pan-Arab summit of 1964 called by Egyptian president Nasser, the gathering of Arab nations considered launching war on Israel over water, and ultimately supported smaller attacks in addition to water diversion projects on the upper Jordan, which helped to precipitate Israel's 1967 decisions about war and peace. Even earlier, Israeli forces attacked Syrian water diversion projects in 1965, clearly presaging the 1967 war.

It was, in fact, at that summit in 1964 that the PLO was born, and its very first military act was to launch an attack on the National Water Carrier in Israel. (Elhance: 115) The situation has only worsened since, with rising population, global warming and water quality problems. Thus, pollution control becomes a driver toward peace, as does birth control and resource consumption control.

national nonviolence

> An old man came out of the barracks across the yard and shuffled towards the latrines. It was startling to see him because no one was allowed outside then. He moved slowly, as if in pain, taking care to stay on the planks, which were slippery. I was impatient, I wished he would move faster before a guard saw him.
>
> He got halfway across the yard and then stood still, looking where to step next. At that moment a guard blew a whistle, but the old man continued looking down at his feet as if paralyzed. Two guards came running through the swirling snow, brandishing their sticks and shouting. They seized him and began to beat him. It is hard for me now, in an era when everyone has seen thousands of beatings and killings on television, to explain how shocking and unnatural this was. I had never before seen anyone hit, let alone beaten; my sister and I had never been spanked or slapped, I had never seen a fistfight or a wrestling match. I stood at the window trembling, unable to take my eyes off the old man, who was pathetically trying to shield his head from the blows of the guards. Blood started flowing from his nose or maybe his mouth, and he cupped both hands over his face, bent his head further and knelt down, receiving the blows.
>
> —Agate Nesaule, Latvian refugee in Nazi prison camp (Nesaule: 45-46)

> *Whether there is or there is not any law in force, the Government cannot exercise control over us without our coöperation.*
>
> —M. K. Gandhi (Gandhi: 85)

Most nation-states have a history of war and violence, but most teach their children to act nonviolently in society. Latvia, a nation that endured Hitlerism during World War II and four decades of Soviet rule following the nazi terror, eventually achieved its liberation nonviolently. If the childhood of Agate Nesaule was a typical Latvian experience, it is little wonder the Latvians were able to avoid the bloodshed of interstate conflict so prevalent from nation-states that train their children to expect and to commit violence.

Subcultures of nonviolence exist all around the world and provide the hope that those who are raised in mainstream cultures will be influenced in some manner by those subcultures of nonviolent option. In Buddhist nations, perhaps the Dalai Lama or Aung San Suu Kyi or Thich Nhat Hahn will present a heroic role model to someone who needs it in a moment of indecision. In the Christian world, a nonviolent nun or priest can present an alternative to a Catholic who is in moral crisis. Gandhi, who first commented upon the **Gita** in 1889 and who did his own Gujarati translation in 1929, felt that this Hindu work was an allegory of internal struggle, not a literal justification for warfare or any other violence. Certainly he helped shape his fellow Hindus' view of nonviolent struggle.

When I visited Larry Morlan in prison in Marion, Illinois, he was a Catholic who had hammered on a nuclear weapon and was serving time in a federal prison for his act. I had interviewed him before his trial and he had told me, "Look, I'm not a hero. When a peasant leader speaks up one time in Latin America, they kill him. That's courage, and that is resistance. Hammering on a bomb in the US is much easier. It's the least I can do."

Larry got out of prison, finished his studies for the priesthood, and became one. He went back and hammered on another weapon, this one a war plane that shot people in the Gulf War. When I brought him to college to talk with my students, he told us about John Ryan, an FBI agent who had been assigned to investigate the movement of which Larry was a part, the Plowshares movement. He showed us the story, with a photo of Ryan, and said affectionately, "He's my FBI agent." Ryan had been told to look into the Plowshares movement and the Veterans Fast for Life as terrorist movements. When he reported that neither warranted any further investigation, that both movements were nonviolent and only practicing open dissident activity with US foreign policy in our democracy, he—a career FBI agent—was fired. (Everett: 215) Larry proudly told us of his friendly conversations with Ryan when the investigation was open and of his delight that Ryan subsequently went on to become involved in the Catholic Worker movement himself. Morlan, a Catholic, had, with other Catholic role models, presented himself to fellow Catholic John Ryan just as the FBI agent was looking for something more substantial with which to identify. The transformation was Ryan's and the mentorship came from those with whom Ryan shared so much spiritual tradition. Our actions do indeed find fertile soil just when we least expect it, just when we believe them to be the most hopeless. At times, we can see the connections, like a bolt of lightning tracing a point from the clouds to the oak tree below. Most times we cannot; the points of interaction sometimes take years to yield effects. But when we know that others have helped people to transform, from person to person, we can develop hope and faith that we, too, may act with some effect, however great or small, when we act in conscience, nonviolently.

Presenting a choice to those with whom we identify in other ways is what these changes are all about. Phil Berrigan and Kathy Boylan—two radical pacifist Catholics who have each acted many times quite boldly to honor the nonviolent Jesus they hold in their hearts—influenced Larry Morlan, who, in turn, influenced John Ryan. How many young activists has John Ryan, in his turn, influenced by his act of witness from within the FBI and then as a volunteer in the Catholic Worker community? Once again, we see an individual's power to help transform society toward what MLK called the long arc of history toward justice.

economies of war and peace

The prevention of deadly conflict has a practical as well as a moral value: where peace and coöperation prevail, so do security and prosperity.

—Carnegie Commission on Preventing Deadly Conflict (Carnegie: 165)

It is not by coincidence that the world's great economic powers also have been the world's political and military powers: overseas dominance by corporations requires overseas dominance of government. A chief purpose of American foreign policy has been to keep as many nations as possible available to the maximum free reign of its corporations by whatever means necessary: loans, grants, technical assistance, treaties, threats, penalties, subversion, military assistance, and as a last resort, direct military intervention.

> —Susanne Gowan, et alia, from the Movement for a
> New Society, 1976 (Gowan: 73)

"Don't take it personally," might be the message from the geo-hegemon to the various identity groups who feel oppressed globally. While the US is constitutionally devoted to freedom within its borders, and to freedom everywhere by its Declaration of Independence, so too was the Soviet Union, for that matter. Pieces of paper seem important at the time, but the reality on the ground is dispositive; when the US trains the Indonesian military for a quarter of a century to commit unspeakable acts of brutal oppression toward its minority population on the illegally invaded island of East Timor, then reading a label that says "Made in Indonesia" may as well say, "Made under coercion by East Timorese oppressed by US-backed military dictatorship." Is the virtual genocide intentionally supported by US consumers, by the US government, by the Pentagon, or are we just innocent sideliners in such a situation?

These are vital, essential questions for those who might wish to help resolve identity conflict globally; we would go a good long way toward such a resolution by eliminating the export of military matériel and training. That initial step certainly wouldn't end identity conflict around our beautiful Earth but it would save some of those conflicts from going past hatred to shooting wars in some cases, which would save untold numbers of lives lost to ethnic conflict annually. Our nuanced, finessed skills at the negotiating table have little value when no one can hear us for the sound of jackboots marching and rockets launching. The end of ethnic conflict is not going to happen in this new millennium, but the replacement of violent conflict management by nonviolent conflict management is possible and is crucial to the endless but nonviolent management of our identity conflicts on our planet.

smart sanctions and a peace economy

> *Sanctions are likely to be most effective when they target the decisionmakers responsible for wrongdoing and deny the assets and resources that are most valuable to these decisionmaking elites. At the same time, care must be taken to avoid measures that cause unintended humanitarian hardships or inadvertently enrich or empower decisionmakers or criminal elements. The essence of smart sanctions strategy is tailoring sanctions to meet specific objectives and focusing coercive pressure on particular groups and resources.*
>
> —David Cortright and George Lopez, Kroc Institute
> peace studies researchers (Cortright: 223)

International conflict

Like a dumb gravity bomb, some economic sanctions are mostly good for terrorizing a population with widespread collateral damage. The results have been most painfully apparent in Iraq. Smart sanctions, on the other hand, can force belligerents to the table by using measures that impact the ruling elites most and the general populace least.

Smart sanctions applied internationally can achieve the desired effect when they include measures that, for example, cut off the arms necessary to keep a ruler in power. Certainly the general populace is only made safer by those, fundamental sanctions. Indeed, using arms embargoes as a first step on a routine basis may pave the way for more regional arms limitation or even elimination agreements, such as that signed by 16 West African nations. In any event, the power of a rogue ruler is weakened sooner or later by an effective arms embargo, even if that embargo is leaky—that is, even if the ruler finds a black market or gray market buyer here and there. Clearly, the stronger the arms sanctions are, the more immediate and more effective the instrument.

Travel bans also affect the elite much more than they do the lowest classes. (Cortright: 223) This kind of measure not only pins down the offending elite, but it stops effective international dealmaking for the business class in the country being sanctioned—or at least vastly cramps it. In this case, care must be taken not to alienate the middle class of the nation in question. This is usually most effectively avoided through serious and honest outreach. This has been effective in the past in nations such as the Philippines, where the middle class grew to feel discouraged with the Marcos regime because it stained all of them with his brutal, militaristic rule. International opprobrium thus weakened the Marcos rule as it caused his own middle class to disaffect from his government.

Freezing financial assets of the offending parties when possible makes an impression almost entirely on those rogue dictators, not on their oppressed people. Due to the murky world of international banking, this is often tricky, but even leaky freezes are more effective and isolating than no attempt to do so.

The tool of economic sanction is not new, but its prominence rose dramatically in the post-Cold War 1990s. From the inception of the UN until the end of the Cold War (45 years), some 647 instances of the use of Chapter VII instruments transpired. In the 1990s alone, there were 620 attempts to affect the behavior of nation-states through the use of such mechanisms. (Cortright: 1) We are now in a period of reassessment and reworking of the principles of such tools; we hope to devise precision instruments to replace the kind of economic bludgeons used against Iraq to such indiscriminate and tragic effect. While sanctions alone may not achieve the desired result, they tend to work best in a milieu of other tactics. Further, the efficacy of sanctions is no more guaranteed than the results of military action. Any action produces winners and losers, with the rare exception of transformative conflict resolution, and sanctions are an attempt to, at the least, cause a lessening of the horrific effects of brutal dictators. They offer some hope and they offer an alternative to bloodshed if designed well.

While most international sanctions are the product, in the end, of a UN resolution, sanctions can be initiated by one individual, or by a small group of active citizens. In July 1985, as South African Prime Minister P.W. Botha declared a state of emergency in 36 magisterial districts of the Eastern Cape, the East Rand, the Vaal Triangle and Johannesburg, the police, army and Special Forces abused this unlimited power immensely, engaging in even more widespread torture, mass arrests and assassinations. As human rights activists in Europe and the US launched boycotts of businesses doing business with South Africa, foreign investors began unloading South African shares. Banks in the US, under divestiture pressure from citizen activists, decided to stop rolling over loans to South African borrowers. (Merideth: 360) A cascading chain of events began to alienate the South African middle class from its own reactionary apartheid government, leading eventually to a transitional government and finally to an end to apartheid. That process was greatly affected by so-called citizen diplomacy, the power of the NGO, the role of those who can't wait, morally, for the entire elected government of a nation or the UN Security Council or the UN General Assembly to take a stand. College students pressuring their Boards of Trustees to divest in South Africa were more important than were the cabinet officials of the Reagan regime, which at that time was stalling, calling its relationship to a bloody rogue government in South Africa "constructive engagement." The people of the US helped start the movement that first began to budge the intransigent South African rulers and also handed Ronald Reagan his first political defeat when Congress eventually voted to end his uninvolved policy.

Learning from similar movements against massive institutionalized injustice elsewhere in the past can help modern movements succeed. We know that these macro-injustices include, for example, slavery and the Jim Crow sequelae in the US, the caste system in India, and others—all of which were supported foundationally by legal, educational and other socially systemic and thus complex institutions. (Ashmore: 232) Gandhi's struggles against the caste system in India informed the US Civil Rights movement and that movement in turn informed hundreds of other movements around the world, including the local, then national, then regional, then continental, then hemispheric, then global movement to end apartheid. Economic sanctions proved critical to many of these struggles.

Sexism and the war system: feminism and peace

> *Arise, then, Christian women of this day! Arise, all women who have hearts, whether your baptism be that of water or of tears! Say firmly:* "We will not have great questions decided by irrelevant agencies. Our husbands shall not come to us, reeking with carnage, for caresses and applause. Our sons shall not be taken from us to unlearn all that we have been able to teach them of charity, mercy and patience. We, women of one country, will be too tender of those of another country, to allow our sons to be trained to injure theirs." *From the bosom of the devastated earth a voice goes up with our own. It says: Disarm, disarm! The sword of murder is not the balance of justice. Blood does not wipe out dishonor, nor violence indicate possession.*
>
> —Julia Ward Howe, *Appeal to womanhood throughout the world*, September 1870 (McAllister: 76)

As the war system became industrialized in the nineteenth century, ironically, it helped to create what is arguably its own most serious enemy: the large class of educated women. Primitive and agrarian societies generally held women down with no hope of betterment, which meant that the war system was essentially impervious to the influence of women. If there is no hope, there is no vision; if there is no vision, there is no action. When women began to get educated, they began the long process of integrating women's values into the decisionmaking bodies of societies.

Feminism began as something of a systemic struggle against war, patriarchy, poverty, classism and inequality. That is what Elise Boulding means by social or humanist feminism. As that initial feminist wave—a long wave, beginning in the US with abolitionist women whose good work preceded the American Revolution and whose leadership might have kept the revolution nonviolent if women had been more widely involved—gave way to the second wave of equity feminism pioneered by the National Organization of Women and others, the social content narrowed. Soon, the sole criterion for some feminists became equal pay for equal work, a worthy but quite tiny step. Women grew shoulder pads and adopted tough corporate behaviors in the name of liberation and didn't use the vote to gain peace but rather justice for themselves within a subculture of elitist global domination. Some of the social feminists—still out to make a peaceable and just world—

were aghast and asked their equity feminist sisters, *Why would you want to be like men? You can do much better.*

In the early days of women's suffrage activism, some men were chary of women voting because they were concerned that the nation would turn soft and be unable to properly wage war. Clearly, with the narrow focus of women's issues since gaining the vote, that has not been the case whatsoever. One might logically ask the ghosts of the women who promised peace once they got the vote what happened. After all, women were in leadership positions in many movements for social change long before they got the vote; some examples include free public education, labor rights, poverty relief, and child labor laws. (Conway: 7) Certainly the formation of the Women's International League for Peace and Freedom—founded before women could vote—was a hopeful portent that didn't materialize in a majority opinion against war.

Founded by ordinary women from countries all around the world during the first World War in 1915, WILPF has a long and distinguished history of acting for disarmament, for justice, and for peace. In fact, they were the voice of sanity, for conflict resolution, for mediation, and they made those views known publicly in Europe when that awful war was less than a year old. (Burkes: 6) Had WILPF been listened to then, not only would WWI been vastly shortened and most of the eight million mortalities averted, World War II would almost certainly been avoided as well. WILPF offered a path to humanity—and still offers it almost 90 years later—that would lead us away from one model of conflict management to a better method. Their members were harassed during World War I, arrested and killed or forced to flee by nazis, and were called before the House Un-American Activities Committee during the McCarthy era. It could be said—admiringly—that WILPF were the witches the disturbed Republican senator from Wisconsin was hunting.

WILPF was instrumental in promoting various international measures that today make up a serious portion of the corpus of law that forbids certain behaviors in war, including the possession of some weapons of mass annihilation. (Bussey: 66)

If anything, the ongoing dichotomy of war and peace in the light of women's vote shows the prevailing split in direction. Individual women—Boserup, Masini, Meadows, Henderson, Maathai, Shiva and more—have made tremendous contributions to the advancement of consciousness. (Boulding: 109) Margaret Mead and Alva Myrdal were two of special significance toward the creation of a peace system. Again, persistence is at the core: "Giving up is not worthy of a human being," said Nobel Peace Laureate Myrdal. (Boulding: 110)

The global sisterhood movement seemed to emphasize the non-hierarchical power with others that tends toward peace and justice. From the

International conflict 115

Hague conferences onward, the hope in these organizations has been realized partially and then dashed, only to be further realized again. The social feminists are working against the war system and towards a peace system in creative ways that are a model for the peace movement as a whole. That they haven't ended the war system is only because they need more women involved, not because they are doing anything ineffectively. They are making the ties between poverty, poor health, infant mortality, justice, a damaged environment, capitalism, patriarchy, central control, hierarchy, and war. These are the connections that need to be made.

The information generated and shared through the global women's organizations "is almost like a new lifeform, encapsulating everything that scholar-practitioner-activist women of the twentieth century have worked to achieve, in an actual systems transformation." (Boulding: 113-114)

The pioneering peace system visionaries whom Boulding describes are models for peace system building. Included are:

- Kamaladevi, the Indian woman who worked to lead *satyagraha* (nonviolent campaigns), community development and interposition. (Boulding: 114)
- Marjorie Sykes, another disciple of Gandhi who joined Vinoba Bhave for a brief time in 1957 when the *Shanti Sena* was reinvigorated, though she elected to train smaller numbers more intensively. (Boulding: 115)
- Muriel Lester, another of the *Shanti Sena* volunteers, did most of her work mediating between Japan and China over the Manchurian question in the 1930s. She was the Traveling Ambassador for the International Fellowship of Reconciliation and did mediation in numerous global conflict areas as a private citizen working for an NGO. (Boulding: 117)

Lester found herself invited to speak in Latin America during World War II and was interred by the British forces there for her antiwar views. Suspected of being a nazi sympathizer—since, in a bloody conflict, all people are labeled as either for or against one or the other side, as though there is no possibility for a third, fourth or fifth position—she was closely questioned when her searched papers revealed, for example, that she had used a German word in her diary: *Zeitgeist*. "I couldn't help laughing," wrote Lester, and she was locked up in a concentration camp in Trinidad in 1941 with others who constituted a dangerous element—mostly traveling German businessmen or, of all non sequitur situations, Germans who had fled nazism, including approximately 150 Jews. Lester was thus imprisoned until FOR in England "raised a fuss" and she was deported home, first to prison in Glasgow, then prison in London, then out when FOR colleagues finally succeeded in obtaining her release, at which time she continued her pacifist speaking and listening tours during the war. (Deats: 216)

weapons of mass destruction or mass instruction?

> *We endeavor to hold life sacred, but in accepting our roles as the victims and the perpetrators of nuclear mass slaughter we convey the steady message—and it is engraved more and more deeply on our souls as the years roll by—that life not only is not sacred but it is worthless; that, somehow, according to a "strategic" logic that we cannot understand, it has been judged acceptable for everybody to be killed.*
>
> —Jonathan Schell (Schell: 153)

> *I stand on the deck of a nearly finished Trident submarine, a household hammer in my hand. I tremble, my knees weaken. What am I doing here? This is the most deadly weapon in the world; more than 2000 Hiroshimas are under my feet. I feel weak, powerless. What can I do? With my sisters and brothers, I, an ordinary woman, can hammer this nuclear sword into a biblical plowshare. In faith I hammer.*
>
> —Marcia Timmel, of her part in the 14 November 1982 Plowshare witness on board the USS Georgia (Gallagher: 47)

As war has worsened historically, or as xenophobia and populist demagoguery has increased the climate of hate and objectification of the Other, military means have degenerated into acts of great barbarism. In World War I, 100,000 were killed in choking, blistering agony by chemical gas weaponry. (Ehrlich: 161) We saw this in World War II, as the hatred for the nazis led Allied forces to bomb civilians—something Roosevelt and others decried early in the war as uncivilized behavior on the part of Italian fascists and German nazis. In the end, the brainwashing of the populace was so complete that it condoned the incineration of entire cities in Germany and Japan, both by waves of conventional bombers and finally by atomic weaponry. Very few military voices were raised internally against these unsoldierly practices, just as very few voices were raised in the media and in society at large.

And as peace movements and antiwar movements have confronted the military with nonviolence, social norms change within the military. We have seen that dramatically with regard to nuclear weapons, which, at the end of World War II were seen as a blessing, as the key to ending the war, as a preventative to the necessity to invade Japan. But the movement to eliminate nuclear arsenals, which began right after Hiroshima and Nagasaki were destroyed, never entirely quit, kept raising the questions, kept resisting with nonviolence, and indeed has been the reason that some are still imprisoned to this day. During the 1980s and the Reagan nuclear build-up, literally scores of thousands were arrested around the world in nonviolent antinuclear actions, while the brains of some of the best and brightest were working to understand the true concept of these weapons in search of a doctrine.

Finally, one by one, at least a part of the military itself has reflected the civilian disenchantment with these obscene tools of omnicide. From the beginning, the nuclear mission following the end of World War II was supposedly deterrence. But deterrence demands credibility and we haven't used a nuke in war since 9 August 1945. In 1960, General Maxwell D. Taylor was still writing about nuclear weapons as unusable and as a deterrent. By 1984, Admiral Noel Gaylor was saying he could imagine "no sensible military use for nuclear weapons" of any size or configuration. In 1992, following Desert Storm, General Norman Schwartzkopf dismissed the idea that nukes would have been used in any conceivable Persian Gulf scenario. In 1994, General Charles Horner declared nuclear arms obsolete and recommended unilateral atomic disarmament. A bit more than a year later, retiring nuclear strategic commander General Lee Butler said the same thing and General Colin Powell actually began ordering the mothballing of several classes of nuclear battlefield weapons. (Schwartz: 167+) The list of nuclear critics from within the military simply depended on changing mores outside the military, in society in general, and upon the transmission of those norms into the military through robust nonviolent action and loving challenge to those who believe in honor. Society is mirror and molder of media and military alike; the dialectic is endless and will go forth to improvement or slide back into violence and immorality if we are not vigilant, as was demonstrated so amply when we bombed Hamburg, Cologne, Dresden, Frankfurt, Tokyo, Hiroshima and Nagasaki from the physical high ground and moral low ground—despite our condemnation of such tactics earlier in the war when employed by the enemy. When Butler made his extraordinary 1996 public declaration against nuclear weapons after a career running that very arsenal, he was joined by 59 other retired senior military officers. (Feiveson: 282) Butler stated that his decision to be public about his disquiet with nuclear weapons was precipitated in part by the brave and aroused nonviolent resisters who made the French decision to continue nuclear testing in the South Pacific so unpopular earlier that same year. He also cited the influence of various nonviolent resisters, who, in their willingness to take risks, demonstrated to him that not all citizens were in denial over the potential effects of "his" arsenal.

Paul Magno and Marcia Timmel, two Catholic nonviolent nuclear resisters, demonstrated their opposition to nuclear weaponry and did so in ways that entailed great risk to themselves. First, Marcia climbed aboard a Trident submarine with other ordinary citizens of conscience and hammered on it in an act of faith and high risk. She could have been shot. She was arrested. She went to prison. She survived and she and Paul—who himself hammered on a nuclear weapon missile in Florida on 22 April 1984 and who served some prison time for his daring act—started a family and lived in a Catholic Worker community. (Gallagher: 49) Paul is a jovial man, joking with us at the Dorothy Day Catholic Worker home in Washington DC and yet, underneath that Italian-American conviviality is a smoldering resolve to act in accordance with his beliefs. Acts like these helped convince Butler that he, too, could take a risk and activate his conscience to some degree.

two brands of tuna

> *We must not be depressed by the election of George Bush. One can hardly argue that the American people have gone wildly conservative when half of them chose not to vote and the other half voted for their candidates with about as much enthusiasm as one feels choosing between two brands of tuna fish in the supermarket.*

—Howard Zinn (Zinn, 1991: 94)

In short, like the practice of democracy, or like the heartbeat of any life, ceaseless activity is required for maintenance of good social behavior. There is no permanent end to human violence, there is permanent opportunity for change in whichever direction we are pulled. That calls us to be pullers, pushers, shakers and movers for some part of the rest of our individual lives.

A caution about feeling in the wake of terrible events that we are too late to do anything. This is never the case. Those who make war prepare the trajectory plan for the next attack with every current attack; only when we stand in their path will we give them pause to consider a different response. Those who favor the commission of such acts of great violence, or the development of new tools of violence, try to accomplish as much as they can before they are discovered so that they can present it as a done deal. "Experience show that most citizens accept a forthright *fait accompli* with little protest or disorder," wrote psychologist Gordon W. Allport. (Allport: v) While Allport wrote this about the advisability of changing segregation laws to integration laws even before *Brown v Board of Education* in 1954, he is making a statement about a phenomenon that usually facilitates a negative, undemocratic action. The need for intervention against violence is crucial anytime, even if in the aftermath, because the cycle is endless unless we intervene. It truly is up to each of us to take moral and active stances or be a part of an apathetic slide back toward the violent behavior that so many are so

International conflict

easily drawn to in a crisis or in a search for profits at any ethical price.

Weapons of mass destruction—nuclear, biological and chemical (NBC)—are weapons of mass instruction every day. We either accept the social norm that it is permissible to threaten to annihilate millions of children or we do not. Platitudes like "freedom" are non sequiturs in association with such arsenals, as Hannah Arendt noted back in 1963. "Downright ridiculous," in fact, "not even hollow." (Arendt: 25) Perhaps it took a German—one who listened to the nonsense about war, glory, *lebensraum*, and that old canard, *Dolce et decorum est, pro patria mori*—"It is sweet and fitting to die for the Fatherland." We either act on the obscenity of the funding, development, testing, manufacture, transport and deployment of such weaponry, or we don't. We are part of that societal decision literally every day of our lives and we are sending a message to the children each and every day that we are silent. The message is, of course, that we accept the decision that it is allowable to kill the Earth and Her creatures, that we may destroy Creation in the name of a transitory offense to our ideological preference, our economic systemic choices. That these arsenals still exist is quite an education for our young people. They are powerful in their lessons and diminish the moral capacity of our society moment-to-moment. Can we threaten entire cities with these weapons—which we continue to do by the deployment of thousands of citybusting nukes—and not expect more attacks on our civilians, such as the terrorism of 11 September 2001? Haven't we deemed such destruction relatively minor by our reliance upon arsenals that, if launched, would indeed not merely dwarf the 9.11.01 attack, but make it a blaring but irrelevant tune-up note to the final atonal cacophony of mass civilian biocidal warfare? What kind of ethical ambiance do these weapons create? They define what we are willing to accept and we accept much worse for our enemies than we do for us, which opens us up in turn as targets.

> *In the autumn of 1962 came the Cuban missile crisis. The mayor of Atlanta wired President Kennedy that all Atlantans supported him (in going to the brink of nuclear war). That could not be permitted to pass, and so a handful of Spelman faculty members together with staff of the Student Nonviolent Coordinating Committee (SNCC) set up a picket line in downtown Atlanta.*

–Alice Lynd (Lynd: 51)

The Spelman teachers took their responsibilities quite seriously that day, and their colleagues in SNCC did too. They helped educate each other, Spelman students, and the Atlantan public. They removed themselves from complicity in the crimes that were being contemplated in the war rooms of the White House. And they helped inform Kennedy that his actions weren't entirely supported by a society so quiescent that it could countenance a meek acceptance of the killing of millions of Russian kids and the inevitable retaliation that would have done the same to us. The truly sad lesson, however, is that so many were so silent during that time.

Kennedy was not bluffing. Daniel Ellsberg was there, in the White House, as an advisor from strategic thinking Rand Corporation, during the entire crisis in October 1962. Not only did he assure us that Kennedy was not bluffing in his estimation, he reported in a workshop that I attended with him in 1984 that he had pointedly asked then-Secretary of Defense Robert McNamara if JFK would have actually gone to nuclear war, and McNamara assured Ellsberg that JFK would have. This kind of brinksmanship was particularly egregious and incredibly risky, but, in a sense, we are a part of that same game daily as long as those weapons are deployed on the fleet of Trident submarines and elsewhere.

Looks like democracy to me

Gossip is the opium of the American public.

—Howard Zinn (Zinn, 1997: 636)

In the aftermath of 9.11.01 the satiric tabloid *The Onion* published a piece that featured fictional interviews with Americans wondering when they'd be able to return to their vapid, superficial lives. The writing was funny because it was tragically true and simply brought the unspoken forward, warning Americans, for example, to possibly hold back on seeing the insipid film *Zoolander* until some healing had prepared us for total shallowness once again.

A quarter century ago, radical historian Howard Zinn made the same notations in a *Boston Globe* column, writing that, *Our most cherished moment of democratic citizenship comes when we leave the house once in four years to choose between two mediocre white Anglos-Saxon males who have been trundled out by political caucuses, million dollar primaries and managed conventions for the rigged multiple choice test we call an election.* (Zinn, 1997: 637)

Voting is the first step in exercising democratic obligations, not the last. Casting our opinion with a hanging chad or scanned digital marker is the least we can do, not the most. In fact, as we learn when we study nonviolent social change, we find that there are 12-year-old girls who accomplish more democratic social change than most "powerful white males" do in their entire adult lives. Children who decide, one day, to get seriously involved in some issue can approach their communities, engage in dialog, persuade people to act, testify, grant interviews, gather petition signatures, make phone calls, lobby and, in the end, cause a shift in public policy—literally years before they are eligible to cast their first official vote in an election. Individual nonviolent determination and persistence may effect more change than checking a box on a ballot, though the leadership may not advertise that to us.

Thus, when the US administration was beating the war drum in 1998, and then-Secretary of Energy Bill Richardson joined National Security advisor Sandy Berger and Secretary of State Madeleine Albright in a national tour promoting another attack on Iraq, they were met by an aroused citizenry at several turns. When Richardson came to Ohio, his speech was marred by a college student literally hanging from the rafters, shouting questions about the situation in Iraq. When Richardson then went to Minneapolis, protesters met him at the University of Minnesota, where Voices in the Wilderness activist Mike Miles dumped a bag of ashes on the speakers' dais, announcing that he had visited Iraq several times, had seen first-hand the lethal effects of American sanctions, and that the ashes represented the policies proposed by Richardson and others. In a television news report of the event, several in attendance were interviewed about Miles' demonstration. "Rude," said one. "Disruptive and childish," said another. But a smiling young man told the reporter, "I'm from the Philippines. It looked like democracy to me." Indeed, after running into mounting sentiment from irate demonstrators across the country, the Clinton administration did not, in fact, go to massive war against Iraq at that time. However temporarily, war was stopped by those who voted with their feet, with their mouths, with their bodies. None would cast an official vote until the next election cycle, but they had joined to alter public policy midterm in a democracy in other, creative, nonviolent ways.

Speaking up is powerful; that power is met by increasing state resistance. High school girl Katie Sierra wore an antiwar t-shirt to her Sissonville High School classes in Kanawha County, North Carolina following the bombing of Afghanistan by her nation—and she was thrown out of school. A local court has upheld the actions of the principal, but her case is now known internationally (if not much in the US), where she has become a symbol for the attack on civil liberties by the warring government of the US. Indeed, it came to my attention via a Serbian professor who found it in *The Times of India*.

Prisoners cannot vote if they are felons; indeed, some states never let them vote again. Does an act of nonviolent witness, that results in felony charges, remove a person from democratic decisionmaking? Dr. King was a convicted felon. It was after his felony conviction, in fact, that the US Congress passed the Civil Rights Act of 1964 and then the Voting Rights Act of 1965, arguably made possible by his leadership.

Even from the deepest bowels of the Bureau of Prisons, nonviolent resisters can influence others. On 9.11.01, many political prisoners were immediately grabbed and shoved in solitary confinement, some say to shut them up, some say to punish all "enemies" of the state. Phil Berrigan was one of those, in prison for hammering on a war weapon. Many of us found out about his additional punishment—for which he had done nothing except prove himself a cogent critic of the state over the years—and we wrote letters of protest to the BOP officials and US elected officials about it. Some wrote media outlets. The net effect of the round-up and lockdown was to prick more of us into action, certainly not the intention of the federal policy at that point. *Dear Tom*, wrote Phil on 23 September 2001, the day he emerged from "the hole," *Thanks to you and your friends. Your greetings came during 12 days in solitary after the tragic events of Sept. 11th. All through the fed penal system, the turnkeys used a broad broom to sweep the naysayers into segregation. Some are still there.* (Berrigan: 1)

Taking the vote from Phil Berrigan was the least effective way to keep him from having an effect on public policy, on the conscience of his fellow Americans, and on his own choices for personal action. Phil Berrigan's resolute, faith-rooted opposition to international violence doesn't stop that violence alone; it provides inspiration to others to work evermore robustly to eliminate war. There are times when, without such individual sacrificial inspiration, a mass movement never coalesces. With the challenge of such witness, mass movement is more likely. Mass movement in opposition to war waged by a nation-state will not, by itself, end the war, but if it is vigorous and nonviolent and has other prongs that extend into the halls of government, into various media, into the schools, into the courtrooms and into faith-based groups, that sum can end war from the bottom-up.

sources:

Aldridge, Robert C., ***First Strike! The Pentagon's Strategy for Nuclear War***. Boston: South End Press, 1983.

Allport, Gordon W., ***The Nature of Prejudice***. NYC: Doubleday Anchor Books, 1958. (original 1954)

Andregg, Michael, ***On the Causes of War***. revised (original 1996) Minneapolis MN: self-published, 1999.

Arendt, Hannah, "Freedom sloganeering as an excuse for war," in: Gioseffi, Daniela, ed., ***Women on War: Essential Voices for the Nuclear Age from a Brilliant International Assembly***. NYC: Touchstone, 1988.

Ashmore, Richard D., et. al., eds., ***Social Identity, Intergroup Conflict, and Conflict Reduction***. NYC: Oxford University Press, 2001.

Berrigan, Philip, personal letter, 23 September 2001.

Boulding, Elise, ***Cultures of Peace: The Hidden Side of History***. Syracuse NY: Syracuse University Press, 2000.

Burkes, Betty, panel discussant, "U.S. Military Bases in Japan: A Japan/U.S. Dialogue," 25 April 1998, Cambridge MA: AFSC New England.

Bussey, Gertrude, and Margaret Tims, ***Pioneers for Peace: Women's***

International League for Peace and Freedom 1915-1965. London: WILPF, 1980. (original 1965)
Carnegie Commission on Preventing Deadly Conflict, *Preventing Deadly Conflict*. Washington DC: Carnegie Corporation of New York, 1997.
Conway, M. Margaret, et al., *Women & Political Participation: Cultural Change in the Political Arena*. Washington DC: Congressional Quarterly Inc., 1997.
Cortright, David, and George Lopez, *The Sanctions Decade: Assessing UN Strategies in the 1990s*. Boulder CO: Lynne Rienner Publishers, 2000.
Deats, Richard, ed., *Ambassador of Reconciliation: A Muriel Lester Reader*. Philadelphia PA: New Society Publishers, 1991.
Ehrlich, Anne H and John W. Birks, editors, *Hidden Dangers: Environmental Consequences of Preparing for War*. San Francisco: Sierra Club Books, 1990.
Elhance, Arun P., *Hydropolitics in the 3rd World: Conflict and Coöperation in International River Basins*. Washington DC: United States Institute of Peace, 1999.
Everett, Melissa, *Breaking Ranks*. Philadelphia PA: New Society Publishers, 1989.
Feiveson, Harold A., ed., *Nuclear Turning Point: A Blueprint for Deep Cuts and De-Alerting of Nuclear Weapons*. Washington DC: Brookings Institution Press, 1999.
Gallagher, Michael, *Laws of Heaven: Catholic Activists Today*. NYC: Ticknor & Fields, 1992.
Gandhi, Mohandas K, *The Essential Gandhi: An Anthology of His Writings on His Life, Work and Ideas*, Fischer, Louis, ed., NYC: Vintage Books, 1983 (original 1962).
Gowan, Susanne, et al., *Moving Toward A New Society*. Philadelphia PA: New Society Press, 1976.
Handicap International, *Antipersonnel Landmines: For the Banning of the Massacres of Civilians in Time of Peace*. Second ed., Lyon, France: Handicap International, 1997.
Lynd, Staughton, *Living Inside Our Hope: A Steadfast Radical's Thoughts on Rebuilding the Movement*. Ithaca NY: Cornell University Press, 1997.
Merideth, Martin, *Nelson Mandela*. NYC: St. Martin's Griffen, 1997.
McAllister, Pam, *This River of Courage: Generations of Women's Resistance and Action*. Philadelphia PA: New Society Press, 1991.
Mitchell, Greg, "Real security: what is it? How can we get it?, in: Shah, Sonia, ed. *Between Fear & Hope: A Decade of Peace Activism*. Baltimore MD: Fortkamp Publishing Company, 1992.
Nagler, Michael, *Is There No Other Way? The Search for a Nonviolent Future*. Berkeley CA: Berkeley Hills Books, 2001.
Nesaule, Agate, *A Woman in Amber: Healing the Trauma of War and Exile*. NYC: Penguin, 1995.
Northrup, Jr., Jim, *Frags and Fragments: A Collection of Vietnam Poetry*. Sawyer MN: self-published, 1990.

Ryan, Charlotte, *Prime Time Activism: Media Strategies for Grassroots Organizing*. Boston: South End Press, 1991.

Schell, Jonathan, *The Fate of the Earth*. NYC: Avon Books, 1982.

Schwartz, Stephen I., ed., *Atomic Audit: The Costs and Consequences of U.S. Nuclear Weapons Since 1940*. Washington DC: Brookings Institution, 1998.

Smith, Perry M., *How CNN Fought the War*. NYC: Birch Lane Press, 1991.

Stoessinger, John G., *Why Nations Go to War*. Eighth ed. Boston: Bedford/St. Martin's, 2001.

Tabb, William K., *The Amoral Elephant: Globalization and the Struggle for Social Justice in the Twenty-First Century*. NYC: Monthly Review Press, 2001.

von Suttner, Bertha Sophie Felicia, "The evolution of the peace movement," in: Thee, Marek, *Peace! By the Nobel Peace Prize Laureates: An Anthology*. Paris: UNESCO Publishing, 1995.

Walter, Eugene Victor, *Terrorism and Resistance: A Study of Political Violence*. NYC: Oxford University Press, 1969.

Ziegler, David W., *War, Peace, and International Politics*. Second ed. Boston: Little, Brown and Company, 1981.

Zinn, Howard, "What does the Bush election mean for the oppressed and for our movements?" in: Farren, Pat, ed., *Peacework: 20 Years of Nonviolent Social Change*. Baltimore MD: Fortkamp Publishing Company, 1991.

———, *The Zinn Reader: Writings on Disobedience and Democracy*. NYC: Seven Stories Press, 1997.

SECTION TWO:

Planetary nonviolent transformation

introduction

> Will the invasion of Iraq really bring us closer to a more peaceful global community? I know from personal experience what the violent death of a family member does to the human spirit. To be honest, I am tired of the violence here and abroad. There has to be a better way.
>
> —Amber Amundson, widow of Craig Scott Amundson (Rai: 206)

> To some degree, the world will be a better and less violent place if each individual makes peace in his or her own life.
>
> —David Barash & Charles P. Webel, "Personal Transformation and the Future" (Barash: 538)

The transformation of one person presages the transformation of society. The power of one is insignificant, except that one person starts each trend, each change, each revolution in how we operate our collective enterprise. One person begins the introduction of each new social norm; one person initiates the movement of the middle, no matter how small that mass movement. Any discussion of the transformation of any nation, any culture, any society, must include a discussion of the transformation of an individual.

Any biologist can describe the "selfish herd instinct," that is, the natural tendency to stay in the middle, to neither risk being the first into the teeth of the unknown or the last straggler who risks being culled by any predator looking for a slow one, a stray one. Humans clearly show this behavior and the level of risk is highest for the brave ones who begin the struggle and the diehards who cling to the rejected paradigm after any great shift. The power of the whole is ineluctably linked to the power of the one. Amber Amundson, the young widow of Craig Scott Amundson, who died in the 9.11.01 attacks, is one of the brave ones saying no to revenge. She is pleading for a new way, looking for new ideas. She knows that she can make her personal peace, that she can refuse to contribute to the cycle of violence, and she wants to know how to proceed toward a systemic response to violence that won't, in turn, precipitate more of the same. Her sister-in-law, Kelly Campbell, described the growing sense of horror that family members felt when, gathered together on the East Coast right after the tragic attack, they were told again and again, "Don't worry, someone will pay for this," and they began to realize that other families were being brought into the gunsights of the US military in other lands, that other families would soon be experiencing the same overwhelming grief and loss that they were going through. They began to recoil. (Campbell)

In a dictatorship, said Ignatzio Silone's protagonist in the 1936 anti-fascist novel **Bread and Wine,** one person saying "No" calls the entire societal acquiescence into question. (Lynd: 113) That is the precise point at which every important sea change in group behavior has occurred in human history; one person says "No." Someone else may figure out what to say "Yes" to, but if nobody has the courage to say no, the phenomenon to which Irving Janis refers, "groupthink," is the prevailing modality for a society, which can lead to compound errors. At some point, dictatorship follows, not only an error itself but a system that produces faulty decisions and erroneous ethics.

It is hard to say no to power, especially because power always presents itself as benign or protective. Woodrow Wilson was elected as the peace candidate. Franklin Roosevelt was elected with a promise to keep the US out of war. Lyndon Johnson was the candidate of peace against warmongering Barry Goldwater. Richard Nixon was elected and reëlected on a platform of peace with honor and then a secret plan to end the war. Bill Clinton was the alternative to more war in the Mideast. Bush was reëlected because neither was the peace candidate. Each of the peace candidates, however, managed to continue or create another war, using rhetoric of peace all the while.

Indeed, Hendrik Verwoerd, elected to rule South Africa in 1948, was the architect of apartheid under the rubric of racial peace. For that matter, global capitalism calls itself free trade. Many innocent people died due to the poverty induced by both systems (apartheid and global capitalism) and both systems used (or use) military might to preserve inequality. By what paths can we bring the rhetoric of the powerful into line with the natural wishes of people for peace and justice? How may we effect transformation rather than simply hope for it?

> *Wishful thinking about the desired transformation of consciousness as an inevitable historical process distracts*

> us from studying the difficult disciplines that will make transformation possible.
>
> –Elise Boulding (Boulding: 55)

Resistance is key, and informed resistance is the beginning of effectiveness. People prefer to believe leaders who tell them nice things and do not normally choose the most bellicose-sounding candidate. Society elects or permits these (mostly) men and then must come to grips with holding them accountable, which is the hard part. Somebody must be the one to begin to first question and then refuse to go along with these leaders or democracy is little more than a husk of the original vision. Being the first to do so is excruciatingly hard. Being the second is still virtually impossible, especially when one sees the revulsion and opprobrium heaped upon the first one.

But each and every person who says no to despotism, to injustice, to pollution, to violence and to the destruction of the human spirit is crucial. Indeed, you are *sine qua non* to the attainment of a critical mass of those who initiate new social mores, evolved social behavior and general human advance. The young woman next door may be the one person who, by saying no today, helps society reach that critical mass that effects change. Perhaps the white-haired gentleman living in the government housing will simply read about a government act that is unjust and he will choose not to be vocal or active in his opposition until tomorrow. Maybe his silence will retard the time when social change occurs by one day and "just" one little girl will lose her chance to go to a decent school, or maybe "just" one baby will contract cancer from pollution because no one said "No" to negative power and "Yes" to justice and nonviolence.

Thus, I think we find, realistically, that each of us are crucial to stopping the bad and starting the good. The weight we individually place on each aspect in our lives is a decision that is quite personal and often makes sense to follow for some time before shifting to another mode. Gandhi certainly showed the world this model, doing nonviolent resistance to the point of incarceration many times and then taking several years to do other peacebuilding and nationbuilding activities he simply called "positive program." He went many years without engaging in a single *satyagraha* campaign while working on local and national self-reliance and intra-Indian comity between religions, communities and ethnic groups. Weaving homespun cloth was more important to him than nonviolent resistance for long periods of time. And when it came time to engage in resistance, he did so with his entire being.

There is always risk. There is risk in silence and risk in active involvement. We choose our personal risk, the level of risk to our loved ones, and the pace of collective change by our level of involvement. Recognizing risk inherent in *all* choices makes it just a bit easier to choose nonviolence and to choose activism, especially when we extrapolate the risks over time and to others.

Does the risk of nonviolent resistance necessarily imply that one ought to accept the legal consequences, even cheerfully with no fight, as Gandhi did? There is a fine line between cheerful acceptance of risk and failing to challenge the correctness of those risks. Legal theorist Ronald Dworkin, writing of the resistance to conscription during the war in Vietnam, noted that prosecutors have great leeway in when and whether to bring charges and could, if they wished, simply stop prosecuting those who nonviolently opposed an unjust government policy. (Dworkin: 51) The law is the law—until it is changed, or interpreted by officers of the court. The law is a basic component of any societal system. The law can be a part of a trend toward war or peace and the behavior of each juridical official and, in fact, every citizen, is important.

When we attempt to determine the role of violence in the affairs of huge groups of people who might shoot at each other, we look at a basic war system. The war system feeds on the human and natural resources of the Earth; it treats the masses of people poorly and pollutes the Earth. It institutionalizes inequality and consumes forests. It causes death by starving the poorest workers, by ruining the environment, and by imprisoning or killing those who work to end some aspect of its rule. It is a system in part because it sets up self-perpetuating cycles of oppression and violence, a reproduction of fighting from generation to generation. (Boulding: 16) Revenge breeds violence breeds revenge. Theft by raw invasion or by thin guise of "law and order" or "fighting communism" is theft that will eventually evoke demands for reparations and uprising. When the theft is accomplished with violence, it naturally elicits the desire to respond in kind, thus a war system of arms racing, arms dealing and periodic arms testing in actual combat. Everything is coldly logical to the war profiteers and hotly needed by those seeking justice by any means at their disposal, the perfect recipe for endless war and war preparation.

Global capitalism is the modern victor in the war system, though the Second World continues to shuffle along, trying to do its part to stay involved—albeit its involvement is more as a subservient host to the war system parasite than as a contending subsystem. While the owners of the multinational corporations live in Europe, the US, or Japan, even communist China hosts some production facilities for the B-6 bomber. McDonnell Douglas and Boeing use Chinese labor and cheaper facilities at the massive Xian Aircraft Company, located in the east-central interior. How, we may wonder, could such a state-owned enterprise be a part of a global capitalist system?

It "was one of the places where the competing multinationals met face-to-face." (Greider: 148) This is how a war system works, in part; there are no true enemies underneath it all, or maybe more accurately it is a truly anarchistic disorder, a Hobbesian world of "war of all against all." War, after all, requires anarchism at the level of relationship where violence is legal. And war requires at least as much coöperation as any peaceful endeavor.

That is the paradox of war; it is both competitive and coöperative. Failing to recognize that is, in the end, to vastly underestimate the ultimate enemy. Give the war system credit. It works, for now, for some. Give it blame. It kills, daily, hourly, by the minute. Resist the war system but realize how to resist it; by any nonviolent means at our disposal.

Peace: a movement, a tradition

> We would not go to war, many of us in the Catholic Worker Movement. Those were terribly dark and troublesome days for lots of us; we read and talked together and prayed together. It wasn't easy. We were opposed to Hitler and Mussolini with all of our hearts and minds. We had warned about fascism, what an evil it was, from the very beginning. We wanted to oppose Hitler; we did oppose him, constantly and actively, in every possible way open to us as Christians.
>
> —Dorothy Day (Coles: 99)

What is the difference between a peace movement and a peace tradition?

A movement is more broad and amorphous; a tradition often provides the small, marginalized prophetic inspiration for the larger movement—and the tradition may be otherwise inactive.

What are some examples of peace traditions?

- religious pacifism

A few minor religions or sects of major religions are pacifist, though they may also be completely inactive in organizing anyone to oppose war or violence. Thus Quakers and Amish both refuse participation in war, but only the Quakers are involved in actively opposing those wars.

- liberal internationalism

One wing of the liberal internationalists believed at one point that free trade and a robust global capitalist economy would bring peace, since war is injurious to most business. This theory proved false but did help to precipitate a minority business ethic toward peace.

- women's peace tradition

From the ancients who explored women's wishes for peace—*The Iliad* is sometimes thought of as a woman's cry for no war, as is certainly *Lysistrata* and other classical expressions of human longing for peace—to the modern origins of Mothers' Day as an antiwar holiday, women have bemoaned the loss of their sons and husbands to war.

- anti-conscriptionism

Many US immigrants fled to the US to avoid conscription, a process begun universally in France in the late 18th century and which spread as other nation-states amassed huge armed forces in response.

- conscientious objection

Several churches will counsel their young men to refuse to serve in armed forces as a religious tenet. The Mennonites, for example, have offered nonviolent noncoöperation to conscription for generations. When Mennonite Elden Birky was drafted in World War II, he refused. One member of his draft board told him that, if the law allowed it, he would prefer to simply shoot Birky and the other objectors. (Sabo: A25) The Mennonites do much more than resist the draft; they are off in large numbers doing service to the poorest of the poor around the Earth. The Mennonite Central Committee sends volunteers to the hot spots—many were immediately called to Afghan refugee camps along the Iranian border at the outbreak of the American bombing campaign—and those volunteers are often times more in harm's way than are soldiers.

- socialist anti-militarism

Part of original socialist thinking was that workers would refuse to be the fodder for the wars fought to benefit business.

- socialist internationalism

When the world was socialist, workers would have no reason to fight their brethren, according to this tradition.

- Comintern peace fronts

To deprive the corporate war profiteers their cynical control was the goal of this tradition.

- radical secular pacifism

Humanist and atheist pacifism is based on respect for the unique intrinsic value of each human life over the value of a border, an argument, an ideology, political control, an issue, a material or a resource.

- anarcho-pacifism

This tradition linked anarchism's value on individual freedom to pacifism's value on the individual life.

- Gandhian nonviolent revolution

A tradition in the sense that few ascribed revolution to Gandhian thinking.

- unilateral nuclear pacifism

A minority believed in unilateral nuclear total disarmament as contrasted to bilateral negotiated nuclear disarmament. Some—e.g. the Plowshares tradition—approached this mainly as a faith-based question.

- transnational antiwar New Left (60s)

This New Left rejected Leninism and the wars of capitalism too.

- ecological movement (70s & 80s) (Young: 229)

Using good organizing principles, we will do best to approach and incorporate these traditions into any campaign for nonviolence, growing a movement by large leaps instead of one person at a time. Who are the leaders? How do we speak to those traditions—do they have publications?

The art of peace: facing the music

"The quality of the peace culture in any given society can found in its art forms," writes Elise Boulding. (Boulding: 103) The arts are a part of the psychocultural identity of any group and are used to exacerbate or mitigate identity conflict in both positive and negative ways. In Nepal, the Movement for Restoration of Democracy, during its successful nonviolent phase, used traditional folk songs—*Jhyaura*—to communicate demands and causes. (Routledge: 349) Indeed, the nonviolent Baltic statehood movements of 1987-1991 refer to themselves as a "singing revolution," for the nationalistic song festivals that helped rally and inspire the end of Soviet domination. (Clemens: 35) Gospel certainly kept the center holding throughout the nonviolent struggles for African American freedom in the Deep South. Danes gathered in increasing numbers all during Nazi occupation to sing national songs in order to keep their sense of national spirit and thus the nonviolent resistance alive.

The military spent more money on marching bands than on disarmament talks during the Reagan regime; the rallying power of military music is well known, from the bagpipes to the trumpets. "Whenever I listen to Wagner," joked Woody Allen in one of his comedies, "I find myself wanting to invade Czechoslovakia." So, too, with nonviolent social movements. From the ballads of Joanie Baez to the South African freedom songs, music stirs elemental emotions and can inspire and empower peacemaking.

During the struggles to reaffirm treaty rights for the Anishinabe people in northern Wisconsin in the late 1980s and early 1990s, I was part of the initial Witness for Peace support for the nonviolent campaign undertaken by tribal folks. At some of the boat landings, where a handful of fishers and supporters were often confronted by mobs of up to 300 or more whites screaming racist epithets, the tribes would send in a drum, which is usually three, four or five members on a single large drum. The singing and drumming was peaceful and centering to tribal members and unnerving to the milling, shouting crowds. As the campaign went on, I began to hear bells, horns and whistles from the white mob, used in an effort to disrupt the drum. (Whaley: 166)

Stopping a war, preventing a campaign of civil resistance from turning violent—these are discrete pieces of a long movement to transform humankind to a peaceful, nonviolent species. We are equally hard-wired for violence and nonviolence, neurobiologically, so the choice is ours and the methodologies are innumerable. Each contributes, especially when seen as part of a greater whole.

humor

> *"Gee, that's a good-looking suit," said Jeff, pleasantly, poking fun at the grim-faced marshal who approached him with handcuffs and waist chain. "Did they have one in your size?"*
>
> —Sam Day, writer and nonviolent resister, of one of his cellmates in prison (Day: 216)

A disarming smile, joke, or wry observation is the heart of some people's approach to nonviolence, whether they call it nonviolence or not. Richard Pryor often said that his humor grew out of his fear and need to avoid being the victim of violence in his ghetto neighborhood. Tibetan Buddhist monks use humor in their political resistance to Chinese occupation. Sarcasm can provide some cushion against rage, just as humoring the oppressor by gently prodding them or by openly patronizing the most overweening of their behaviors can invite them to change.

At a large social event held at a Catholic Worker farm in preparation for an act of nonviolent resistance to a military base, Sam Day held forth in the center of the crowd, greeting old friends and offering endlessly humorous bits to all. One by one, he greeted each of us; Sam was quite blind the last several years of his remarkable life and so was keenly attuned to surprise. How could he be so ready to speak so personally to such a bewildering variety of people who simply said who they were once in earshot of Sam? I wondered. We usually have the advantage of visual warning first and thus have time to mentally prepare to exchange greetings, views, news and wit with the other person. Sam started from scratch each time, with a half-smile on his face, as though each person was The One with whom he could finally let down his (mostly non-existent) hair. I watched as Sam was greeted by a nonviolent resister fresh out of prison, wearing an electronic monitoring bracelet. Sam asked if he could feel the bracelet, which was on the woman's ankle. When she lifted her foot high as she could, she told Sam to bend over, to find the bracelet, and Sam did so, grabbing the woman's foot and earnestly speaking to the bracelet, "Hello, officer? Officer? Listen! We're having a great time here! We have plenty of food and good company! Come join us! Over and out, sir!" and Sam let the ankle go.

Sam wrote very serious articles for many years as editor of the *Bulletin of Atomic Scientists* and then as managing editor for The Progressive. His research was impeccable and his journalistic ethics were redoubtable. His fearless confrontation with militarism and repeated trips to jail and then to prison for nonviolent resistance are memorable in aggregate. But when I think of Sam Day, I think of the man who told a screaming two-year-old child in mid-tantrum whose mother seemed incapable of dealing constructively with the situation, "Carl: tuck it." I think of the old codger working a crowd for donations for some worthy group, making a great show during his transition to blindness of donating his magnifying glass to this organization, since it was so worthwhile and since he had such little money. Sam's memory lives most sharply in my heart in his combination of courage and humor, analysis and humor, persuasiveness and humor.

I've enjoyed a great deal of prisoner humor over the years. During a particularly long, tense day on the cellblock, skinny CJ rushed to the door to the outer hall, grabbed the bars and spoke for all of us when the guard came around at long last. "Hey, Big Tony! I want the phone!"

The guard looked at CJ, all 123 pounds of him, as CJ made his bold demand. As he turned to leave we all knew he would continue ignoring our request for the phone as he and the other guard had for the past several hours. CJ yelled at the burly guard—a man pulled from road duty for excessive violence, a man with a volatile temper and the demonstrated capability to react under the influence of that temper—"Tony! Don't *make* me come out there!"

We held our collective breath. Tony's visage darkened and he reached for his keys, taking a step toward the door where CJ gripped the bars. I laughed, hoping to draw attention to the humor of the moment that held so much threat for the ne'er-do-well recidivist CJ. CJ laughed and stepped back, "Just kidding, Big Tony," he said, hands in a palms-up shrug pose, as if to say, "I had to get your attention some way; we are really needing the phone and I thought being ridiculous might help. Are you going to continue to be ridiculous too, or can you laugh at my predicament and grant us the phone?"

Tony hesitated, lifted an eyebrow toward CJ as if to say, "That was ridiculous, since we both know I hold all the power here, so I'll choose this time to take your humor as temporary insanity and I'll get you the damned phone," which he then did.

Humor knocks the intimidator off-track. Humor gives our companions a breathing moment, some relief from the tension of the situation, a moment in which we can alter the expected trajectory of an event. By itself, it cannot achieve a nonviolent victory. But humor can open the door to places we need to go, even if that door swings shut again, and can give us a glimpse of what might be beyond.

CHAPTER SIX

Nonviolent histories,

transformative training

> One evil empire down, one to go.
>
> —Howard Zinn quoting a Michael Moore film (Zinn: 142)

> *These things are called ideals as long as they exist in the realm of ideas; they stand as achievements of progress as soon as they are transformed into visible, living, and effective forms.*
>
> —Bertha Sophie Felicia von Suttner, Oslo, 1906 (von Suttner: 214)

Human capabilities

> *The theory of evolution has been used to justify not only war, but also genocide, colonialism, and suppression of the weak....It is scientifically incorrect to say that war or any other violent behavior is genetically programmed into our human nature.*
>
> —*Seville Statement*, 1986 (Groebel: xiii-xiv)

Are humans hard-wired for war or for peace? The answer is yes. Fine minds bring considered conclusions to the question, but those who come down on one side or another are ultimately revealed to be only half-right, if that. Albert Einstein and Sigmund Freud, generally thought to have a few smarts between them, exchanged a few letters ruminating on this topic and came down on the side of war as an inevitable part of human nature. They were right about human nature and wrong about inevitable. The evidence proved them wrong when Margaret Mead—who was just as respected in her field of anthropology as the two guys were in their fields—pointed to tribal peoples who engaged in other methods of conflict management. A theoretical physicist can posit and prove the nature of matter. A theoretical psychiatrist can research and help us understand intrapersonal and interpersonal human emotional drivers, causes, and effects. But an anthropologist can show us exactly where some societies act in ways that are outside our normal understanding of human range, which is what Mead found and reported. Thus, it turns out that, as Boulding tells us, Mead showed that humans can construct a war system or a peace system. (Boulding: 3) It is not possible to say that it must be one or the other. Nobody can categorize the human mind that completely, as the eminent scientists told us in their joint statement from Seville.

Our attitude and aptitude toward making violence or making peace is then some combination of genetic predisposition and learned behavior—nature and nurture. (Boulding: 4) Indeed, a leading expert on how humans react to danger says it goes well beyond fight or flight, that we also can pose, submit or create a clever redirection. (Grossman) In short, we are hard-wired for creativity, for an unlimited number of responses. We are humans, and whatever our failings, we have more intellectual possible responses to danger than does any other species we have studied.

Options are in fact the human condition, unless we don't perceive them; perception is reality when it comes to choice, if not to natural consequence. That is a part of the bedrock philosophy of nonviolence; we can always choose to act nonviolently ourselves and the reaction of others is up to them. I can choose to dismantle a component of the arsenal of weapons of mass destruction—as I have, twice—and that is behavior for which I am responsible. Others who have accepted positions in the field of law enforcement are accountable for their responses to my act.

Similarly, each people collectively is responsible for its own behavior, its means of struggle, its conflict management methods. A people can be led to act viciously, violently, oppressively, unjustly—or the same people can be led to act with nonviolence, with compassion, with a fiercely confrontive but non-harmful modality.

The Druze—a tiny sect of fewer than one million, an offshoot synthesis of Shi'ite Islam with Christian, Hellenic, neo-Platonic and other influences—tend to live in the mountainous regions in the Middle East, from the Chouf Mountains of Lebanon, the Mount Hermon range crossing Lebanon into Syria, and the Carmel range in Israel, including the Golan Heights, an area lost by Syria to Israel in the 1967 war.

The Druze fighters have been highly regarded in the anticolonial war against the French in Syria, in the IDF and in the armed uprising in Lebanon against the IDF in the 1980s. When, in 1981, Israel tried to cajole, then compel, Druze in the Golan Heights—an area the UN said did not belong to Israel—to accept Israeli citizenship, most Druze refused, and one said, "Israel can do whatever it wants to us: they can confiscate our land. They can kill us. But they cannot tell us who we are. They cannot change our identity." (R. Kennedy: 196) Druze struck, many losing their jobs, they violated curfew to harvest crops, when gathered in crowds and told to disperse or risk being shot they refused, the nonviolent forces protected vulnerable IDF troops from harm, and this nonviolent campaign—waged fearlessly under mortal threat—was on the verge of victory when the Druze in Lebanon began to attack the IDF there. Israel cracked down on Druze everywhere, including the Golanis, and brutally forced identification cards on people so that they could move about, work and simply have a society. The Golani Druze have not engaged in violent uprising—so far. But they are an example of people deciding to wage combat either nonviolently or violently—and are an example of a warrior culture that switched in some places to a fierce nonviolence, disciplined and almost victorious.

There are many other examples of a warlike people who have undertaken to learn and practice militant nonviolence—examples of true transformation. The Pashtuns—not merely a warrior culture but a people who seemed to thrive on, and even seek out, violent conflict—led by Badshah Khan, were Gandhi's Muslim allies in the nonviolent liberation struggle against Britain. The "Servants of God," some 100,000 Muslims, were loyal to their nonviolent code, a transformative loyalty which, in turn, won Gandhi's loyalty to them, and provided him with much of his wish for a non-partitioned, independent India. The mountain people of what would become Afghanistan and Pakistan did not prevail in this regard, but independence from Britain was, in part, won with nonviolence by a people who loved to wage war.

We are all just people in the end; we all have failings but we can all be persuaded to try nonviolence and we can all learn how to make it more successful.

nonviolence and brutal tyrants

> On their first encounter, Dorothy was tired from her travel and wanted to focus on family needs rather than talk with an unexpected visitor. After a brief

> *conversation, she suggested Peter return another time. He was back the next day, animated with his plan to provide Dorothy with an entirely new education.... He wanted her to look at history in a new way which centered not on the rise and fall of empires but rather on the lives of the saints. He was certain that sanctity was at the center of what really mattered, and. that any program of social change must emphasize sanctity and community.*
>
> —Jim Forest on Dorothy Day and Peter Maurin, founders of the Catholic Worker movement (Forest, 1997: 56)

When those who believe in nonviolence meet the usual challenge, "What about Hitler, huh?" it often reduces our arguments to some form of faith-based absolutism. We have to admit that we don't know how on Earth to stop a Hitler with nothing but nonviolence.

Which is a sad moment for our logic circuits. We can do better. If we can't *imagine* how to resist Hitler, then we can read about how others did. Learning history is a bit like the scene from **The Hitchhiker's Guide to the Galaxy**, when one character—who is pointing a weapon at another—says, "Imagine I have a blaster in my hand and I'm pointing it at you." The other character says, "You *have* got a blaster in your hand and you *are* pointing it at me." The first one says, "Yeah, well, I didn't want to tax your imagination too much."

When the Catholic Workers were a tiny minority of oppositional pacifists during the grand mobilization to halt Hitler and his allies, they were reviled by most, seen as traitors to freedom, thrown into US prisons with scorn.

And yet, at the very same time, virtually every time mass organized nonviolence was attempted in confrontation with nazis, it succeeded. The non-Jewish women who sought to free their Jewish husbands from the SS prison in Berlin during the height of the roundup of all Jews nonviolently stormed the prison for days. They were warned they would be shot. They paused and fell back into the alleyways, and regrouped. They keened, they pressed forward and they exhibited a love that even hate-filled nazis couldn't resist. The Jewish husbands of these Aryan women were all released and were never bothered again.

And, when the nazis tried, in late 1936, to replace the crosses in churches with swastikas, the Christians in Oldenburg erupted in a "storm of indignation" and the order was eventually rescinded.

Further, protests by families stopped the gassing of the *Untermenschen*— the insane or those with birth defects—forcing Hitler to order a cessation of that direct killing, though starvation diets and lack of heat in winter quarters

Nonviolent histories 139

contributed to the decentralized killing of many additional victims. Still, there were no mass murders of those "undesirables" after 1941 as a direct result of outrage by the German *Volk.* (Stoltzfus: 92)

Similarly, the teachers in Norway defeated the Quisling nazi puppets by their absolute refusal to teach nazism, even when they were rounded up themselves and shipped to the far north to die in prison camps. And when the King of Denmark responded to the order of the occupying nazis that all Jews must wear a Star of David, he donned one too, starting a national movement that helped foil the roundup of Danish Jews.

Violence hadn't worked particularly well for the Danes. Their forces lost the entire country in one night; on 8 April 1940 the nation was still independent and by the next morning it was in German hands, overrun by nazi troops who captured 70 Danish soldiers without firing a shot at the Citadel in ancient Copenhagen, ending Danish hopes that Hitler meant it when he had signed a nonaggression pact with Christian X, the Danish king, in May 1939. Indeed, with the handwriting on the wall following Germany's invasion of Poland later that year, Denmark actually reduced its armed forces—the only European nation to do so during that war year.

The Danish perception—at least at the level of public discourse—was that Hitler would have smashed tiny Denmark into a bloody rubble-strewn pulp if she had resisted violently, and that the nonaggression pact could lead to a policy of *samarbejdspolitik*, of coöperation and limited retention of sovereignty. It appeared as though Hitler might win a short war for dominance over Europe and that the best policy for the society was to allow Germany to essentially take imperial control of the nation while Danes survived the ordeal. The king felt as though economic and political capitulation for the time being would allow his people to live in more numbers in a society with more infrastructure and with some shred of dignity instead of enduring humiliation and bloody annihilation.

German policy responded favorably to this mature attitude and the occupation of Denmark was in fact much less traumatic than any other in Europe. Troops were ordered to treat Danes as more or less junior partners in racially superior, civilized, nazi-led Europe.

Individuals, however, began to develop commonsense nonviolent resistance. 17-year-old Arne Sejr typed up and distributed his version of what it meant to be a good Dane during the occupation:

1. *You must not go to work in Germany and Norway.*
2. *You shall do a bad job for the Germans.*
3. *You shall work slowly for the Germans.*
4. *You shall destroy important machines and tools.*
5. *You shall destroy everything which may be of benefit to*

>   the Germans.
> 6. *You shall delay all transport.*
> 7. *You shall boycott German and Italian films and papers.*
> 8. *You must not shop at Nazi's stores.*
> 9. *You shall treat traitors for what they are worth.*
> 10. *You shall protect anyone chased by the Germans.*
> *Join the struggle for the freedom of Denmark!*
> (Ackerman: 212)

Sejr's Ten Commandments became a nationwide, sacred document of nonviolent resistance to the most brutal empire to sweep across Europe in centuries, perhaps ever. The spirit of resistance was also found in cultural expressions, such as widespread singing of Danish songs of national pride, and in journalistic rebellion to German censorship.

1941 saw a tightening of German internal power in Denmark and a lesson that resounds through history about the safety and power of violence versus nonviolence. When—upon Germany's invasion of the Soviet Union on 22 June—the Danes were ordered to round up all communists, they did so, justifying the arrest of more than 300 by noting that communists had a philosophy of exporting violent revolution and committing acts of terrorism. Even as the Danes were collectively powerless at that point, they continued to display nonviolent resistance; property destruction of nazi war matériel increased. Unexpectedly, the Germans handed the Danes a chance to collectively express themselves by allowing an election on 23 March 1943, and Danes did so in record numbers, spurning the Danish nazi party almost entirely, which got barely three percent of the vote. This awareness of national unity led to strikes, crippling German exploitation of the Danish economy. Sadly, one strike turned violent and Hitler ordered harsh measures inflicted on the Danes, now outlawing strikes and calling resistance organizing a capital offense. On 15 September 1943, SS battalions began arriving in Copenhagen to initiate the long-delayed roundup of Danish Jews. Nazi plenipotentiary Werner Best commanded the process and chose Rosh Hashanah—Friday, 1 October 1943, when Jews would be home—for the major thrust. One German nazi and many individual Danes made the famous rescue of the Danish Jews possible.

Georg Duckwitz, a German, was a confidante of Best's, and when he heard of the Rosh Hashanah plan, he phoned Danish friends, the Danish rabbis were notified, and virtually all Danish Jews immediately went into hiding. Danish fisherpeople began a heroic boat brigade to Sweden with Jews, saving 7,220 and losing 472 to German pursuers in early October.

Following a widespread continuation of Danish resistance, a German officer informed Christian X that the swastika would now be raised above the Danish castle, to which the king replied that a Danish soldier would then take it down.

> "That Danish soldier will be shot," the officer replied.
>
> "That Danish soldier will be myself," the king responded.
>
> The swastika never flew over the castle. (Ackerman: 229)

Others can recount the mass murders committed by nazis against a population of that tried its own form of accommodation, the Jews, but, as we have seen, all Jews were not rounded up alike. Even they were treated differently, depending upon nationality. Still others will tell of individual heroes who opposed nazism nonviolently, fearlessly, out of a deep Christian faith, and were summarily executed.

That was the case for Franz Jägerstätter, an Austrian born in 1907, who refused nazi conscription and was beheaded in 1943.

Jägerstätter was not political, but seriously devout in his Catholicism, and was the only person in his small village to vote against the Anschuluss, the German take-over of Austria, on grounds of religious freedom. He was drafted in February of 1943, refused to don the German army uniform, and was arrested and taken to prison at Linz, and then on to Berlin, where he stood military trial 6 July 1943. His letters just before his death reveal someone struggling to coöperate with authorities but simply unable to resist his own conscience. He wondered why God endowed humans with free will, for example, if they were then to blindly obey their government without criticism or question. He questioned his own worth as a father and husband—he had three little daughters—if he could love his family so much that he would go against what God wanted him to do. Jägerstätter also wrestled with what some call psychic numbing—the give-in to mass action and repetitive mass cultural acceptance of clearly objectionable behavior. And, in the end, he noted in a preserved notebook, a person of faith is held accountable for action as an individual. (True: 140) Jägerstätter died in obscurity, forgotten to history, yet another lesson in the futility of lone nonviolent action in the face of overwhelming violent power of the state.

Well, not quite.

Gordon Zahn, an American sociologist, ran across Jägerstätter's story in his research on German Catholic coöperation with nazis, and Zahn then wrote about the Austrian. Daniel Ellsberg, the brilliant Rand Corporation analyst who advised Kennedy during the Cuban missile crisis and who helped construct the Vietnam policy in the mid-1960s, came across the story of Jägerstätter and it stuck with him. Along with the challenge of another draft refuser, Randy Kehler of the US—whom Ellsberg heard speak just before Kehler's imprisonment—Jägerstätter influenced Ellsberg to release the Pentagon Papers, a stunning body of information on the truth about the US war in Vietnam that helped turn around public opinion on the war and thus ended the war sooner. (Hallock: 316) We are then left with the question, How many American and Vietnamese lives did Franz Jägerstätter save, some 25 years after his "pointless, futile" death? It is this kind of question based on this set of historical facts that calls into question the effectiveness of conscience even under extremely dubious and apparently hopeless circumstances.

So, *what about Hitler, huh?* Well, with a much more robust and widespread use of mass nonviolent noncoöperation, perhaps even nazism could have been stopped with nonviolence. It will forever be unknowable, but it is not beyond the imagination.

The problem with using nonviolence against fearsome, ruthless, beweaponed aggressors isn't that it doesn't work; it is that it is so counterintuitive that it is seldom tried, and when it is the success that might follow is regarded as a lucky fluke.

oppressed help others

Historically, the Huguenots have been an oppressed minority in France. When the Germans invaded and easily took over France early in World War II, most French coöperated with scarcely a murmur, allowing the Nazis to rule without committing many of Germany's resources. Even when Hitler ordered the round-up of Jews, the French coöperated.

Except in the Huguenot region. In the tiny region of Le Chambon, approximately 5,000 citizens risked their lives hiding an approximate equal number of Jews. Within that oppressed minority community, the most oppressed of all—women—were key in this effort. They were often the direct providers of food, shelter and security for Jewish children, women and men who were otherwise doomed to Nazi extermination camps. (Holmes: 81)

Thus, even during the darkest days of Nazi occupation and oppression, the lamp of liberty was kept lit, not just by chest-thumping violent men with arms but by those who understood through experience how to live with as much freedom and dignity as possible under any circumstances. By working to save the vulnerable ones, the people of Le Chambon were the spark of liberation for the entire nation of France, even though few have acknowledged it since. The French have been eager to ignore the far braver behavior of a small minority who clearly held to a standard much higher than most of the rest of her citizenry. That's one way nonviolent struggle is left out of the pages of history texts.

It is possible for a nation to live without a violent military—but it may not be possible for a nation to survive without some kind of defense force, which leaves us to consider a nonviolent force, a kind of disarmy. We are not, as we have seen, genetically programmed to wage war, but certainly conflict is ubiquitous. From the discovery of the Tasaday people on the island of Mindanao in the Philippines in 1971—who used no elements of war in their conflict management—(Yost: 65) to the Seville Statement of international experts in anthropology, psychology and sociology, as we know, humans are no more hard-wired for shooting than for singing, no more for slashing than for dashing, and no more for making war than for making love. War in the Philippines in 1986, had it occurred as a result of the two armies about to clash—the rebels and the Marcos faction guarding the presidential palace—would have been termed "inevitable," just as predictable as the bloody black-against-white war in South Africa. *Those wars never happened despite all conditions pointing toward war in both cases.*

If a people have a history that doesn't include using a military or any other form of violent collective self-defense, they have just disproven the theory that humans are biologically programmed to only resort to war to resolve conflict or deal with threat. If a people use mass nonviolence one time to achieve a social goal—national liberation, civil rights, freedom to practice religion, defending a sacred space, achieving democracy, winning a labor strike, getting the franchise, shutting down harmful businesses (drug dealers, slave traders or worker-exploiters, polluting industry)—the successful use of mass organized nonviolence disproves the claim that nonviolence cannot work.

There are many sources that document nonviolent successes; for much more, explore the source list following this chapter. We will look briefly at a few case histories (mostly India and the US Civil Rights movement) and we ought to solidly understand that nonviolence may be regarded as a faith-based philosophy—faith in observable, provable, documented history. Other faiths may lead to nonviolence and other faiths may bolster the tendency toward a strategic acceptance of nonviolence, but faith and philosophy ultimately are secondary for the bulk of the population in question; they are concerned with what works to gain themselves dignity and justice. "I know," wrote Gandhi, "that a whole people can adopt it without accepting it as its creed and without understanding its philosophy. People generally do not understand the philosophy of all their acts." (Gandhi: 189)

India

> *Gandhi used the traditional to promote the novel; he reinterpreted tradition in such a way that revolutionary ideas, clothed in familiar expression, were readily adopted and employed towards revolutionary ends.*
>
> —Joan V. Bondurant (Bondurant: 105)

India used nonviolence to gain national liberation from the British empire. The struggle lasted from approximately 1914 until freedom in 1947, some three-and-one-half decades. Hundreds of *satyagrahis* lost their lives. The counterfactual questions: *how many Indians would have been killed had they used violence? How long would it have taken?* India (1.27 million square miles) is half the size, geographically, as the US, and had several hundred million citizens during its independence struggle. A much smaller nation, Guatemala (42,042 square miles), used mostly violent methods to oust its military dictator. It took almost exactly the same amount of time, from 1954 until 1996, and approximately a *quarter million* Guatemalans lost their lives, many of them noncombatants. A similar comparison could be made to El Salvador (a mere 8,056 square miles, which lost 75,000 from a nation of 5 million in a two-decade civil war) and other nations who have engaged in long and bloody guerrilla wars for national liberation. Indeed, any look at any reputable historian's guide to the greatest wars and atrocities of the 20th century doesn't include India liberation or any variant thereof—the number of mortalities never rose to the level at which it was considered a war (usually at least 1,000 in any given year qualifies the conflict for status as "war.") The partition between India and Pakistan took half a million lives and Gandhi was absolutely opposed to it happening. Liberation from Britain of the entire population of the second-most populous nation on Earth didn't even register with the statisticians who compile these records. To contrast, a less-populous nation—Russia—lost 8,800,000 in its war of liberation. And the Soviet model was exported, willy-nilly, as being the best.

> *Perhaps the most persistent element in Gandhi is the recurring theme that non-violence is truth-creating....Means and end in Gandhian satyagraha are distinguishable only temporally. ...Non-violence becomes both the means and the end, and the terms become convertible.*
>
> —Joan V. Bondurant (Bondurant: 193)

Some say, well, the British empire only left India because it was weakened by World War II. This argument fails on three important counts.

First, that same argument is precisely the case for those militaries that gain victory; there is usually a nonviolent component to whatever war we wish to examine, and it could just as easily be claimed that the nonviolent factor was the reason for the military success. Historian Paul Kennedy recounts a complex set of such factors in his comprehensive *The Rise and Fall of the Great Powers: Economic Change and Military Conflict from 1500 to 2000*. The outcome of conflict is virtually never a simple set of variables; we might argue that the only reason Hitler lost Europe was that the nations of the world began boycotting his regime. He couldn't keep up, industrially, with the war materiel needs, but while he could, he was militarily victorious. Thus, nonviolent methods defeated his violence. No one would seriously credit nonviolence with winning World War II for the Allies, but the logic is just as compelling as the claim that nonviolence didn't win independence for India.

Second, irrespective of World War II, Gandhian nonviolence had weakened British resolve to maintain the imperial hold on India and it had been eroded from the bottom up by Gandhi's persistent and highly successful outreach to British citizenry even as he continued his outreach to his own people.

Third, violent revolution had been tried against the Brits and had only succeeded in stiffening the resolve of the empire in India. It could be argued persuasively that violent guerrilla warfare retarded the day of independence by providing the will and excuse to the British rulers to continue an increasingly unpopular situation of domination over a peace-loving and respectful people who only wanted independence.

As Kennedy points out, defeating the indigenous army is but one aspect of attaining and maintaining control over an area. When Napoleon scattered the Spanish army in late 1808, the success of his invasion looked "decided" to him. Then the peasants decided differently; they denied his troops access to food by any nonviolent means at their disposal even as Spanish business shifted their posture from hostility toward Britain and friendliness toward France. The combination revealed Napoleon's imperialistic overstretch and his hubris made it necessary to commit some 353,000 troops to Spain by 1811 to overcome local and nationalistic noncoöperation. Thus, while the Spanish army failed to stop Napoleon, the people helped to reduce his imperial advance. When that noncoöperation was repeated by the Russian people after their army was defeated by the French, the end of French imperialism in Europe was at hand. (P. Kennedy: 135+)

Of course, history as taught to us focuses on the Duke of Wellington, but without citizens engaging in nonviolent noncoöperation, the Duke would likely have failed to stop Napoleon at Waterloo. The reverse is also true; citizen coöperation will assist a budding imperialist every time. Without the enthusiastic support of the French people, Napoleon could never have raised

From Reconstruction to civil rights

The Old Man to the young

*Ain't gonna let nobody, Lordy, turn me 'round,
turn me 'round, turn me 'round,
Ain't gonna let nobody turn me 'round,
I'm gonna keep on a walkin', keep on a talkin',
Marching up to freedom land.*
—Traditional song, adapted by the Albany Movement, 1962 (Carawan: 62)

When a quarter million US citizens came to Washington DC—many of whom had been to jail for attempting to act like citizens, to vote, to mingle in public places—on 28 August 1963, one old man found the day particularly sweet. He was, after all, the man who dreamed the event. His dream made it possible for Dr. Martin Luther King Jr. to express to the world that he, too, had a dream.

Asa Philip Randolph was born in 1889, as black people were entering the long, dark oppression of post-Reconstruction Jim Crow segregation. As a young man, he rose through the ranks of labor and founded the Brotherhood of Sleeping Car Porters in 1925. He became the Vice-President of the AFL-CIO and a civil rights leader. Naturally, the state of oppression suffered by black Americans was generally glossed over and conveniently ignored by most of white majority society for most of Randolph's life. In 1928, as Randolph gained prominence in a world divided, popular commentator H. L. Mencken noted the opacity and duplicity inherent in race relations within the context of US America's self-image: "Every American is taught in school that all Americans are free, and so he goes on believing it his whole life—overlooking the plain fact that no Negro is really free in the South…In the same way he is taught that religious toleration prevails among us, and uncritically swallows the lie. No such thing really exists." (Mencken: 211)

Randolph was a strategic genius. He knew Mencken was right and was finally afforded an opportunity to develop gains as a result of the extreme disparity between paper democracy and reality for blacks. In 1941, as the war economy sprang from the ashes of the Great Depression, A. Philip Randolph watched his people stay mired in a ruined economy and he grew restive and then enraged. He delivered a message to the president: Either make sure that all monies spent by US taxpayers on goods from private corporations do not support unfair hiring, or face a "thunderous march" on Washington, the likes of which this nation has never seen. Franklin Delano Roosevelt caved at the thought and issued the FEPC order to do business only with corporations that practiced equal opportunity hiring. Randolph had just proven the deterrent value—the threat power—of nonviolence. Indeed, his march was more bluff than real threat, as little organizing had happened and it was only a week away when FDR had met with Randolph.

He continued to dream of such a march as he watched the war for democracy—fought by US soldiers of all colors—come and go, while segregation remained in the Deep South and the last hired, first fired ethos continued to keep northern blacks in general poverty. He talked about the march. Few were interested.

As the Civil Rights movement moved from its post-Montgomery boycott semi-quiescent period through its 1960 sit-in and equal-access phase and finally into the voting rights era, Randolph continued to clamor for his march. Now that the movement was beginning to reach a national audience, now that the results of the struggle could affect national politics by enfranchising a large disenfranchised constituency, a march on the nation's capital was making more sense.

Then Birmingham, Alabama, boiled over in the early summer of 1963, the battle lines were drawn, and the movement's five major organizations recalled Randolph's idea. Congress of Racial Equality, SNCC, NAACP, SCLC and the Urban League named Randolph director and asked him to do this thing. He brought Bayard Rustin on board—a hotshot organizer who had spent World War II in prison as one of the relatively few African-American conscientious objectors. Randolph, then 74, and the much younger Rustin went to work, delegating, contacting, and built a coalition of 1,500 groups.

28 August 1963 didn't just spring forth with a public notice; it was a massive organizing effort that changed history. It was a prong in a multi-tined attack on legal discrimination that emanated from the courts, from the streets, from the churches and synagogues, from the halls of legislatures, from the media and from the schools. The March on Washington attempted to catalyze a shift in the system and it succeeded. It took place in an atmosphere of 20,000 civil rights arrests at approximately 800 civil rights demonstrations in the nation during the ten week period leading up to it. (Lewis: 203) From it flowed the Civil Rights Act of 1964 and from it came an address that stirred the conscience of the nation and the world, Dr. King's *I Have a Dream* speech.

One man dreamt that march for a quarter century or more. He lived to be its titular head, its lead organizer. He was born with no vote in an era of terrorism in African-American communities and he lived to help bring change to his nation through mass nonviolent power. (Saunders: 4)

People Power in the Pacific

Democracy came to the Philippines in 1986 on the heels of mass nonviolent action.

The example of the Philippines is illustrative of two principles. First, that training pays off if we hope to substitute nonviolent people power for armed might. Second, that an imperialistic power can be evicted just as a colonial power proved to be evictable in India.

When the rebel troops of Defense Minister Juan Ponce Enrile and General Fidel Ramos were rumbling down the *Epifamio de los Santos Avenue*, the 10-lane main highway in Manila, Philippines, in late February 1986, the world was certain that we were about to witness the beginning of a civil war. After all, the tanks and troops loyal to US puppet Marcos were waiting around the presidential palace, prepared to defend their commander-in-chief. Imagine the surprise of the rebel troops when they were met by tens of thousands of Filipina citizens, determined to stop the threatened bloodshed by keeping the belligerents apart. Imagine the relief of the loyalist troops. Imagine the bewilderment of the international community at this unprecedented example of nonviolent interposition. Four days later, the government of Marcos—and thus the not-so-invisible hand of the imperialist puppetmaster US—fell. The international press offered no real explanation for this phenomenon and moved to another news story without ever explaining why.

Turns out that the nuns and priests had been offering nonviolent trainings and doing community organizing toward this day for about a decade. When the crisis came, Cardinal Sin himself got on the radio and called for the people to protect the armed forces from each other, and the nuns in habits and priests in robes led the people into the streets. (Diokno: 26) Like a military success that comes from endless exercise, drill, and training refinements, nonviolent people power is more likely to happen with trainings and planning and outreach to the citizens—even if it is on a very local basis. *Especially* if it is on a local basis.

Later, after the democracy was in place, elected properly and functioning, the Philippines asked the US military to leave, which they did. That, of course, was a great deal of why the people there wanted Marcos out, so that

Nonviolent histories 149

they could at last rid themselves of the imperialist armed forces, but there was essentially zero chance of doing so with armed force. It was incalculably more adaptive to do so nonviolently, achieving the same result with zero casualties that would have been a bloody and doomed proposition otherwise.

Increasingly, the notion of the citizenry "by-passing the national governments" (Glossop: 298) in order mitigate or eliminate violence is being used to great effect. The most salient example is the ban on landmines, a major international treaty achieved in record time by a coalition of non-governmental organizations and which took effect 1 March 1999. Other such coalitions are forming, e.g., the Hague Appeal for Peace, and 1997 Nobel Peace Laureate Jody Williams calls this phenomenon "the new superpower."

born to lead

> I think the first prerequisite of nonviolence is for the nonviolent person to assume that there are other feelings and not to impose. Trying to impose is a mistake a lot of non-activist nonviolent people fall into, just as they fall into the trap of thinking nonviolence is a land of milk and honey. Nonviolence is really tough. You don't practice nonviolence by attending conferences—you practice it on the picket lines.
>
> —Cesar Chavez (Forest, 2000: 227)

Cesar Estrada Chavez was born on March 31, 1927, into a poor family of Mexican-Americans who had homesteaded near Yuma, Arizona two generations before, but who lost the land during the Great Depression. His role in life was to work the agricultural fields, which he did beginning at age 10 as his family struggled through the loss of their land and into their life as migrant laborers. Cesar Chavez harvested the power of the people who had no power, he gathered it and shaped it and gave it all back to them, organized and nonviolent. More than any other factor, Cesar's nonviolent spirit and gentle guidance brought new rights to those who were told from birth and from entrance into the US that they had no rights.

Like many nonviolent leaders, Chavez began in a moderate, service-based organization and outgrew it. He worked for the Community Service Organization from 1952-1962, based in San Jose, California, providing information and advocacy services to Chicanos immigrants. Over this decade of experiential growth and classical organizing—CSO was begun as a spinoff from Saul Alinsky's Industrial Areas Foundation—Cesar began to see that one path to success for entire classes of people—not just individual holding actions—was to organize a migrant laborers' union. The CSO didn't support him in that, so he started the National Farm Workers Association, registering more than 17,000 families in the first three years. (Figueroa: 68)

Chavez united people with his persistence, his fearless field organizing in the face of hired thugs, and his experiential valuation of each person's and each family's ownership of the union and its methods. He went to the poorest of the poor and insisted that they support the union with money that they really didn't even have. This helped to guarantee buy-in, participation and devotion that in turn guaranteed effectiveness. Simply, Chavez saw the power latent in the organized people and tapped into it. Key to his success was his coalitional weaving of consumers to minorities, agricultural workers to students, and ethnic groups to each other (specifically Filipinos to Chicanos). (UCLA)

He also saw the power of the boycott in Montgomery, as Rosa Parks and Martin King sparked and led a movement that brought economic and then political pressure to bear upon forces that appeared invincible at first. Cesar initiated a boycott against the agribusiness growers and their products that spread across the nation, making it impolitic to eat table grapes or to drink certain brands of wine (no Gallo for nonviolent imbibers). He undertook several lengthy fasts and invited others to join him for all or part of them, including politicians, film stars and other high-profile message-amplifiers such as Bobby Kennedy and Danny Glover. The UFW remained nonviolent in the face of brute attack and realized most of its goals over a series of campaigns that continued through Chavez's entire life. A little man, born poor and destined for stoop labor and illiteracy, Cesar Chavez gave the world a lesson in empowerment and hope, persistence and steadiness. His faith in nonviolence was built on action and his action came from his faith in nonviolence.

principles demonstrated by UFW organizing

- get buy-in from everyone
- practice absolute nonviolence
- use economic pressure
- organize very locally
- organize nationally
- be inclusive and coalitional
- use creative, sacrificial tactics (e.g. fast)
- organize the organized (e.g. go to churches)
- use the moral language of the culture for nonviolence (e.g. Catholic church)

- promote nonviolence as a pragmatic and effective method
- get celebrities involved

The nonviolent history success stories are numerous and prove that humanity has a choice in how we strive for independence and freedom. Indeed, a military model makes a society more violent, more retributive, more prepared to give up civil liberties in favor of technical "security," and more willing to ignore all other damage inflicted on our lives, lifeways and livelihoods by the military. Nonviolence, by contrast, will gain us fewer material possessions, but honest people don't want other people's goods. Nonviolence is possible and its more honest, more democratic, more based on human rights, more ecological and much more life-affirming. And one person—no matter how long it takes—can dream a pivotal event that changes history toward justice, toward nonviolence.

sources:

Ackerman, Peter, and Jack DuVall, *A Force More Powerful: A Century of Nonviolent Conflict*. NYC: St. Martin's Press, 2000.

Barash, David P. and Charles P. Webel, *Peace and Conflict Studies*. Thousand Oaks CA: Sage Publications, Inc., 2002.

Bondurant, Joan V., *Conquest of Violence: The Gandhian Philosophy of Conflict*. Rev. ed. Berkeley CA: University of California Press, 1965.

Boulding, Elise, *Cultures of Peace: The Hidden Side of History*. Syracuse NY: Syracuse University Press, 2000.

Campbell, Kelly, presentation, Portland OR, June 2002.

Carawan, Guy and Candie, *Sing for Freedom: The Story of the Civil Rights Movement Through Its Songs*. Bethlehem PA: A Sing Out Publication, 1990.

Clemens, Jr., Walter C., "Baltic independence movements, 1987-1991," in: Powers, Roger S., and William B. Vogele, *Protest, Power, and Change: An Encyclopedia of Nonviolent Action from ACT-UP to Women's Suffrage*. NYC: Garland Publishing, Inc., 1997.

Coles, Robert, Dorothy Day: *A Radical Devotion*. Reading MA: Perseus Books, 1987.

Day, Samuel H., *Crossing the Line: From Editor to Activist to Inmate—a Writer's Journey*. Baltimore MD: Fortkamp Publishing, 1991.

Dworkin, Ronald, "On not prosecuting civil disobedience," in: Kempton, Murray, et al., *Trials of the Resistance*. NYC: The New York Review, 1970.

Figueroa, Maria, "Chavez," in: Powers, Roger S., and William B. Vogele, eds., *Protest, Power, and Change: An Encyclopedia of Nonviolent Action from ACT-UP to Women's Suffrage*. NYC: Garland Publishing, Inc., 1997.

Forest, Jim, *Love Is the Measure: A Biography of Dorothy Day*. Maryknoll NY:

Orbis Books, 1997. (original 1986)
Forest, Jim, "People are willing to sacrifice themselves..." in: Wink, Walter, ed., *Peace Is the Way: Writings on Nonviolence from the Fellowship of Reconciliation*. Maryknoll NY: Orbis Books, 2000.
Gandhi, Mohandas K, *The Essential Gandhi: An Anthology of His Writings on His Life, Work and Ideas*, Fischer, Louis, ed., NYC: Vintage Books, 1983 (original 1962).
Glossop, Ronald J., *Confronting War: An Examination of Humanity's Most Pressing Problem*. Jefferson NC: McFarland & Company, Inc., 1987.
Greider, William, *One World, Ready or Not: The Manic Logic of Global Capitalism*. NYC: Simon & Schuster, 1997.
Groebel, Jo, and Robert A. Hinde, *Aggression and War: Their Biological and Social Bases*. Cambridge UK: Cambridge University Press, 1989.
Grossman, Lt. Col. David, lecture, COPRED/PSA conference, Bethel College, April 1997.
Hallock, Daniel, *Hell, Healing and Resistance: Veterans Speak*. Farmington PA: The Plough Publishing House, 1998.
Holmes, Robert L., *Nonviolence in Theory and Practice*. Belmont CA: Wadsworth Publishing Company, 1990.
Kennedy, Paul, *The Rise and Fall of the Great Powers: Economic Change and Military Conflict from 1500 to 2000*. NYC: Random House, 1987.
Kennedy, R. Scott, "The Druze of the Golan: a case of nonviolent resistance," in: Holmes, Robert L., *Nonviolence in Theory and Practice*. Belmont CA: Wadsworth Publishing Company, 1990.
Lewis, John, *Walking with the Wind: A Memoir of the Movement*. San Diego: Harcourt Brace & Company, 1998.
Lynd, Staughton, "Marxist-Leninism and the language of *Politics* magazine: the first New Left...and the Third," in: White, George Abbott, *Simone Weil: Interpretations of a Life*. Amherst MA: University of Massachusetts Press, 1981. (111-135)
Mencken, H. L., *H. L. Mencken on Politics: A Carnival of Buncombe*. NYC: Vintage Books, 1960.
Rai, Milan, *War Plan Iraq: Ten Reasons Against War on Iraq*. London: Verso, 2002.
Routledge, Paul, "Nepal, Movement for Restoration of Democracy, 1990" in: Powers, Roger S., and William B. Vogele, *Protest, Power, and Change: An Encyclopedia of Nonviolent Action from ACT-UP to Women's Suffrage*. NYC: Garland Publishing, Inc., 1997.
Sabo, Matt, "Standing against the flood: Harrisburg's Mennonites," *The Sunday Oregonian*, 18 November 2001. (A 21+)
Saunders, Doris E., ed., *The Day They Marched*. Chicago: Johnson Publishing Company, 1963.
Stoltzfus, Nathan, "Dissent in Nazi Germany," *The Atlantic Monthly* September 1992 (86-94)
True, Michael, *To Construct Peace: 30 More Justice Seekers, Peace Makers*. Mystic CT: Twenty-Third Publications, 1992.

UCLA Chicano Studies, 'Cesar E. Chavez" website: http://clnet.ucr.edu/research/chavez/bio/
von Suttner, Bertha Sophie Felicia, "The evolution of the peace movement," in: Thee, Marek, *Peace! By the Nobel Peace Prize Laureates: An Anthology*. Paris: UNESCO Publishing, 1995.
Whaley, Rick and Walter Bresette, *Walleye Warriors: An Effective Alliance Against Racism and for the Earth*. Philadelphia PA: New Society Publishers, 1994.
Yost, Jack, *Planet Champions: Adventures in Saving the World*. Portland OR: BridgeCity Books, 1999.
Young, Nigel, "Peace Movements in History," in: Barash, David, *Approaches to Peace: A Reader in Peace Studies*. New York: Oxford University Press, 2000.
Zinn, Howard, *The Future of History: Interviews with David Barsamian*. Monroe ME: Common Courage Press, 1999.

CHAPTER SEVEN

Drill it in:

training like the nonviolent military

> Throughout that wet and bitterly cold night, I thought about what it means to "wage peace." I first pictured centuries of soldiers sitting in rain and cold as we were that night. People have always been ready to leave their families, go to faraway places, endure incredible hardships, and even die in order to wage a war. Is it conceivable, I wondered, that the cost of peace could be less? What if we were willing to sacrifice for peace as others have sacrificed for war?
>
> —Jim Wallis (Wallis: 1)

Unless and until the primary military function has been replaced by nonviolent options, it will continue to be the only choice made by nation-states, the sole exception of Costa Rica (no military) notwithstanding. That primary function, of course, is to wage war and thus coerce other governments into acting in manners approved by the warring nation.

How could it be possible to truly wage peace, as Jim Wallis puts it?

First, as Wallis calls for in his moving introduction to the 1982 classic, **Waging Peace**, we as individuals must come to the same realization that Gandhi's *satyagrahis* did; nonviolence is not an easy path, but the sacrificial path will be taken by *someone*. Will it be by young soldiers, tricked by recruiters or pressured by society into learning the skills of killing and the glory of dying for the flag? Or will the path of sacrificial defense of the vulnerable ones and our land be undertaken by those who wish to use nonviolence to engage those who threaten us?

I've talked with many active-duty military men over the years as a peace activist and one of the first things I acknowledge to them is that unless and until enough of us commit to serious nonviolent action with all the risks and commitment that involves, we will hire soldiers to do it violently. They are all mercenaries, even if they as individuals are committed ideologically to violent defense of the country, because the Pentagon is paid for by those who would rather pay others to kill and die than take that risk themselves—the US taxpayers.

The fact of life is that conflict is inevitable and that it is oftentimes risky. As a society, we must fully recognize that and make choices based on pragmatism, which is exactly what we do now, and we have the most fearsome military that history has seen as a direct result. In fact, it usually gets its way without having to go to war because it demonstrates periodically how ruthless it will be in a shooting match. The US American military has taken soldiering to a relatively high point—in a relatively low field of endeavor.

And so, allowing ourselves the necessary indulgence of envisioning, how do we replace that particular means to the end of protecting the people and the land we love—no matter which country we are from? Replacing the military means with nonviolent means will be our most daunting task in developing a peace system to replace the war system. To economically pull back from a war system will be very hard, as it not only means losing some jobs and manufacturing, but it means that unjust resource capture cannot be defended, and this will be the greatest economic equalizer the world has ever known. Changing the media to analyze toward nonviolence instead of using words and concepts to prepare us for more war will be another large but doable job. Changing education toward peace will naturally occur insofar as academics honestly search and report findings. Religion will simply need to honestly shift from justification to accurate interpretation of their wisest teachers from antiquity to the present. Families will more easily make the transition as mothers ascend to decisionmaking roles and military service is seen as enforcing injustice, not as a socially mandated role for their male children.

But actually implementing a change to national nonviolence will take immense logistical and preparatory work rivaling that of the armed forces. Retraining an army to use nonviolence—becoming a "disarmy," if you will—will not just involve the troops but will change every member of society into a reserve member of that disarmy. Nonviolent resistance to invasion, for example, will require mass noncoöperation in order to make any interpositioning force work properly. In other words, a mass boycott of social, industrial, information and other societal services is what each and every citizen must be prepared to undertake. We have, then, a need for two types of training, beginning with an active and committed citizenry. And the frontline troops—those who actively seek conflict in the name of nonviolent resistance to injustice—need intensive and extensive training. How can this be accomplished?

retrain to restrain: the arsenal of nonviolence

Taking an oath of nonviolence is easy; practicing it is difficult. "To feel anger and fear while participating in a nonviolent action is natural. In order to succeed, though, nonviolent activists need to restrain themselves from using violence, even when violence is used against them." (Terkel: 67)

Endless training marks the military life; education and drill also mark the life of the nonviolent warrior. Rosa Parks was a seasoned and highly trained activist when she sat down on the bus in Montgomery, Alabama, on 1 December 1955. She worked daily on NAACP issues and had received training at the Highlander Folk School in Tennessee, a center for union organizer training. Dr. Martin Luther King, Jr. also attended Highlander in preparation for his role in further social change. (Terkel: 68) Using *ad hoc* nonviolence can work, especially in a single campaign, but it is a rare culture that can produce an ongoing nonviolent force without specific nonviolent training.

spectators or participants?

The willingness to sacrifice will follow the recognition that it will be not done in vain. Soldiers keep a record of wins in their minds and are thus able to generate hope that they will not only win the war, but that they will personally survive too. How can members of society come to know that nonviolence could work to defend the land, lifestyle and people we love?

It is entirely possible that society will never know that if society is built on the US American model of hyperconsumerism that is inevitably taking natural and human resources from others around the planet at unfair prices. The only way that our society can maintain our lifestyle is by an armed and dangerous military which will provide weaponry and training to the local armies, who in turn will maintain control over the populace so that, for example, unions never gain a foothold. When a union leader is assassinated in a nation from which we get cheap materials, we are to blame in two ways—both of which are in our power to remedy.

First, we provide the weapons and training to the military of the nation that uses them to repress laborers who cannot bargain for decent wages and conditions. If all else fails, the US military itself may be forced to do the job, though that's a distant and nonpreferred option. We may remedy that in two ways. One, stop paying war taxes. Two, elect a government that will stop providing weaponry and training to armed forces.

Second, we buy the goods in question unquestioningly. We vaguely hear about some objection to certain products coming from certain countries, but most pay little attention to how they direct political and military activity through their purchasing power and consumer choices. Obviously, the remedy is to stop buying these products and services and to urge groups and governments to cease such purchases.

negotiation: a security function

Militaries threaten war. Militaries wage war and train others to do so. But militaries have a tertiary function, at times.

Norman Schwartzkopf negotiated the ceasefire at the end of Desert Storm. Douglas MacArthur negotiated the surrender of the Japanese in August 1945. The military negotiates peace sometimes. Of course, presidents send their State Department negotiators afield as well, but all national negotiations have armed might as the backup threat. Those who believe in nonviolence are thus called to learn about negotiation that doesn't involve that kind of threat. Indeed, the fields of Peace Studies and Conflict Resolution—while emanating from common roots in the 1940s and 50s, have split and we are finding that they need to rejoin.

Those who practice nonviolence, wrote Dr. King, must learn to use that nonviolence to bring the parties to the table. However, the table is often regarded with deep suspicion and aversion by activists. This is more due to lack of skill than honest principled rejection of the method. Similarly, those who practice mediation fail almost universally to recognize the potential of nonviolent direct action in bringing the sides to the table. This mutual ignorance and failure is crippling the speed of social change needlessly.

"Time and patience are power." So says a practitioner and trainer of traditional negotiation. (Karrass: 48)

Nonviolent citizen soldiers: civilian-based defense

> *If the government doesn't stop the war, we'll stop the government.*
>
> —antiwar slogan leading toward Mayday actions opposing war in Vietnam (Albert: 229)

We all participate in the war system, even if only as taxpayers—indeed, Osama bin Laden asserted that US citizens were now legitimate targets *because* they pay taxes and are thus complicit in what the US has done to the Muslim people. What would happen if we all participated in the peace system? Could we defend a nation? A country? Anthropologist and conflict researcher William Ury gives us something to go on when he notes that "For the great bulk of our time on earth, coexistence has been more the norm than coercion. Human beings are just as capable of living in peace as they are of living at war with one another. Getting along is perhaps even more rooted in human nature than is fighting to the finish. We are *Homo Negotiator*." (Ury: 197) What can we do with this knowledge?

First we can develop hope, and then, perhaps, faith (reversing the religious process in this case). Hope raises expectations and motivates us to work toward a goal that would remain an undiscussed fantasy without the spark of desire for something we sense is attainable. Give us an inch of nonviolence and we'll take a mile of disarmament. As Jessie Wallace Hughan pointed out in her 1942 writings, using violence even in defensive war means breaking the Ten Commandments and using nonviolence does not. (Hughan: 318) "Thou shalt not kill" is so basic—it is key to believe it's possible. Without hope, then, we abandon ethics, values, elemental tenets of civilization. Indeed, wrote Cicero, *Inter arma silent legis*—In war, the law is silent. (Barash: 112)

If our laws, the Ten Commandments and even Just War doctrines and all the rudiments of human belief become irrelevant during war it is reminiscent of Ammon Hennacy's rueful observation that being a pacifist between wars is akin to being a vegetarian between meals. We have values or we do not. *Now is the time to be bold for peace,* says Devorah Brous, Israeli peace activist during the most furious time of IDF occupation and Hamas and Islamic Jihad suicide bombings, ***now****, when it's hardest is when it's most important.* (Brous)

Hughan and others challenge us to devise potential for victory in the penumbra of our ethics, thus making them, at last, real. The vision of a force that will not shed blood has long been regarded as so unrealistic, so utopian, that it is merely the stuff of inspired religious verse: "Now...the trumpet sounds with a mighty voice," wrote Clement of Alexandra, "calling the soldiers of the world to arms, announcing war; and shall not Christ, who has uttered his summons to peace even to the ends of the earth, summon together his own soldiers of peace? Indeed, O Man, he was called to arms with his blood and his word and army that sheds no blood; to these soldiers he has handed over the kingdom of heaven." (Egan: 35) Nice prose—nearly poetry—but always relegated to the dreambin of history—where it has been dusted off by Gandhi and now scholars say it just might be possible—not only in the Next World, but in this one.

As the first to suggest such a possibility in the 20th century based on a practical set of steps, Gandhi was prepared to advance his theories and practices, representing the full flower of his mature thought, when he was killed. His vision, as recalled by Narayan Desai—who grew up on Gandhi's ashram with his *satyagrahi* parents—consisted of three steps. First, disarm and befriend the world, thus presenting a nation-state nonviolent posture. Second, highly disciplined *satyagrahis* would offer themselves as bodily resisters and spiritual opposition at the border of the country. Finally, if all else failed, all citizenry would noncoöperate in an attempt to block a successful takeover of that which society produced. (Desai: vii)

Gene Sharp has done the germinal research in the field of nonviolent civilian-based defense since Gandhi's original vision. His Albert Einstein Institution at Harvard and his Civilian-Based Defense Association are two academic and activist organizations, respectively, that study, promote and practice these methods of intranational and international conflict management. But his pioneering thinking has not stood stagnant. Nonviolence International coördinator Yeshua Moser-Puangsuwan notes: During the last two decades of the twentieth century, cross-border nonviolent action initiatives, specifically focused on intervening in civil conflict, have been pursed with greater energy, resources and organization than at any other time in human history. (Moser-Puangsuwan: 319) These have been small efforts, usually involving one or a few volunteers, but have been numerous enough to offer us data and examples. These individuals are helping us learn new models of sensitive yet robust cross-cultural justice work and transformation.

We have several considerations when we think of the possibilities of nonviolence. Primarily, how may we substitute nonviolence for violence? That question involves two main areas; what functions of violence (or the threat of violence) can nonviolent forces serve and what can nonviolence not accomplish? A separate set of functions are those that nonviolence serves that violence never addresses at all. Thus, we have three subsets of conflict management within the comparison and contrast of violence and nonviolence:

- The tasks that violence and nonviolence can both perform.
- The functions that only violence can serve.
- The operations suitable only for nonviolence.

Our next task is to determine the range of possible desired roles of our conflict management organizations. What follows is one set of those:

- defend national borders from invaders
- protect government from overthrow

Drill it in: training like the nonviolent military

- guard human rights
- prevent property theft or destruction
- invade other nations
- conquer indigenous peoples
- steal natural resources from other nations
- maintain an unjust economic advantage over others
- promote global siblinghood
- reduce fear and suspicion
- reduce the desire for vengeance
- topple an unjust regime
- conduct a coup on behalf of a ruling elite
- protect natural resources
- prevent war

Clearly, there are some of these operations that can be accomplished by the use or threat of either violence or nonviolence. Some of these items of business cannot be achieved through nonviolence at all and some cannot happen using violence. Hughan makes this point in positing a nonviolent US: "Before it disarms it will, of course, have removed all trade restrictions on its own raw materials and will have completed the process of setting free its few imperialist possessions." (Hughan: 320) Once we group them we must then decide what are the most important considerations and choose our methods accordingly. But that choice is uninformed and premature until we come to understand which kind of power can accomplish which ends.

achievable only by violence:

- invade other nations
- maintain an unjust economic advantage over others
- conquer indigenous peoples
- steal natural resources from other nations
- conduct a coup on behalf of a ruling elite

doable only with nonviolence:

- promote global siblinghood
- reduce fear and suspicion
- reduce the desire for vengeance

what either violence or nonviolence can accomplish:

- defend national borders from invaders
- protect government from overthrow

- guard human rights
- prevent property theft or destruction
- topple an unjust regime
- protect natural resources
- prevent war

I propose that most humans are most interested in the set of objectives that are doable with either, i.e., the third subset. Most of us are neither overwhelmingly greedy nor are we totally altruistic. We generally want security and justice. The father of Civilian-Based Defense theory, Gene Sharp, notes simply that, in order for CBD to succeed, "'Human nature' need not, and most likely will not, be changed." (Sharp, ***Dilemmas***: 746)

How, then, may we substitute nonviolence for violence in order to achieve those ends, the goals of most of humanity at one time or another?

Our inclusive range of choices (using either violence or nonviolence, recognizing that some believe in a separation of means and ends) includes:

- raise an *ad hoc* army to do the job by physical destruction and psychological terror.
- maintain an armed force in anticipation of periodically needing to use it to accomplish those objectives by means of attack or credible threat of attack
- use *ad hoc* overwhelming nonviolent people power to shut down governments or cripple economies and threaten further disruption until goals are met.
- develop and maintain mass training and commitment to using nonviolent methods in order to achieve the ability to powerfully negotiate favorable terms with any opponent through a combination of respect and fear of not only diplomatic consequence (bad publicity), but of a noncoöperative grinding of society and the economy to a halt.

The law of the nonviolent jungle

Humanity has chosen the first two options so many times to such drastic but observable ends that the second two options are seldom pronounced possible. And when the second two methods are used, if they fail that is proof positive that they "never" work and are impractical—though that same assertion isn't made about violence when it inevitably fails for at least some of the participants. If, on the other hand, nonviolent methods succeed, they are often regarded as a fluke, an anomaly, an aberration of history.

These anomalies are what Gene Sharp calls Citizen-Based Defense. The disarmy. *Shanti Sena*. Nonviolent PeaceForce.

Like the constant preparation for armed conflict undertaken by armed forces, those who organize for nonviolent conflict resolution are called to a kind of *prévenance* for peace, an anticipation of how conflict might be guided toward nonviolent methods of management. CBD can be used to achieve the ends that most people favor, provided the people are prepared to sacrifice in order to obtain those objectives. Those ends will almost always be just, though the CBD methods could perhaps theoretically be used to achieve injustice, such as the suppression of the rights of a minority by overwhelming majority nonviolent action, but that scenario is essentially a hypothetical with little to no historical precedent or logical underpinning—majority oppression of minorities has been a violent practice in the past. When we consider CBD we essentially consider mass nonviolent action to preserve or obtain the good for most or all of society. The ultimate beauty of CBD is that, even when mistakes are made, all errors are much more correctable when no one has been killed making them, which is the usual result of CBD. This further breeds the atmosphere of openness that helps lead to trust and fear-hate-violence reduction. The more the method is used, the more effective it becomes, a positive feedback loop that builds a part of a peace system.

> Gandhi was of the opinion that progress was impossible without the right to err, and an essential of political organization was 'freedom to err and the duty of correcting errors.' This concept follows from the Gandhian philosophy of conflict where 'truth' is relative and satyagraha serves as a technique for discovering truth in a given conflict situation."
>
> —Joan V. Bondurant (Bondurant: 163)

That disarming psychological advantage is the edge, the wedge, into the opening of sympathy, however grudgingly given, first by the courageous minority of the dominant society and then by the majority of the members of that society. Unlike the mechanical considerations of armed conflict (do I have a bigger, faster arsenal?), the true power of civilian-based defense begins with a frankness, an announced humble fearlessness in the face of apparent vulnerability. It is openness, lack of either secrecy or clandestine maneuvering, that sharpens that very spearpoint of effectiveness. (Sharp, **Dynamics**: 482) Transparency plus humility—even in the face of a natural tendency toward introversion—will go much further in the pursuit of a fair resolution of conflict than will the hubris-filled arrogance of the violent forces. Indeed, some of our greatest nonviolent practitioners were extraordinarily withdrawn, even timid, people. "This shyness I retained throughout my stay in England," wrote Gandhi of his London student years. "The presence of half a dozen people would strike me dumb." To that, however, Gandhi added, "My shyness has been my shield and buckler. It has allowed my to grow. It has helped me in my discernment of truth." (Gandhi:

27) While no one feared Gandhi, he and his *satyagrahis* coerced governments nonetheless. About the openness of the movement he noted that "secrecy has no place." (Gandhi: 67)

The history of CBD is the history of peace, though it is not called CBD. Gandhi and his troops called it *satyagraha*, truth-force, and used it in their independence campaigns. (Sharp, **Gandhi**: 131) The Indians eventually drove out the invaders, the foreign troops, in defense of their homeland. In another historical example, for nine months in 1923, masses of impoverished Germans nonviolently noncoöperated with occupying French and Belgian armed forces, winning some victories through what we now might call CBD—mass strikes and slow-downs (McDonald-Morken). Those victories were sadly wiped out when the resistance turned violent and reprisals then escalated, which is a story repeated in history again and again. Mass nonviolence and CBD are all-too-often an *ad hoc* proposition, done almost instinctively by a people who see where their true power lies. "Only periodically aware of itself," says Michael True, "it is sometimes halting and contradictory in its development." (True, 1995: *xxiii*). Clearly, the episodes of mass nonviolence practiced by disciplined warrior cultures, such as the Israeli Druze or the Pathans under the Badshah Khan are examples of this phenomenon. (Holmes) McDonald-Morken cites several more historical examples of nonviolent resistance to invasion, oppression and military coup. As we learn and progress, the obvious hope is to "connect the dots," to learn to anticipate, to train, as George Lakey helped to do with Solidarity in Poland in the early 1980s and as his Training for Change institute continues to do.

Advocates for nonviolent CBD are frequently challenged by the historical examples of the worst genocidal maniacs; the first of which to be rhetorically trotted out is Hitler and his Nazis. But the record reveals numerous instances of the successful use of CBD against apparently unstoppable Nazi forces, from the failure of the Quisling forces against the churches or the teachers in occupied Norway to the release of the Jewish husbands of non-Jewish women right in Berlin in the most frenzied part of the war and genocide. Sharp recounts one little known example of the successful nonviolent defeat of the attempted deportation of 20,000 Jews from Bulgaria to Germany in early 1943, when Jews and non-Jews filled the Jewish quarter and refused to allow the removal of those residents. (Sharp, **Methods**: 153)

CBD proponents ask the provocative question, *What if nations cut their military budgets and devoted some of that to developing the training necessary to create a populace prepared to practice CBD when necessary?*

In 1995, 4.8 million men and women were on active-duty in the US military. Millions more were in the reserves and all of us paid for that activity with our individual and families' daily work for money, since most of the military budget comes out of federal income taxes. Further, in the summer of

2001, huge tax rebates were given in vast disproportional fashion to the rich—averaging $45,000 each. Then, following 9.11.01 terrorism, corporate lobbies secured passage of the so-called Alternative Minimum Tax, which would nominally make all corporations liable for some taxes—minimal indeed. Mostly, however, the law will actually *return* taxes already paid by corporations, going all the way back to 1987, including some amazing totals, such as $1.4 billion to IBM, $1 billion to Ford and a package of billions more to various major corporations. (Jackson) At the same time, the US Congress gave a whopping $20 billion to the Pentagon to wage war in Afghanistan for a few months, above and beyond the already well-stuffed DoD budget. What would the counterfactual show us, give us?

Even in the domestic arena, we can look to women's suffrage, a totally nonviolent success; we examine the Civil Rights movement, which created several national laws in the 1960s, making racial discrimination illegal. These national laws were preceded first by mass nonviolent resistance and noncoöperation and then by a slow but certain positive response by the opponents on a local and state basis—not by the beneficent national government, as myth has it (e.g., the abandonment of *de jure* school segregation by 35 southern cities *before* fed legislation) (Cooney: 159). The United Farm Workers nonviolent campaigns of direct action and consumer boycott were successful in gaining numerous rights for migrant farm workers. Several years of mass nonviolent witness finally won the unfettered treaty rights of the Anishinabe people of northern Wisconsin and Michigan. Long before, a form of implicit CBD was practiced by enslaved Africans, brought here in chains, who, faced with tremendous brutality and oppression, took the natural nonviolent mass lifestyle and culture of resistance. "They showed their refusal to submit by running away. Even more often, they engaged in sabotage, slowdowns, and subtle forms of resistance which asserted, if only to themselves and their brothers and sisters, their dignity as human beings." (Zinn: 32) This is a common, natural element of CBD, practiced by individuals from our first stirrings of natural nonviolent resistance, when we refuse to eat what we don't like, when we use "barely conscious ways to express discontent," and we carry that forward from individual reaction to group sense of victimization and response, "for example, in employment relations they dislike, they may come in late, be absent, work slowly, or act ineptly." (Kriesberg: 52) A psychologist may label such behavior passive-aggressive and a sociologist may call it incipient rebellion.

It is even be possible for a small, invaded and heavily colonized country to achieve a form of autonomy using CBD. Some Canadian natives have done so. And the eventual nonviolent success in South Africa ought to be a beacon for Tibet and other invaded, colonized nations.

The South African example is certainly an illustration of the ability of the people to adapt to the removal of the "leadership." They went to prison. They always do; that ought to be part of the plan. When it is not (it's usually not), those left usually go through a period of insecurity and "lack of definition in the situation," as participant and journalist Maris Cakars noted of a major antiwar action at the Pentagon in 1967. (Lynd: 277)

Sharp's thesis is simply that the power lies with the people and they can choose to give it up to rulers or they can choose to take it back. Others hold parallel views based on a theology.

> *Gene Sharp...argues that even under tyranny, people are only ruled over if they let it happen...The underdog does not come to know that 'I am somebody' by ascription. He is somebody by right...I know it by virtue of the incarnation.*
>
> —John Howard Yoder, "Burden and Discipline" (Hawkley: 35)

At times, it may appear to the student of nonviolence that we as a society willfully overlook and dismiss the possibilities of a new definition of defense, that which we could call Civilian-Based Defense. The lessons are clear; what we often lack is the political will, the education, the courage and, most crucial of all, the imagination to risk nonviolence.

> *We're gonna plant some seeds*
> *We are the seeds*
> *We need some sunshine*
> *We are the sunshine*
> *We need some spirit*
> *We are the spirit*
> *We need some changes*
> *We are the changes*
>
> —P.J. Hoffman (Gowan: 296)

Mass nonviolent action puts immense pressure on any government; when 932 peaceful protesters were arrested and put on trial together in British Columbia, it was the largest mass trial ever held in the western hemisphere. (MacIsaac: xi) And it was done to protect our human right to a pristine environment, to beauty, to natural wonder, to observe and enjoy Creation. That event, to become even more effective, could have been followed by a campaign pressing the lines established from the Montgomery bus boycott of 1955-1956, the UFW table grape boycott of the late 1960s-1970s and the INFACT successes boycotting Nestles, GE and Philip Morris (to force those corporations to quit making infant formula, nuclear weapons and tobacco products, respectively). One of the keys to civilian-based defense is just what the UFW and INFACT have done with publicity and recruitment; take those immediately affected and reach out to involve many others, elsewhere. That is also the secret of the power of accompaniment as practiced by Peace Brigades International and others (Mahony: 54)

To conclude, we need to recognize that we will develop the willingness to sacrifice that soldiers have so admirably demonstrated over the millennia and still do—except our troops will be willing to die, but not kill. We also need to charge everyone with the role of noncoöperater at times of great need. And then we ought to prepare for this transition to nonviolent force by training constantly.

sources:
Barash, David P., *Approaches to Peace: A Reader in Peace Studies*. New York: Oxford University Press, 2000.
Bondurant, Joan V., *Conquest of Violence: The Gandhian Philosophy of Conflict*. Rev. ed. Berkeley CA: University of California Press, 1965.
Brous, Devorah, lecture, First Congregational Church, Portland OR, 11 August 2002.
Cooney, Robert and Helen Michalowski, *The Power of the People: Active Nonviolence in the United States*. Philadelphia: New Society Publishers, 1987.
Desai, Narayan, *Foreword* in: Moser-Puangsuwan, Yeshua, and Thomas Weber, *Nonviolent Intervention: Across Borders, A Recurrent Vision*. Honolulu: Spark M. Matsunaga Institute of Peace, 2000.
Egan, Eileen, *Peace Be With You: Justified Warfare or the Way of Nonviolence*. Maryknoll NY: Orbis Books, 1999.
Gandhi, Mohandas K, *The Essential Gandhi: An Anthology of His Writings on His Life, Work and Ideas*, Fischer, Louis, ed., NYC: Vintage Books, 1983 (original 1962).
Gowan, Susan, et al., *Moving Toward a New Society*. Philadelphia PA: New Society Press, 1976.
Hawkley, Louise and James C. Juhnke, *Nonviolent America: History Though the Eyes of Peace*. North Newton KS: Bethel College, 1993.
Holmes, Robert L., *Nonviolence in Theory and Practice*. Belmont CA: Wadsworth Publishing Company, 1990.
Hughan, Jessie Wallace, and Cecil Hinshaw, "Toward a national defense," in: Sibley, Mulford Q., ed., *The Quiet Battle: Writings on the Theory and Practice of Non-violent Resistance*. Boston: Beacon Press, 1963. (Hughan's original 1942)
Jackson, Jesse, "Raiding the treasury," email, 15 November 2001.
Karrass, Dr. Chester L., *Effective Negotiating: Workbook and Discussion Guide*. Santa Monica CA: KARRASS, 1991.

Kriesberg, Louis, ***Constructive Conflicts: From Escalation to Resolution.*** Lanham MD: Rowman & Littlefield, 1998.
Lynd, Staughton and Alice, ***Nonviolence in America: A Documentary History.*** Maryknoll NY: Orbis Books, 1995 2nd edition).
MacIsaac, Ron and Anne Champagne, editors, ***Clayquot Mass Trials: Defending the Rainforest.*** Philadelphia PA: New Society Publishers, 1994.
Mahony, Liam and Luis Eguren, ***Unarmed Bodyguards: International Accompaniment for the Protection of Human Rights.*** West Hartford CT: Kumarian Press, 1997.
McDonald Morken, Colleen, "Nonviolent Civilian-Based Defense," paper presented at Martin Luther King Jr. observance, Sigurd Olson Environmental Institute, 17 January 1998.
Moser-Puangsuwan, Yeshua, and Thomas Weber, ***Nonviolent Intervention: Across Borders, A Recurrent Vision.*** Honolulu: Spark M. Matsunaga Institute of Peace, 2000.
Sharp, Gene, "Civilian-Based Defense: making the abolition of war a realistic goal," in: Ringler, Dick, ed., ***Dilemmas of War and Peace.*** Madison WI: University of Wisconsin-Extension, 1993.
Sharp, Gene, ***The Methods of Nonviolent Action: part two of: The Politics of Nonviolent Action.*** Boston: Porter Sargent Publishers, 1973.
———, ***The Dynamics of Nonviolent Action: part three of: The Politics of Nonviolent Action.*** Boston: Porter Sargent Publishers, 1973.
———, ***Gandhi as a Political Strategist.*** Boston: Porter Sargent Publishers, 1979.
Terkel, Susan Neiburg, ***People Power: A Look at Nonviolent Action and Defense.*** NYC: Lodestar, 1996.
True, Michael, ***An Energy Field More Intense Than War: The Nonviolent Tradition and American Literature.*** Syracuse NY: Syracuse University Press, 1995.
Ury, William, ***Getting to Peace: Transforming Conflict at Home, at Work, and in the World.*** NYC: Viking, 1999.
Wallis, Jim, ed., ***Waging Peace: A Handbook for the Struggle to Abolish Nuclear Weapons.*** San Francisco: Harper & Row, Publishers, 1982.
Zinn, Howard, ***A People's History of the United States.*** New York: Harper & Row, 1980.

Appendix to chapter seven

Sample nonviolence training

Note: In conflict resolution trainings, John Paul Lederach teaches the elicitive model, a method of communication that draws from others and uses the buy-in and the information to further the process, to define the path, to honor each participant fully and thus to tailor each event to the people involved. I am convinced that his methodology is best for nonviolence training as well. He calls the opposite workshop design "prescriptive," and that, of course, is a cookie-cutter "we know what's best for you" approach. (Lederach: 47) The Procrustean one-size-fits-all Bed is a starter, something to compare to and build from, and that is what follows. I encourage trainers to offer more nonviolence trainings to as many diverse groups as possible, to take feedback from all, and to learn to elicit from each individual the emotional and informational data needed to construct increasingly customized trainings. Doing enough of these will prepare the trainer for cross-cultural trainings that are key to promotion of effective nonviolence. Experiment, elicit and improve each time.

Trainer prep: for trainings that will extend more than a half-day, bring certificates only missing the name of the participant. Fill those in at the conclusion of the training. You will be asking much of those who take part and more will be expected of them following the training. They ought to have some authentication that will verify that they have undertaken to learn some techniques that can help them personally and professionally. Even if they are taking your training for college credit—as many of my students do—a special, frameable document stresses the importance of this training and will, if displayed, offer something for others to think about into the indefinite future.

What follows is one version of nonviolence training. The first time I offered nonviolence training I assisted Marv Davidov, who learned his nonviolence techniques from his participation in the Deep South during the Civil Rights movement. Davidov called many elements of his training "SNCC." This refers to his involvement with the Student Nonviolent Coordinating Committee, which grew out of the original sit-ins in Nashville, Tennessee and Greensboro, North Carolina. Over the years, I've tried to add components of the theories and practices from Communications, Conflict Resolution, Negotiation and Mediation. Elements of a nonviolence training reflective of such a synthesis might include the following, though your time may limit you to choosing just one or two (I write in the first person as trainer toward the participants):

- *introductions and stated goals of each participant*

This training is occasionally robust; the idea is to help prepare participants to learn to respond nonviolently when conflict or potential conflict arises. We aim with this training to change lives, however greatly or slightly, to change our directions to the degree we can toward nonviolence, away from violence. To change our perceptions is to change our direction is to change our lives, and in that sense, we view this nonviolent training as life-altering. This is not to make claims that nonviolence will get you out of every pickle you ever get into, nor is it to claim that, following this training, you will be prepared to neatly and nonviolently resolve every instance of attack or intimidation. What we do offer is a chance to learn some of the techniques of nonviolent conflict management, some of the information that gives us a different estimation of the potential power of nonviolence and some of the possible reasons for this school of thought and action.

You will be safe throughout the training. This is not a martial arts class, nor is it even a training for physically handling belligerents or the violently mentally ill. There will be no physical rough roleplaying, though some of the roleplays may be emotionally tough—but we will debrief each one, to allow for your reactions and to allow you to ask the group for the support you need to make the most of this training. Except for roleplays, we expect courteous communication and the trainer is just one of the facilitators. Each participant is asked to assist in the facilitation through support for all members. We expect no interruption, no personal insult or attack on character—except during defined roleplays. This is meant to be a safe zone of community-building interaction. Those who have taken nonviolence training are indeed a community and we are all about building a small portion of that community in this training. For the duration of this training, you are part of a combat unit, a nonviolent battle squadron, and it is entirely appropriate and necessary to regard each other as co-members of a fighting group. We are simply learning a different way to fight.

Our first activity is to go around and express to each other what we hope to gain from the general study of nonviolence and, in particular, what we each hope to take from this training. As facilitator, I'll be taking notes. I don't keep time; tell us what you need to tell us in the time you need. We all attend enough meetings in which someone is asking us to wrap up. Instead, we will try to be wrapped up in each other—though we will finish this session when we promised, on time, so this is trust that all of us will honor that promise.

nonviolent theory: soften the target (William Penn's Letter to the Delaware)

When we think about using nonviolence, we are obviously replacing a different set of responses, a set of options that we learn to leave behind as we learn a different, more centered response to threat, to attack, or to intimidation. We are, in the main, concerned with replacing violent response with nonviolence, and one tactic we use when we learn violence is softening the target. In the military, this is usually achieved by long-distance weaponry, such as aerial bombardment, missiles, rockets, or anti-personnel devices delivered or planted secretly. Similarly, we can soften the target in our nonviolent approach. We can prepare the Other—the aggressive co-worker, the domineering boss, the bitter spouse, the surly teen-ager, even the drunken

Drill it in: training like the nonviolent military

stranger—by launching a long-distance message. One historical example is William Penn's *Letter to the Delaware*, in which the English Quaker leader, who had been granted colonial control over vast lands in what eventually became Pennsylvania, reached out across the ocean to touch Native Americans before he even set foot on the ship that was to take him here. In that letter, Penn assured the Delaware leaders and tribal members that he and his people intended to befriend them, to be nonviolent, to negotiate fairly, and to reach agreements that all parties would find fair. This target-softening might have been scoffed at by other English; it might have been seen as fairytale naïve, as an invitation to be robbed and killed by savage natives. But that's not how it worked; the Quakers maintained cordial and productive relations to the Delaware even as the Delaware ultimately waged war on the English. No Quaker family that maintained its wilderness homestead with open nonviolence was hurt during that war; the only civilians hurt were the ones who sought shelter in the armed forts. The contract agreed to by the earliest Quakers with the Delaware held for as long as the Quakers held onto nonviolence, which was for almost the entire colonial period, essentially until they became a state of an armed United States. The target-softening worked then and it can work again. It is not always possible, but it generally helps when it can be done.

roleplay: soften the target

Needed: two participants. Others observe and comment during the debrief. Situation: You are at work, in a meeting to discuss staff performance goals. A co-worker who considers himself in competition with you and others frequently uses these meetings to subtly and not-so-subtly attack others, including you. The meeting is in ten minutes. You have a brief opportunity to soften the target.

- *debrief*

How did the potential victim of attack try to prepare the potential attacker differently? Everyone offer observations, including what seemed to work, what might not, and how this experiment might be altered to try something else.

nonviolent theory: employ the counterfactual

> *Miri Heatherwick: Don't you think your faith in political support from the international community is futile since business interests and money will always take priority over morals?*
>
> *Dalai Lama: And then I ask you, if we used violent methods, are you sure many governments would come to*

help us? No, I don't think so. The situation would be even worse. (Heatherwick: 11)

Consider the counterfactual; what if the vast majority of Europeans had approached the original people here in the US in the manner Penn did? Our nation's history and our cultural baggage would be quite different; it is entirely possible that, for example, we would have essentially no pollution problems, no significant war history, certainly no slavery in our past and that we would feel immensely safe in our neighborhoods.

Nonviolent theorist Dr. Michael Nagler writes of the educational, child-training counterfactual. What if we trained children to be compassionate? He cites a study from the *Journal of Abnormal Social Psychology* in which two groups of children were conditioned to either react aggressively or coöperatively—no matter what their previous upbringing had been, since they were selected for their groups randomly. They were then brought together for an exercise in frustration and response. As might be expected, when they were all promised a movie and candy and then abruptly hustled off to another classroom and told that neither would be available, the children who had been encouraged to be aggressive started fights and were noisy and disruptive. The other children, who had previously been encouraged to be coöperative, actually throve during this experiment, intensely focusing on consoling others and becoming more coöperative than ever. (Nagler: 24) We have to ask the counterfactual: what if all children were trained to be compassionate, caring and coöperative?

I often hand out an excerpt from Barbara Deming's essay *Revolution and Equilibrium*, which is a bit dense and may need its own brief frontload. Use whatever makes sense to you; you are introducing them to the writings of nonviolent thinkers and you are creating a quiet window of time for yourself, during which you can review what these good people have told you about their goals for this training. Use your time to do two things. First, make the linkages and create a set or sets of commonly held similar goals and generally examine what bonds the group and what bonds the group—as it is presenting itself—to you. Then think about your plans and how to set them into this new information most effectively. You may, for example, take more time and offer more stress to the group-to-group nonviolent conflict resolution discussions and roleplays if that is the general sense of what the group is looking for. Or you could spend more time talking about nonviolent self-defense in response to personal attack or threat of attack, if that seems to tie the group together more.

When the group seems to be done reading, ask for questions and comments and then offer your thoughts on what coheres in the group as you have been able to see it. Stop for additional comments or observations but

Drill it in: training like the nonviolent military 173

don't necessarily do a go-round. They are more time-consuming and there will be several more of those chances.

- **establish ground rules**

Explain which rules are imperative to you and which might be discretionary, depending on the will of the group. For example, I won't teach or lead groups unless everyone agrees not to interrupt and not to engage in personal attack—except when roleplaying and not physically roughly even then. Other facilitators are able to flow with interruptions and are able to use personal attack as teachable moments. I prefer to be able to challenge violators on the spot. Other facilitators may have other ground rules that I don't absolutely need—e.g., no language that may be politically incorrect. This is a matter for you do determine ahead of time. To formulate and then decide on your ground rules, it is necessary to make your group's unalterable rules consensual. This requires a go-round or at least asking for a show of hands of anyone who cannot continue with your inflexible rules. If there are rules you must operate under and one or more cannot agree to follow them, you must decide whether to continue, or ask someone to leave the group, or ask the group to decide. You absolutely do not want to be into a training and have your basic rules violated and a debate to erupt at that point.

On confidentiality: At times, I train people who are required by law to report what they hear if they strongly suspect a crime has been committed. It is best to clear that up ahead of time so that everyone feels safe about that and so that no one is labeled a snitch. I simply inform the group that, while I intend to respect confidentiality, and while I am going to ask the group to agree to the same, we cannot expect that confession of a crime or naming the perpetrator of a crime—no matter how distant in the past—will necessarily remain in the group, since many of us have obligations to society to take such information to someplace for possible adjudication, or at least investigation. Assure the group that the intent is not to squelch depth of discussion but rather to assure all participants that this group is operating out of a sense of duty to humanity, and part of that duty is to bring violators of our social codes to accountability. Clearly, this discussion is malleable; I might well report a sexual crime or violent crime divulged in what may be the victim's cry for justice (though this is hypothetical personally, since I've never had that happen in any training), but I've trained many groups to prepare to break the law in acts of nonviolent civil resistance, and so cannot and will not reveal that information to anyone to whom the group doesn't wish it revealed. Even then, however, openness and transparency of intent ought to be discussed, so that paranoia is eliminated. I often tell them ahead of time what I have said for many years in response to paranoid talk in such trainings or meetings: It would be an honor to be a defendant with each of you in a trial in which we are charged with conspiring to spread nonviolence. It gets the worst fear out in front and embraces it, which can be liberating—or at least a reality check for all.

- *hassle line*

Everyone lines up in two equal lines opposing each other. The first line represents those who are holding one position—for example, in favor of some basic human right, or some piece of legislation—and the others hold a mainstream point of view. The mainstream group heckles and derides those who have come to make their statement. The challenge to the first group is to keep the situation nonviolent. This exercise may be repeated periodically throughout the training in one permutation or another (e.g., one line comprises activists and one comprises media out to get the story, with some media friendly, some hostile, some diffident, some strictly professional).

- *debrief*

Hear from everyone on reactions, or ask specific questions and go-round, or ask questions of specific participants who seemed to you to represent one noteworthy item. If you do go-rounds, be aware that they eat up lots of time—but can also be quite secure for those who wish to express themselves and aren't good about asserting themselves. You will probably do well to enforce the no-interrupting ground rule early and with vigor during your first go-round, since that will set the tone for the rest of your training. If you choose to just hear from one or two during this debrief, it is usually best to preface your next debrief or your next discussion with something like, "Let's hear from those who haven't been talking much." Always give the chance to pass—to not respond—but try to at least give equal opportunity to all and extra encouragement to those most reticent.

worst case demonstrations

This is where I offer my fall-back, default settings of response to rapidly escalating attack. For me, they are in response to three explosive situations and I have them at the ready at all times. Others need to think about what they might do.

1. Display of fierce temper and irrational, shrill excited verbal aggression on the part of the attacker, overwhelming my considered, rational, calming approach. I simply say Peace be with you, brother (sister). I open my palms and take a step backward, if there is space for that, allowing some calming space to come between and to settle, hopefully, on both of us.

2. Obvious intent to jump to physical attack. I sit down on the floor or ground while maintaining eye contact with the perpetrator and am as calm and non-threatening as possible. If there is audio room for it, I also offer a peaceful invitation. I keep my hands visible, palms up and open.

3. Physical attack. If it is beyond pushing or virtually rhetorical shoving (again, sitting will usually work in that case), and if actual hard blows are being delivered, the so-called SNCC (pronounced "snick") position is the end of the line. This is a curled-up on the floor or ground position designed to protect as many vital organs as possible. I usually demonstrate this quickly and do not ask for anyone else to do it, since it is entirely memorable and we need not dwell on it. Stress that none of these defaults are desirable and should only be employed when all else is failing. Dropping to the floor or the ground, for example, is radical and ought to be done only in the face of radical threat. It will appear overblown otherwise and, in the case of the SNCC position, could even elicit the predator-prey reaction and invite the actual beating we are trying to avoid if done during tension but before the tripwire to violence has been crossed. I usually mention how ridiculous one might seem if one used these two physical reactions if they weren't absolutely necessary, which reassures the participants that they won't leave the training expected to hit the streets prepared to sit on sidewalks every time they engage anyone in rigorous discussion. It is also helpful, I think, to note that, for me personally, I've only had to deal with the SNCC position a very few times over 35 years of activism and nonviolent resistance and only had to do unplanned sitdowns a few times. These are emergency measures and, we hope, our lives are not lived in constant emergency. Further, the techniques we are learning will tend to help us avoid such emergencies.

- **explanation of when nonviolence has succeeded historically**

This is the time to establish the bona fides of nonviolence as a realistic response to even the most oppressive attacker, invader, armed occupation force, mugger, rapist, belligerent cop, surly drunk or hostile youth. Having heard something of your participants' stories and hopes, you can tailor this section to discussions of most interest to the group in aggregate with special references to history that might go more directly to the interests of one or more participants who are looking for something different than the others.

- **talk about research into rape response**

When research is examined critically and it appears as though a particular kind of nonviolent approach is best, that understanding goes to one of the most dramatic questions that people have about nonviolence, i.e., But what should I do if someone is trying to rape me? While this is used as a rhetorical given by those who argue against nonviolence, the question is now one that can be completely turned around; evidence indicates that the nonviolent, assertive response may be not only the most effective but also the least likely to result in harm to the potential victim.

- **roleplay a confrontation, focusing on passive acceptance**

Set up a situation in which a smaller, more apparently vulnerable person is verbally intimidated by a larger, aggressive assailant. The vulnerable one should passively, virtually silently accept his fate, perhaps whimpering a bit now and then. The others ought to watch with instructions to be formulating observations, criticisms, suggestions and questions.

- **debrief**

Go around the circle and offer everyone a chance to talk about what they have seen in the light of what they know. Answer questions directly put to you and allow participants who did the active roles to answer questions put directly to them, but otherwise make sure that the entire group is heard from, uninterrupted, in turn. Summarize learnings at the close of this circle.

discuss the differences between assertion and aggression

When does assertion cross the line to become an invasion of another's emotional space? When that line is crossed is the line, arguably, between assertion and aggression. Another way to look at it is that assertion is standing up for one's rights in the context of standing up for the rights of all, whereas aggression is trying to bring another person into a position of submission. The distinction may sound subtle but the line is quite bright in real life. Crossing it is dangerous and not going right up to it is dangerous. In other words, conflict avoidance can work under many circumstances but only permits injustice and violence in too many situations or relationships, whereas reacting with rage and the apparent desire to dominate or hurt is perceived as an attack on the dignity of an individual. Being attacked as a person means becoming defensive. Having behavior attacked as unprincipled while still honoring the core value of the attacker is an assertive response that is most likely to elicit a more just outcome, however grudgingly granted by the perpetrator.

- **roleplay an aggressive response to attack**

One person simulates an unjust attacker or cruel dominating authority figure or a threatening criminal, while the other represents the outraged, objectifying, insulting counter-attacker who feels wholly justified in an aggressive response to unjust attack.

- **debrief**

What happened? Did the perpetrator suddenly come to his senses, smile, apologize profusely for any inconvenience and stroll away never to bother

Drill it in: training like the nonviolent military

innocent folks again? Probably not; it's not the way of the world, and it is not how we seem to react to counterattack. Did the initial attacker stiffen his resolve and come back again with an even more dominating attack? If so, why do we think that happened? Could it be that any humiliation only breeds the seeds of the next conflict, the deepening desire to best the enemy?

- **roleplay an assertive response to attack**

One person attacks another unjustly and the innocent victim stands up for her rights very boldly and forthrightly, demanding that the perpetrator live up to a code of honor, to a code of just and fair behavior. For every injury, she struggles to maintain dignity of both herself and her attacker and she is relentless in asserting her right to be treated like a full human being.

- **debrief**

How does the assertive victim's response affect the perpetrator? Does the conflict tend to escalate or deëscalate? Why do people think that this simulation is different in tone and outcome than the previous aggressive roleplay? Anybody have a story that might show something similar from real life?

discuss humanizing the opponent through personalism

Ask the group how they each feel when they feel as though someone expects the best behavior possible from them under the circumstances? If they are interacting with someone who seems to see them as possessing great qualities and high potential, do they feel as though they tend to live up to it more often?

Helping an attacker to humanize you will help to save you; helping an attacker humanize himself will help to save you and everyone who interacts with him in the future. This is not to claim that good work done to develop the capability to humanize you cannot or would not transfer onto another person, but the connection isn't as direct. Further, it is usually easier to help another to humanize himself—to believe himself capable of what you are assuring him are superior norms and achievable norms by him. Clearly, overcoming internalized self-oppression is a part of that struggle, but it can be achieved in a short-term fashion with a surprise tack that can bolster that unexpected self-image. Essentially, the message you need to deliver is: You know, and I know, and I know that you know, that you are a basically good person who truly would rather not do an act of violence that would hurt another person. This may mean that you need to rise above your pain that you had been hoping to mitigate through sharing it with another, but that is part of what makes you a fine person, when you do rise above that.

How you deliver that message is unique to your circumstances, your communications style, the ability of the opponent to hear you and many other internal and external factors; in short, context. But it is the message you are advised to deliver by any nonviolent means at your disposal. Social workers do that daily when they come across clients who might otherwise hurt them. So do cops and probation officers as they enter other people's turf and attempt to deal with conflict. If an unarmed parole officer can enter a convict's home and assure him that he is a bigger man than the relatively little man who just violated the terms of parole and that he must come along peaceably to jail and back to prison for another year—and parole officers do this as a part of their jobs—certainly the rest of us can begin to learn to do that.

- **roleplay a commonality-seeking response to attack**

One person is insulted because of her identity. She responds by asking questions that immediately trigger a realization of a possible commonality. For example, a carpenter who is protesting a nuclear bomb facility can respond to riot-dressed police with comments about working conditions, fair pay, lousy hours, no credit for a job well done, and, besides, who makes all the money? The nuclear arsenal manufacturers, who are never on the front lines of anything except at the Pentagon, picking up their fat checks for millions. Maybe the cop has a brother who pounds nails, or maybe he used to. The rich will all be living high on the profits and the poor will pay with their health by working with this poison, as usual. It's a bit like the veterans who went to DC to protest and walked silently, with dignity, and when the cops were arresting them, it was done with great tenderness.

- **debrief**

How can the use of identity be used in a positive way, that is, to bring the attacker into your identity group, or to enter his? When objectification becomes impossible because the attacker is brought to the point of closer identification with or grudging appreciation for the victim, the attack withers away. Is there at least one participant with a story that might illustrate this principle?

bring in conflict resolution theories of principled negotiation

Explain the four elements of principled negotiation—1. separate the people from the problem. 2. focus on interests, not positions. 3. invent options for mutual gain. 4. insist on using objective criteria. (Fisher: 15)

- **roleplay attack response based on insistence on fair practices**

Drill it in: training like the nonviolent military 179

There is a neighborhood argument over children playing too loudly in the vacant lot. A man who says he is interrupted incessantly by their "damned noise" lives next to the lot and has threatened the children with bodily harm. When one of them curses at the man, he comes out and chases them. One of them, the son of a single mother, lives in a small home on the other side of the vacant lot. The mother is outside at the moment and she sends the child straight inside. The man yells a threat at her as he strides toward her, fists clenched and a snarl on his face. She stands up to him and demands that he not trespass on her yard. He slows very slightly as he walks onto her grass and shouts at her about the "brats" that "he's gonna hurt." She takes a step toward him and asks him if he thinks he has a right to come onto her property and threaten her child with harm. Eventually, they actually talk and she and he work out what they each regard as fair.

- **debrief**

How did the dynamics seem to change when the man heard the woman stand up to him so intrepidly about the trespass? And how did they change again when she refused to be intimidated by his sturm and drang?

discuss identity conflict and core protection

From the theories of identity conflict, we learn that everyone has an identity—indeed, a series of identities. From communications theory we learn that everyone has a core that no one can get to, that they reserve for just themselves. And, we also discuss the use of non-antagonistic language that respects the identity of the other while making a claim for one's own identity and, in fact, anyone else's.

- **roleplay attack on identity and face**

An African-American child is insulted and called a racial name in the park by a high school aged boy; one adult is a witness. The bigger child is with two compatriots; all three are dressed like antisocial tough guys and all are menacing. The witness stands up for the attacked child and is surrounded by the three belligerent young men. Using a variety of "I" messages, honoring and acknowledging techniques, and gentle challenges to be the very best that they can be, the witness defuses the situation, even though no one is necessarily visibly transformed on the spot and even though none of the tough boys loses face or necessarily admits to error. The racial insult is not repeated and the child obviously feels safer and also validated.

- **debrief**

Is it necessary to intervene in such a situation? Why or why not? Is "victory" possible and what defines victory? How were the identities and thus the faces of everyone protected, or were they?

explain current mediation theories

Voluntary agreements reach through mediation have a much higher rate of compliance than do judgments rendered by an authority. The basic process teaches the mediator listening skills and communications skills that are then used to facilitate a process that is likely to lead to an agreement to which both—or all—parties voluntarily agree. Key to the process is the initial opportunity to tell the story, something that simply never happens in court. During a courtroom proceeding, all communications are tightly controlled by a ritualized, precedent-reliant, heavily prescribed and proscribed filter system. Spontaneity and the sense of having said one's piece simply never happens, whereas in mediation that is the quid pro quo; I will listen to your pesky version of the story because I know I'll get to give mine. No interruption is not an option in this phase of mediation; it is a generally accepted requirement that frees all parties to potentially hear the other side. The best mediations—the ones that make progress in conflicts that have proven intractable and perduring—elicit transformations based on one side at last hearing and ultimately sympathizing with the other side.

- **roleplay focusing on questioning, listening to stories**

In a professional meeting of six colleagues working for a non-profit organization, one irate member attacks the character, the work habits, the quality of work and the quantity of work of another colleague. The attacked person doesn't respond immediately, but his friend rises to defend him, counter-attacking the initial attacker, amidst interruptions and steadily rising voices, personal statements and generally slashing commentary. As the tempers flare all around, one colleague asks the first attacker a question, seeking information or seeking sources, and continues asking questions of each party in turn, stressing each time that she is just looking for information, just trying to understand. As she is interrupted, she valiantly goes forth, gently probing. At some point, when possible, she asks if the group can allow each person to take 10-15 minutes to completely clear the air. One-by-one they agree.

- **debrief**

Did the emotions generated by the attacker nearly preclude any chance for listening? Did the person who gathered facts reduce tension or channel it more appropriately, more usefully?

discuss working with people with mental health problems

Drill it in: training like the nonviolent military

It is clearly necessary to use special techniques if someone if violently mentally ill, but psychiatrists, psychologists, nurses, orderlies and counselors have to do so daily. The vast majority of those patients—either in locked-down units, in-patient open units, out-patient treatment or intaking emergency rooms—are managed without physical force and when force is used it can be done without inflicting pain. Basic redirection skills are key—using refocusing tactics to knock intense dysfunction loose from its destructive track.

- **roleplay based on redirection**

It is a border check in a country suffering from civil war and the attendant violence directed at leaders of the civilian opposition. The guard is quite authoritarian in a shrill way, fingering his automatic weapon and capriciously barking orders. His fellow guard, his immediate superior, remains less visible, in the guard shack. One person is accompanying another who is in danger if she is detained. The accompanier has a letter from a higher authority which theoretically gives the two of them freedom to pass, but the isolated border checkpoint is not in view of anybody who can intervene in case of emergency. Suddenly a third guard exits the shack and approaches the local human rights worker who is being accompanied. He roughly demands identification and calls her a communist, a troublemaker, and a danger who is with the guerrilla forces. He begins to manhandle her and the accompanier approaches him, asking if he can offer any information, asking if he can help with his connections to some governmental official, preferably military, pulling the letter from his pocket in a non-threatening fashion. The letter generates suspicion and curiosity and is eventually used to get the attention of the superior officer, who lets the group pass after he is properly deferred to and placated.

A nonviolence training can take place in a half-hour or over a period of several months. Our skill levels and depth of understanding will be reflected in the time and creativity we devote to these trainings. Any training is good; more training is better. When someone says, "I don't need nonviolence training; I did that a few years ago at the blockade of the nuclear waste truck," or some similar statement, they need to be asked if they see nonviolence as a preferable method to violent resolution of conflict. If they do, they then should consider how one method of conflict management can replace another without greater and greater commitments to deeper training and repetitive training. Soldiers march and handle weapons, drive tanks and shoot ordnance. Nonviolent forces need to respond quickly and professionally to conflict or risk losing any chance for success. The very same is true if a person is using nonviolence training to prepare for potential conflicts on the job, in a neighborhood, amongst a clientele, or in a family. The notion that a policewoman could walk or drive a beat and handle outbreaks of violence using her weapons and physical defense skills without constant training is ludicrous. A person who does nonviolent work in that milieu is much better prepared with ongoing training, debriefing, and more training.

On the other hand, those who work in situations where they may suddenly be expected to know CPR—but rarely if ever actually perform it in reality—are only required to undergo a two-four hour annual recertification training. Nonviolent response to attack or to intimidation may be something that one rarely, if ever, needs to actually employ for some who simply wish to be exposed to the skills. Those people can perhaps be adequately served with short, periodic refresher trainings to help keep them a bit more prepared in case of emergency.

sources:

Fisher, Roger and William Ury, **Getting to Yes: Negotiating Agreement Without Giving In**. NYC: Penguin Books 1981, 2nd edition, 1991.

Heatherwick, Miri, "Against the action, not the actors," Peace News, June-August 2000. (11)

Lederach, John Paul, **Preparing for Peace: Conflict Transformation Across Cultures**. Syracuse NY: Syracuse University Press, 1995.

Nagler, Michael, **Is There No Other Way? The Search for a Nonviolent Future**. Berkeley CA: Berkeley Hills Books, 2001.

CHAPTER EIGHT
National liberation & terrorism

In the end, the people have all the power. They can withhold coöperation, they can redirect coöperation, they can resist, they can give and they can take. They can stay away or they can overwhelm. The Pentagon, for example, is the world's largest office building, and fields millions of personnel around the world, yet, as Air Force veteran and former Black Panther George Edwards notes, "There are tens of millions of us, and yet we're at risk because of them. We think that they have all the power, and yet we do; we just don't realize it. But we don't dare to cross that threshold. We don't dare, but if we wanted to, we could shut down the Pentagon." (Hallock: 257)

The power to stop war, achieve justice, gain liberation is all about political power and public policy. Nonviolence is what happens when hope and courage are added to sober analysis of cost and benefit.

It is when people dare, when they realize their power, that hope rises and with it the possibility of liberation. In a world of thousands of nations but only 191 official nation-*states*, "national liberation" can mean a lifestyle, a state of being and a respected collective identity—sustainably recreated with nonviolent power. We see examples and illustrations all around the world.

> [The] *"support of the black majority for international sanctions and the broadly nonviolent movement to end apartheid helped bring the white government to the realization that the status quo could no longer be maintained."*
>
> —Carnegie Commission on Preventing Deadly Conflict (Carnegie: 126)

Indeed, the power of nonviolence to achieve national liberation has been studiously ignored by most of those responsible for teaching the next generation of national leadership, even though that generation—and the next, and the next—has had the nonviolent model available since the British lost the crown jewel of the largest empire history has ever seen. When India became free in 1947, military apologists were quick to claim that only because Britain was reeling from the effects of World War II was India able to push over and prod out such an erstwhile imperial power.

True enough. And the reverse can be claimed with equal truth; without nonviolent resistance, most armed national liberation struggles would have been doomed to failure.

The colonists had been increasingly withholding coöperation from the British before and during the American revolution. Had the citizenry coöperated generally with the imperial masters, the revolution almost certainly would have failed.

When the Sandinistas won freedom from US-backed Somoza in Nicaragua in 1979, their victory was made possible by a widespread pattern of citizen nonviolent opposition to the military government of Somoza. (Jeffrey: 164)

More to the point is the question *How did nonviolence achieve that particular Indian liberation at that particular time and what general lessons can we learn?*

Richard Gregg spent years in India studying and working with Gandhi and Gandhi's successors. He initially wrote a short book, **The Power of Nonviolence**, in 1934, and then updated it after more time in India and more occasion to apply nonviolence to then-current psychological theories. His works remain vital and informative, though the language is dated.

Gregg compared nonviolent power to martial arts that use the force of the attacker in the defense of the attacked. He called it psychological jiu-jitsu, and what he meant by this term was what he saw happen again and again in India, when the mighty armed force of the British Empire was repeatedly a liability to its own success, due to tactics, strategies and philosophies practiced by nonviolent Indian liberation fighters. The British tried heavy-handed methods and those methods only served to strengthen the resolve to withdraw coöperation, and thus made their imperial investment less and less profitable while at the same time increased the overhead, the capital investments that the British thought necessary to enforce the requisite rule.

Part of the reason for this nonviolent success is that the morale of the British troops was constantly undermined by the nonviolent but very assertive reaction of Gandhi's forces, which served to make it virtually impossible to remain angry enough to commit violent injustices. Anger is exhausting. (Gregg: 45) It is also a poor companion to respect, which the Brits felt more and more for the heroic self-sacrificing *satyagrahis*.

When no fresh reasons are injected into the situation, it is hard to evoke past outrage and it is hard to maintain troop willingness to use violence against an enemy that offers neither the predator-prey relationship nor the no-holds-barred warrior competition. Once fear and rage subside, reason has a chance.

Terrorism, military action, or law enforcement?

> *Terrorism is sometimes a tool for revolutionaries and nationalists, but it is most frequently used by governments to maintain state power.*
>
> —Jonathan White, professor of criminal justice and author of *Terrorism* (White: xx)

> *Terrorism has often been the preferred methodology of marginal or disenfranchised groups. There is appropriate concern that the technical capabilities of terrorists are increasing.... Yet groups employing terror have often failed to achieve their stated goals in any reasonable time frame. This fact may lead populations that have formerly sheltered terrorists to the rediscovery of other approaches, including the strategic use of nonviolent action.*
>
> —Peter Ackerman and Christopher Kruegler, scholars of nonviolence (Ackerman: xxii)

The losing effort to stop terrorism illustrates the futility of trying to stop the gush of hot water from a bathtub spigot by using rags and fingers—or in smashing at the spewing scald with a sledge hammer—when the clear answer would be to reach for the faucet control above the spigot instead of focusing solely on the precise point of visible emission. Nonviolent peacebuilding is not merely the best way to address terrorism; it is, at some point, the only path with a chance for sustainable success. While much was made of the great sense of relief at the end of 2002 that no new al-Qaida attacks have brought US office buildings crashing down, we may be assured that the sense of anti-US grievance is only rising around the Earth, and that, in the upcoming period, we can expect either more terror attacks on US soil or a wider and wider war as we attempt to apply US hegemony everywhere, an intimidation rightly called terrorist by many. With national leadership almost casually talking about US abilities to destroy two separate nations at the same time, can we place ourselves in the targeted nations and ask how that feels? Thousands of bomb sorties on the way? That is a rain of terror, a reign of imperial brute force.

As Jonathan White points out, states use terrorism—indeed, states virtually own the concept and merely loan it to private parties, who then get all the credit or blame, glory or scorn. Lenin advocated for it and practiced it. The US certainly used it during World War II when the cities of Hamburg, Cologne, Dresden, Frankfort, Tokyo, Hiroshima and Nagasaki were attacked indiscriminately and mercilessly, with the avowed, announced intent not to reduce military targets to unusable rubble but rather to demoralize the enemy. Such terror attacks are a direct outflow of Carl von Clausewitz's theory of total war, which itself is an extension of the ancient—and even then controversial—practice of laying siege to a city. The civilian casualties inflicted by states have always vastly outnumbered those exacted by irregulars. History will name those irregulars terrorists, anarchists, freedom fighters or the Fathers of nations, depending on who writes the history books and how the campaigns turned out. Similarly, some so-called law enforcement looks exactly like terrorism, as does some military action. Simply, the use of violence or credible threat to use violence in order to induce compliant behavior by causing fear is frequently terrorism, though the more popular understanding associates the word with violence against targets at best peripherally—and oftentimes not at all—associated with the adversary to be influenced. (Kriesberg: 114)

"You cannot say terrorism when it occurs in New York is bad terrorism and when it occurs elsewhere is good terrorism," said Jaswant Singh, Indian External Affairs Minister, speaking of the alliance between Pakistan and the US against Afghanistan's Taliban, when India considers Pakistani actions in the Kashmir terrorist. (*Newsweek*: 21)

Most would consider the violent overthrow of an elected government to be terrorism; indeed, many in Chile and Guatemala regard the US government as a terrorist state, since that is precisely what happened to them in 1973 and 1954 respectively, at the initiation of the United States Central Intelligence Agency. The Allende and Arbenz governments were in power because of the expressed wishes of the people of Chile and Guatemala and the US replaced both in bloody takeovers, replacing both with military dictators answerable to Washington, friendly to transnational corporations, and brutally repressive to their indigenous labor and human rights leadership.

> *The punch to my stomach and the torture bed again. Stop it...please! Like a caged animal...I can't turn around; my kidneys are mangled. Today, I saw blood in my urine.*
>
> —Alicia Partnoy, former political prisoner in her native Argentina, ***The Little School: Tales of Disappearance and Survival*** (Partnoy: 94)

> One wishes only that more legislators voting on [Latin] American aid...would listen to Partnoy's song of freedom.
>
> —Julia Alvarez, Foreword, *The Little School: Tales of Disappearance and Survival* (Partnoy: 10)

Scholars sometimes mark the difference between the terrorism of the challenger and terrorism of the recognized state as a siege of terror waged by the former and a reign of terror executed by the latter. (Walter: *vii*) In reality, there is a vast difference, though not to the people actually attacked in the moment, especially if they are "collateral damage." The asymmetry of power means nothing to particular victims. Though the Israelis can kill three times as many Palestinians because they have superior firepower, courtesy of the US, it does not diminish one iota from the grief and pain of those attacked by low-tech explosives or AK-47s. Concomitantly, it ill-serves us to deny that the innocents dying on the ground are each sacrificed by push-button warriors and chickenhawk politicians.

> *"Air campaign"? "Coalition forces"? "War on terror"? How much longer must we go on enduring these lies? There is no "campaign" – merely an air bombardment of the poorest and most broken country in the world by the world's richest and most sophisticated nation. No MiGs have taken to the skies to do battle with the American B-52s or F-18s. The only ammunition soaring into the air over Kabul comes from Russian anti-aircraft guns manufactured around 1943.*
>
> —Robert Fisk, journalist, *London Independent* (Fisk)

The dead Afghan child or the dead Washington DC postal worker are just as gone, though they weren't the direct, announced targets of the smart bombs or smartly produced anthrax-laced envelopes. It is hard to imagine a more precision weapon than one with an actual address written on it, yet the mail room personnel die in these battles—and they react angrily, knowing that their deaths are regarded as merely incidental, evidenced by the extreme caution taken initially in the halls of Congress and the lack of concern about the postal station until two workers died. Can we fathom the corresponding anger felt by the Afghan people who get in the way of US "precision munitions" as they lay in their hospital beds? "The longer this war goes on the worse it is going to be not only for the millions of people in Afghanistan but also in the estimation of the 1.2 billion Muslims of the world and the 57 Muslim states in the world," writes Francis A. Boyle, professor of

International Law, University of Illinois-Champaign Urbana. (Boyle)

> *The duration and the sharpness of the American bombing campaign was beginning to shore up support for the Taliban inside Afghanistan, where their popularity was clearly on the wane before Sept. 11.*
>
> *Repeated reports by the Taliban of American bombs' killing civilians appear to have intensified the feeling among Afghans that the United States has attacked Afghanistan, not just its rulers. The Taliban have found much of their support among simple, uneducated people.*

—reporter Jane Perlez, *New York Times*, 24 October 2001. (Perlez)

During a siege of terror (e.g. a bombing campaign or al-Qaeda attacks), the elite and the military are most fearful because they are the usual intended targets, though everyone is living with some apprehension. During such a siege, it is easy and—for the elite and for the military—desirable to get the populace aroused and angry at the Other. Under a reign of terror (e.g. Taliban rule, Saddam Hussein rule or US puppet Shah of Iran rule), most of society lives in daily paranoia at the potential pain of even the wrong utterance or improper association. People have a much harder time speaking out loud during a reign of terror and are erroneously seen by outsiders as being less critical of their authorities. Naturally, one of these types of terror tends to enable the other, which usually means societies which suffer from the one are also in the midst of the other, making distinctions trickier.

The series of occurrences in the US around the 11 September 2001 attack were different in the sense that, while much of the world identifies the US with the support or creation of reigns of terror now and in the past—from Iran to Guatemala to Israel to Indonesia to the Philippines to El Salvador to royal regimes in the Mideast to Chile and on and on—most of the citizenry of the US were and still are utterly, blissfully, confusedly, unaware of that. Instead, they associate the notion of reign of terror with those in enemy nations—the terror inflicted by Lenin and Stalin upon the peoples of the Soviet Union, by Saddam Hussein in Iraq, by Kim Chong Il in North Korea, or the terror of Hitler in Germany. Thus, US citizens were dumbfounded when those engaged in a siege of terror struck back in the name of all Islamic peoples suffering under repressive governments propped up by the US—from Jordan to Saudi Arabia to Egypt and so forth—as well as in the name of followers of Islam under direct attack from the US in Iraq or living in territories occupied by the lead recipient of US military aid, Israel. At some point, if those of us who are educating and writing do our jobs, the US Americans will, like the

British vis-à-vis the IRA, understand the complaints against them. They—like the British—will no doubt continue to engage in an armed response of vicious proportion, but they will do so with the knowledge that their attackers have their own reasons. The door to discussion thus opens a crack.

At this point, US Americans still exhibit great confusion and cannot grasp motives as they consider the desperate suicide attacks by zealots from the Mideast and Central Asia. Why, we wonder, do they commandeer civilian airliners to fly them into tall buildings in the US? Why strap themselves with explosives and board a bus in Jerusalem or walk into a pizza joint there? Why are they so willing to sacrifice themselves? According to one US CIA official, "To get somebody to fly an airplane—to kill himself—somebody paid his family a hell of a lot of money." (Hersh: 35) Others cite religious fervor and more point to oppression and revenge.

Most analysts also look specifically at Islamic frustration with westernized Arab regimes. (Congressional: 369) To be clear, the term "westernized" is a euphemism for the partnership between the center nation elite and the periphery nation elite; thus, "westernized" can be translated into a number of predictable characteristics: rich, autocratic, patriarchal, violent, terrorist (on the part of the state toward indigenous leadership that challenges policy), and, most of all, a corrupt client of the US war manufacturers. Terrorism is routinely committed by "westernized" states against their own minorities or their own dissidents and it is facilitated by arms and training from those Western powers. Thus it happens that recruits for organizations like al-Qaeda can come from the ranks of Muslims who are from nations that have been so exploited. One pundit labeled the rule of periphery elite Mobutu Sesi Seka in the colonially formed Congo a 31-year "kleptocracy," and that label could as well be affixed to all states controlled by and used by the rich domineering elites. Those governments in the so-called developing world enable violence and destruction on a rampant, systemic scale as they funnel all the wealth into the US-European region, keeping only enough to satiate the local despots.

Debt forgiveness to any people who manage to throw off these rulers would be at once minimally fair and in the enlightened self-interest of those who see a more just world as a more nonviolent and sustainable world. The major lenders have the reserves to handle such debt elimination. (Roodman: 65) And when those poorest of the poor nations have recently thrown off repressive governments left over from the Cold War—such as that in Mozambique or Nicaragua—debt relief ought to be seen as compassion for those who suffered long enough from the ravages of an East-West armed struggle, a struggle that has left so many poor nations in such bad economic shape. Nicaragua, victim of such geopolitical battles, owed $5.7 billion to outside lenders even before the devastation of Hurricane Mitch. When international lending bodies trumpeted their responding "debt relief," others revealed it to be largely postponement, something Roman Catholic Archbishop of Tegucigalpa Oscar Andres Rodriguez called a "stay of execution." (Abramovitz: 48) Clearly, the post Cold War economic structures will either radically readjust or merely serve to bolster increasing levels of conflict as generations unborn are inflicted with past debt.

War and extreme violence—acts that are life-taking and life-risking—are always much more complex than one easy lead graf in a popular press or one Big Interview with an official.

When facing its own population, the US government doesn't acknowledge that the majority of the world is aghast at the plight of the Palestinians and at the oppression heaped upon them by Israel. Despite UN resolutions, the US supports Israel in its crushing deprivation of a people who were in the way when the Israeli state was born—a state with its own bloody birth, midwifed by terrorism. In retrospect, the hotels blown up by Israeli freedom fighters in attempts to kill British officials and thus terrorize them out of the region looks a lot like the World Trade Center attacks which are similar attempts to get Western capitalism out of the Muslim world.

Here is part of the core issue—and that central issue for most terrorists who come from the Muslim world is that they have been treated like subhumans too often and too long by US-Europeans for them to forgive and forget—that we simply don't hear about: the US doesn't recognize that much of the territory controlled by the Israeli military and now settled by Israelis is recognized internationally as belonging to the Palestinians. The very name for the uprising against Israel is the *intifada*, which translates roughly into the "shaking off," presumably refers to Israel's presence in areas that do not belong to them except as spoils of war. Like the stony Sinai Peninsula, the Gaza strip is not coveted land but rather a bargaining chip that Israel would love to trade for peace—that poor run of sand is so abused that it is parching and polluting its own population into ill health constantly as it sucks its aquifer to depths so low that the sea has invaded beneath and ruined much of the potable water. (Homer-Dixon: 90) By the time Israel fully gives up Gaza, it will be almost absolutely unfit for human habitation.

Nonetheless, Israel is occupying another nation's land just as surely as Saddam Hussein occupied someone else's land upon invading Kuwait on 2 August 1990. Indeed, because of irredentist considerations, some would argue that Iraq had more of a claim on Kuwait than Israel does on the Gaza or West Bank or even the Golan Heights. Whatever the legitimacy of the competing claims, the US won't mention this to its own people. (Said: 132) Thus, we miss a vital body of information that might go to some glimmer of understanding of the rage driving the storm of relentless and recurring terrorism.

Understanding the roots of any terrorism is important. Understanding the cancer cell is important to the medical researcher; this doesn't mean those who search for the cure favor cancer. Learning the reasoning of the terrorist will help us establish experiments toward eliminating terrorism in the classic MLK fashion: by making them our friends. We will not eliminate terrorism by jumping on the bandwagon of one side of the other, by cheering on the terrorists, for example, in Hamas—who are explicitly saying that their suicide bombers kill civilians out of revenge—or by supporting the reign of terror coming down on the Palestinians from US-sponsored Israel Defense Force. At some quiet point in the *sturm und drang* those of us who favor nonviolence might do well to honor the few who cut themselves out of the mirror-image violence of both the intifada and the IDF.

What are other roots of this phenomenon? They are many and deep, as is true whenever and wherever we honestly investigate.

Some say the very existence of Israel would never have happened in modern times except for Hitler, the Holocaust, the subsequent clamor for a homeland for Jews. Without the creation of the state of Israel, obviously, most of the Palestinians in refugee camps would never have been forced off their land—indeed, there are several generations of Palestinians living in those camps, some of whom have never seen their homeland. Thus, some might say, we can try to analyze what caused Hitler and the German populace who brought him to power? We can then blame the Treaty of Versailles for its punitive reparation requirement of Germany, mostly insisted upon by the French, who also linked some coal-rich border territory to Germany's compliance with that odious treaty—and the subsequent irredentist German claims on land occupied by Germans living in Austria, Czechoslovakia, and Poland. (Kegley: 163) We can then—if we really wish to pursue this—return to the retributive peace accords following the war of 1870, which made France seethe for half a century or more after its bitter defeat as the belligerent in that six-month war with Prussia. Just as in interpersonal conflict, there is always one more bit of blame to cast upon another. It makes just as much sense to say that it is the fault of Napoleon, for what his actions did to the European community, or to point the finger at Columbus, for that matter, for his role in facilitating a major expansion of colonial power and wealth so that Europeans could exert hegemony over all others.

Coming closer to the present, one of the prime causes of terrorism was fueled by the 1967 war, a blitz by Israel (one of many tactics the oppressed learned well from the oppressor) that ended almost as it began. It left the citizens of the region in a fog of disbelief and nonacceptance—not unlike Europeans in the aftermath of the German invasion of Poland in 1939. Nothing about the war seemed permanently real to anyone and, indeed, the lives of those in the region have often been given over to readjustment and efforts to rectify the situation ever since.

The essential conclusion that one might come to is that violent control of the Palestinians hasn't worked for the Israelis and violent uprising hasn't worked for the Palestinians—both of them hanging on to their dysfunctional methods since the founding of Israel in 1948—but neither side has recognized that nonviolence might provide the solution so desperately needed. (Rigby: 32) While dialog in the internal communities has been officially initiated since the 1950s—most of the early efforts were municipally based in places like Haifa and Jerusalem under the aegis of the Hestadrut (Jewish Labor Union) and others—the national government didn't pay much attention to the question until the Khana antidemocratic fundamentalist Arab-hating Jewish movement rose to prominence in the early 1980s. (Abu-Nimer: 37) Arab leaders in the region have historically toed the line, opposing Israel, participating in war.

Exceptions are rare but significant. Though he was part of the military coalition arrayed against Israel, King Hussein of Jordan eventually made a unilateral peace with Israel. It was hard for him to do so on the one hand. He announced Jordan's entrance into the war against Israel just before midnight on 5 June 1967 and it was before 3 a.m. just a bit more than a day later that he received word from the great pan-Arabist Nasser that Jordan troops should withdraw from the West Bank, thus losing territory instead of gaining it as planned. By the 9th of June Nasser had resigned and Palestinians—citizens just the day before and refugees now—were trudging across bridges from their homes in the West Bank to the East Bank. (Abu-Odeh: 134) The camps—already home to so many following the 1948 war—swelled with yet more desperate, defeated, doomed Palestinians destined to dance in the streets upon hearing of a successful suicide bomber.

In a sense, the Palestinian question is the most vexing because most parties recognize the Palestinians right to a homeland but very few of those parties actually wish to see it.

Similarly, most parties recognized the Jews' right to a homeland, but few actually hoped it would happen, and no one wished to be near it. The original Zionists, who met at their first conference in 1896 in Basel, Switzerland, were considering Argentina and Uganda as possible locations for that homeland, but eventually settled on Palestine. (Spencer: 25) When Zionists began to settle in Palestine in the late 19th century, they brought an Eastern European culture of moneymaking success and robust economic achievement with them, slowly eclipsing traditionally paced Palestinian lifeways. When the rate of Israeli occupation increased and an independent Israel was looking much more likely—even before the outbreak of World War II—Arabs were already looking at Jewish prosperity and economic hegemony in Palestine not as good news but as a threat to an indigenous way of life and a bid to take over. Violence between Arabs and Jews in the region erupted periodically, including bloody riots in May 1921 and more violence emanating from Jerusalem in August 1929 and spreading nationwide, driven by the winds of hatred. At the core is identity, with all the baggage it carries, illustrated by the long-simmering conflict over holy places, each one a symbol, each one at the heart of territory coveted by at least two peoples, and usually at least three or four. (Idinopulos: 192+)

Simply, Israel is perceived as a nation of ancient foes of the Arabs who have conquered the heart of the holy land, who are armed and ready to drive off all who approach ancient holy sites, and as a population willing to exert humiliating control over those who wish to live on their ancestral lands in traditional patterns. It is also seen as a bastion of US imperialism, a place from which to monitor the oil fields and from which to launch or coordinate military attacks on Arab and Persian nations. Conversely, Israel is seen as an outpost of last-ditch survival of a persecuted people. Truth resides in both.

What can one person do?

On the negative sides we have Osama bin Laden and George Bush. Osama bin Laden always refers to the same issues when he is interviewed. "His pan-Islamic ideology seems particularly compelling to followers with the continued presence of U.S. troops in the Arabian Peninsula, sanctions against Iraq and a stalled Mideast peace process in which the United States is widely identified as furthering Israel's interests at the expense of Palestinians." (Loeb: 92) George Bush reacted to the attack on the US exactly as bin Laden thought he would, exactly as he hoped he would. The two need each other to maintain their cherished positions as "leaders," when, in reality, neither would be a leader worth much without their visions of destruction and identity group air of dire emergency.

On the positive side we find Noam Chomsky, one man, not an elected official, researched the Palestinian question and offered a stinging and thorough critique of US involvement in the issue. His scholarship has taught the teachers, empowered the activists, informed the mediators.

Mubarak Awad, a Palestinian not elected to any office, wrestled with his identity and his conscience and started offering nonviolent training to fellow Palestinians.

Some Norwegians undertook to connect high-ranking Israelis and Palestinians, ultimately resulting in the famous handshake on the White House lawn in September 1993. Those Norwegians were nongovernmental individuals.

In Seattle, on the day the World Trade Center towers were destroyed, more than 100 folks gathered downtown to demonstrate against any military retaliation—and two weeks later there were thousands in the streets calling not for inaction but a positive program of peacebuilding to replace a violent response. These demonstrations are public calls for nonviolent measures, for a cessation of the cycle of violence, for a complete change in direction. When we make those calls forcefully, we interest at least some of our fellow citizens and we offer an alternative to jingoistic, shrill calls for blood. When there are a million in the streets instead of one hundred, policy will change.

Dr. Zahir Wahab is a professor in the graduate school at Lewis and Clark College in Portland, Oregon, where he teaches sociocultural foundations of education, critical theory, multiculturalism, contemporary issues, contemporary studies, and political economy of education. He has degrees from American University in Beirut, Columbia University, and Stanford University. Dr. Wahab is originally from Afghanistan and is a four-time Fulbright Fellow. In addition, astonishingly, Dr. Wahab is on staff at the Goose Hollow Family Shelter at First United Methodist Church. He works as the custodian and sends his wages to support family members still in Afghanistan. During 2001, Dr. Wahab traveled to Afghanistan, Pakistan, and others parts of Central Asia. (Interfaith) In the aftermath of the events of 11 September 2001, Dr. Wahab was a hyperactive community speaker, reaching out to church groups, activists, academics, students and anyone who would listen, offering himself as a resource on Afghanistan, evidence that these are intelligent, compassionate people who simply wish to gain freedom and live in peace. His history, and his warm smile and caring demeanor earn him a place as a citizen goodwill ambassador from a maligned and attacked nation.

Arundhati Roy—Indian architect-turned-writer-then-activist—used her pen to address both her own people and then the entire world when her country and Pakistan did their ill-advised nuclear tests in 1998. She first challenged the rest of the world to rise from its complacency and its long history of assuming that it could take its time resolving its nuclear question while freaking out over the notion of a bomb on the subcontinent (*Can the Blacks handle the Bomb?*). (Roy: *vii*) Then, in a series of essays, she addressed her own people on the issue, resulting in a small book, **The Cost of Living** and subsequent books of original writing. She has become part of an international movement of writers who are attempting to continue their voice of reason and conscience above the inane media frenzy and political fray.

snowballing compassion

Reaching out to individuals and groups who are identified as somehow culpable for an act committed by individuals utterly unknown to them is a positive, healing step in a crisis. Jennifer Terry, then a student of mine, called her Muslim friends back home in Kansas during the World Trade Center crisis, offering her loving impulse into a fearful situation. While her act alone is the snowball-in-hell scenario, any snowballing of that kind of response can result in a different picture. One can mentally see the flames of hatred and fear retreat in the face of millions of such gestures. Each of these small acts battles the human tendency since time immemorial to lump all similar strangers into a group of offenders in a crisis. From the days when *the only good Indian is a dead Indian* to the Japanese internment camps to a modern Muslim dread, it is a phenomenon that goes to the need we have to understand danger. Military responses against the innocent are a tragic historic commonality. (Blalock: 227) Jennifer offers hope.

Nonviolent response to terrorism

> Nonviolent action...may not permit them to act out their hatred for others by taking revenge; but it allows—it requires—them to act out all the truth they feel about what the other has done, is doing to them, and to act out their determination to change this state of things. In this very process, one's hatred of the other can be forgotten, because it is beside the point; the point is to change one's life.
>
> –Barbara Deming, "On revolution and equilibrium" (Deming: 185)

Peacebuilding takes commitment by individuals and by organizations to prepare the way for governmental peacebuilding. Huge war budgets hamper such efforts, but "it is also clear that peace processes, particularly the components related to conciliation and mediation, depend more on the development of new relationships, increased interdependence, trust, commitment, and proper timing than they do on dollars....It must simultaneously be long-term slow and short-term intensive." (Lederach: 130+)

Since Aristotle, philosophers have been wrestling with the question of Just War—when is it permissible to go to war and what ought to be our conduct while waging it? Augustine codified the Christian code after the Christianization of the imperial Roman army in the fourth century CE—Christians needed an official excuse and the Bishop of Hippo devised one. Aquinas carried on the refinements one thousand years later and our democratic lawmaking bodies continue to grapple with this issue. The concept of *jus ad bellum*—when recourse to war is permissible—involves a list of seven conditions.

- **just cause**: the danger must be real and certain
- **competent authority**: only legitimate governments can wage war
- **comparative justice**: do rights and values justify killing?
- **right intention**: avoid unreasonable conditions, avoid civilian casualties
- **last resort**: have all peaceful options been exhausted?
- **probability of success**: don't kill or die unless there is a reasonable chance to make it worth it
- **proportionality**: does waging war respond to commensurate threat? (National: 412+)

For those who believe that nonviolence is the first and last choice, we are called to construct a parallel but different list. That list would be all the items that the Just War adherents forget to place before the putative "last resort."

There are many potential elements in a nonviolent response to terrorism, some of which are counterintuitive, some are long-term, some are best if done by governments, some components are best done by NGOs, some may be accomplished by either, some are addressing the causes and some tactics go straight to law enforcement, which can be done at least technically nonviolently. Several of these possible actions are discussed elsewhere in this book. A partial list—some of use in certain scenarios, some in others—might include:

- massive aid to the poorest citizenry
- massive influx of nonviolent workers as deterrent to violence from all sides
- citizen-based diplomacy
- debt relief to poorest nations
- sanctions that primarily affect elites
- education about terrorism
- education about nonviolent power
- global opprobrium
- ruling by International Criminal Court
- tracking and capturing suspects
- trial at International Criminal Court
- require adherence to International Court of Justice
- negotiation with all involved governments
- negotiation with all aggrieved parties
- mediation amongst all stakeholders
- reconciliation
- complete cessation of arms trade
- disarmament negotiations for states and irregulars

- interposition
- new economic guidelines and practices
- support for indigenous nonviolent groups
- support for indigenous pro-democracy elements
- end support for autocracies
- initiate cultural exchanges
- promote culturally and ecologically sensitive tourism
- promote nonviolent resistance to war or retaliation

massive aid to the poorest citizenry

> Bin Laden's activities in Sudan did not stop at arming and training a disparate gang of Afghan Arabs. A consummate networker, he was training terrorists and simultaneously telling politicians he wanted to help develop the country and improve Sudan's crumbling infrastructure.
>
> —Simon Reeve, *The New Jackals: Ramzi Yousef, Osama bin Laden and the Future of Terrorism* (Reeve: 178)

If terrorists come to the aid of a nation, spreading money throughout, they can be regarded by many as a friend to whom shelter should be offered. The US military response to this, whether to Libya, Sudan, or Afghanistan, has been to bomb those nations until they realize the costs of harboring terrorists, even generous terrorists. But a more long-term and helpful way to approach that struggle for the hearts and minds is obvious. Aid agencies stand ready to head into the poorest parts of the world with food, clothing, medicine, building materials and other necessities of life. Many of these places are war torn, desolate and the perfect breeding ground for new terrorists. The sheer goodwill generated by massive aid will not only obviate the thirst for inchoate rage and revenge in the present, but will change the ecology of what will produce the next generation of terrorists. If terrorists actually do spend a bit on the people in their version of trickle-down economics, isn't that better than the rain-down of bombs? And if the poorest are the recipients of massive aid, they will resolve their own complicity in terrorism because they will have so much more to lose.

massive influx of nonviolent workers as deterrent to violence from all sides

A publicly visible wave of humanitarian workers, peace activists,

International Solidarity Movement troops and others would—if numbers were large enough or certain celebrities were involved—almost provide a human shield against bombing and would tend to dampen local violence in the interest of public relations all around.

citizen-based diplomacy

"Of course," writes pundit Arianna Huffington, "when it comes to acting on our patriotism, we don't have to wait for our leaders. If they won't lead, we can just step around them." (Huffington: F5) Huffington was referring to trading in fuel pigs—SUVs in particular—for lean machines that will make the US less dependent on foreign oil. She could have said the same for countless other efforts undertaken by citizens unwilling to wait for their governments to begin doing the right thing. Citizen diplomacy handed Ronald Reagan his first major domestic defeat when it forced a reluctant US Congress to emulate its sanctions on a vicious apartheid regime in South Africa, as one of many such examples.

debt relief to poorest nations

Most of the nations that harbor terrorists are in debt to international lending agencies and most of that debt is left over from the previous ruling power's poor decisions and blatant theft. Thus, for example, the Philippines are in extreme international debt (Roodman: 17), due almost exclusively to the theft of the former US-sponsored dictator Ferdinand Marcos, and the Philippines are fertile terrorist recruiting grounds for al-Qaeda and other violent groups. Should the poorest people continue to pay for the thievery of former rulers who were clients of the richest nations? This simple matter of justice shows us one notch on the key to defeating terrorism through nonviolence.

sanctions that primarily affect elites

Smart sanctions are much more understood following the decade of sanctions since the end of the Cold War. None should imitate or even approximate the killer sanctions that so decimated the people of Iraq—while leaving their leadership intact. If sanctions related to human rights, then what of sanctions against the Saudi government, for example, which has not only managed to either alienate bin Laden or support him, depending upon which report you believe, but also terrorizes its own citizenry by anyone's definition. Ought the citizens of the world permit beheadings and amputations—the Friday fare in Saudi Arabia—or ought we somehow devise sanctions that target the obscenely rich thousands of Saudi princes and the theocratic terrorist House of Saud? Of the 19 hijackers that committed the 9.11.01 massacre, 15 were

Saudi nationals. Did they go despite or because of their homeland government, a ruling body kept propped up by US armed force? Global policeman, sanction thyself...

education about terrorism

Lifelong peace and justice activist Bradford Lyttle attended a workshop I offered on Nonviolent Responses to Terrorism and pointed out that the history of suicide attacks—which produce their own variety of terror—show that, when the attackers escalate to that level of commitment, their effectiveness increases. After Pearl Harbor, the Japanese in World War II were largely unsuccessful in their attacks on US warships until they desperately turned to kamikaze attacks by air and small submarine. Those strikes sunk more than 30 US warships and introduced a kind of awe-struck terror amongst US troops. (Lyttle) When has terrorism been effective? Irgun, the Zionist group that blew up the King David hotel in a bid to force the existence of the state of Israel, obviously used terror "successfully." Is it ever a military tactic as legitimate as, say, a warship, or a bomber aircraft? Is it understandable?

global opprobrium

No force, governmental or irregular, can long operate internationally in the face of unremitting negative opinion by the vast majority of the world's people. Any organization using violence to achieve its ends—from the largest nation-state or coalition of nation-states on down to the most marginal groups relies on reaching allies with news of its victimhood and its righteousness. To the extent that anyone can check the record and find that violent groups are not acting righteously or with proportionality, global outreach will not support the recruitment of more terrorists and will indeed tend to cut its ranks. It has taken every blunder that George Bush and Company could make to help Osama bin Laden to first avoid total condemnation from around the world—which he essentially had initially—and then to enjoy huge approval in places that learn of US bombing of poor Afghan and Iraq villages, wedding parties, and of US massive support for IDF rockets that kill Palestinian children. It is absolutely no accident that a war response to the suicide attackers of 9.11.01 infamy were followed by an increase in suicide bombing in Israel and the Occupied Territories. Part of that is the green light to Ariel Sharon from the US and part is the growing admiration for "martyrs" that gets vindicated each time another US bomb kills another three-year-old Muslim child.

ruling by International Criminal Court

The emerging ICC will have a large role to play in future indictments of war crimes suspects, whether those suspects are in the employ of a nation-state or whether they are acting outside that framework. If a president of a state orders violent activity against civilians, for example, the ICC will increasingly be able to call that offender to the bar even as its *ad hoc* version has called Slobodan Milošević. The advantage to the new ICC is that it will not be the tool of the powerful nations, unlike many others of its precedents, and slowly, if it is done with impartial fairness and complete probity, will come to be regarded as the venue for registering extreme grievances. If the former—or current—president or cabinet member of a large nation is committing crimes against humanity, that person must be accountable to the world, just as we expect an irregular such as Osama bin Laden to answer to the law. Sadly, the US government has chosen instead to pervert the law: "In the place of fair trials and due process he has substituted a crude and unaccountable system that any dictator would admire. The tribunals Mr. Bush envisions are a breathtaking departure from due process. He alone will decide who should come before these courts. The military prosecutors and judges who determine the fate of defendants will all report to him as commander in chief. Cases can be heard in secret. Hearsay, and evidence that civilian courts may deem illegally obtained, may be permissible. A majority of only two-thirds of the presiding officers would be required to convict, or to impose a death sentence. There would be no right of appeal to any other court." (*The New York Times*)

trial at International Criminal Court

Nonviolent sanctions against terrorists of any stripe include action in courts. Anne-Marie Slaughter, professor of international law at Harvard, says that, since 1996, the US Congress has made it much more feasible to take foreign parties to domestic US courts to sue for damages suffered as a result of terrorist actions. The catch is that the party needs to be brought to the bar in person. (Toobin: 41)

tracking and capturing suspects

Intelligence is a precious yet delicate matter rarely left to transnational bodies that owe allegiance to the people of the planet more than to any nation or coalition of nations. An organization meant to facilitate enforcement of international law needs to be international—or non-national—and needs highly trained cadres of actionists skilled in tracking and apprehending suspects that may or may not be shielded by—or even part of—a government. Envisioning: this body can use already developed techniques for handling the violently mentally ill when the moment of capture comes and ought to use its increasingly excellent reputation as its entree into places on the planet where terrorists used to operate as saviors but are seen more and more as illegitimate offenders. We made need to construct some kind of modern equivalent to the Simon Wiesenthal nazi hunter style of "bring-'em-back-alive-so-they-can-stand-trial" nonviolent commando force. Terrorists captured by the same techniques, for example, that we use to restrain violently mentally ill patients—using physical force but still non-pain compliance—could work, conceivably. At some point in human evolution, we will classify anyone committing any act of violence against other humans as insane by definition.

Not only is the incipient ICC a potential venue for airing initial grievances, it will be a place of trusted judgment and dispensation if it is linked to some kind of rehabilitative process, not retributive. When those injured feel as though they will be heard, they will be supported, and the perpetrators will be offered rehabilitation for their cruel and unjust ways while they are justly incarcerated, the ICC will gain immensely in the eyes of the peoples of the world and terrorism will be further isolated and will wither on its formerly well-watered vine.

require adherence to International Court of Justice

The ICJ ("World Court") is only beholden to the UN member nations, to the system of nation-states, and is thus a poor-to-limited venue for individuals, groups, ethnies or any party which is not in fact one of the 191 recognized nation-states on Earth. Nonetheless, their rulings are at least an effort at global opinion and ought to be followed by the nation-states themselves. Thus, when the ICJ finds that the US may not mine the harbors of Nicaragua, and the US government rejects the ruling, that undermines the very concept of law and order. It makes the US into a scofflaw nation. This is a dangerous place to be for a country that uses international law to justify bombing other nations, as it did with the air wars on both Belgrade and Baghdad, for example. Following the mandates of the ICJ is to allow for the rule of law instead of the rule of the terrorist—whether that terrorist is a guerrilla force or armed force of a nation-state. And when, in 1996, the ICJ ruled that "States must never make civilians the object of attack and must consequently never use weapons that are incapable of distinguishing between civilian and military targets," the US and the entire nuclear-biological-chemical WMD club became even more explicitly violative of international law. (Wilkie: 7)

negotiation with all involved governments

The history of nation-states suggests that when all governments are involved in negotiations germane to their past, present and future, agreements are more stable. This is a basic principle of mediation and one that applies to all legitimate bodies of governance as well.

negotiation with all aggrieved parties

Whoever claims grievance deserves to be heard, even if it is concomitant with law enforcement against its leadership. Thus, for example, tribal leadership of the peoples of Afghanistan would need to be at the negotiating table in any discussion of enforcing international criminal laws in their areas of traditional control. Negotiations need complete support, even if it means creating temporary communities of diaspora so that leaders can speak freely and forcefully. The extent to which commitment to such negotiations is demonstrated will be reflected in the honest and complete participation by the victims from all involved backgrounds. If a party feels it needs to commit an act of terror to get to the table, something is wrong. If we say we will never negotiate with terrorists, we operate in historical ignorance. Peace comes when warring parties meet to discuss terms. Nonviolence mandates talking first, if possible, to avoid war.

mediation amongst all stakeholders

Often, negotiations need to be preceded by virtually therapeutic mediation techniques developed in the past decade or so by practitioners in the mediation profession. Stories heard and absorbed by all on a voluntary basis—from other injured parties to the charged perpetrators—will often go so deeply and elicit such pain that the victimhood of all can be, for once, acknowledged by all. Once that happens, honest negotiations can proceed. (Rothman: 28) This will go to developing an environment in which terrorism is attacked at the roots, which include powerful emotive reaction to the impression—true or false, but real in any event—that no one is listening and that the Other is uncaring and unjust. Deep work in the long, early phases of such mediation is just emerging as a skill that can address certain heretofore unreachable elements of protracted, violent conflict.

reconciliation

The conflict resolution continuum begins with armed force, then adjudication with armed force back-up, then arbitration, then negotiation, then mediation and, finally, in transformative work, reconciliation—which is the least understood of all. (Assefa: 37)

complete cessation of arms trade

There is no substitute for reducing arms to all sides in a conflict, from the AK-47s to nuclear missiles. Oscar Arias has initiated one project that is a combination of education and international political measures. The UN is crucial in this effort, as are monitoring NGOs such as the American

Federation of Scientists.

disarmament negotiations for states and irregulars

The US spent more than $1 billion per month to wage war against Afghanistan and $1B per week to do the same in Iraq. (Dao) This includes many cruise missiles at nearly $1 million each, many of which are going to destroy stone huts or Red Cross warehouses in nations sliding down a slippery slope to mass famine and collapsed government. These million-dollar missiles could each translate into a million meals, or 100 brand-new homes for Afghans in recovery from the devastating war of the 1980s. Each F-14 that sorties its rain of terror on poor Afghanistan is running a $30,000 pricetag on each sortie, the result of which will produce misery for Afghanistan and strengthen the recruitment capabilities of terrorist networks. The initial allotment given by Congress to the Pentagon was $20 billion, spent in just 4-5 months as more weapons are deployed into Central Asia. It was even more costly and ghastly in Iraq. This militarization of the region will reduce the standard of living both in that region and in the US as war costs occlude a peace-oriented budget that used to begin to serve human needs and is now redirected to war and violence. As long as the US war machine is the most heavily funded and globally active, we can expect some type of violent reaction by the irregular forces. This has been the historical case from Northern Ireland to Colombia, from Angola to Vietnam. Disarmament is one significant step along the only path away from violence, and guerrilla or terrorist forces see themselves as legitimate. They cannot be made to disarm; they will find arms in a world awash in weaponry. When the US begins to disarm, we will convince others to begin.

interposition

Without this element, nonviolence is a dead letter, though it is also doomed if tried out of context, without a host of other measures. Even Gandhi failed to see how this might work until he was an old man; he recruited both noncombatant and even combatant troops amongst Indians, for the British war effort in spring of 1918. (Bartlof: 14) Later in his life he proposed a large, nonviolent sort of disarmy he called the Shanti Sena ("my Peace Army") in order to meet potential invaders and possibly to intervene or interpose elsewhere to dampen contact between belligerent forces. Today, the most robust iteration of this idea is the Nonviolent Peaceforce.

new economic guidelines and practices

Global justice is a movement to hold corporations accountable for the damage they have done and continue to do in the name of free trade. The alternative—fair trade—doesn't end international movement of goods and services, but it does make them answer to human rights and environmental laws and standards. Thus, when it is against WTO guidelines to trade goods that come from areas where armed force stifles or eliminates collective bargaining, for example, WTO will be closer to fair trade. Violations of human rights are a direct driver to terrorism; alleviation of those abuses by economic fair trade will remove yet another link in the terror chain weighting us down.

support for indigenous nonviolent groups

When a local group proclaims that it seeks justice using nonviolent methods, that local group ought to be able to rely on national and international bodies for support, including the UN. Indeed, if US foreign aid went in part toward nonviolent groups who are clamoring for justice and we concomitantly cut and eliminated arms aid, terrorism from irregulars and especially nation-states would lessen. One major example of which was the Kosovar Albanians during the 1990s under the leadership of Ibrahim Rugova, who was left twisting by the international community and thus his people were vulnerable to whatever Milošević felt like doing. Once terrorism from nation-states lessens, terrorism from irregulars will decrease too.

support for indigenous pro-democracy elements

This is a citizen option, whether we are acting to influence our own governments or in support of NGOs working to offer direct support to such movements. Thus, during the long effort to gain the vote for blacks in the Deep South during the mid-20th century, people from the northern US would send aid to those organizations or go in person to help. They didn't wait for the US government to intervene; they didn't merely plead to the federal government to act; they acted independently of any government and they paid some prices and they advanced the cause of freedom. Bradford Lyttle, as a young man in the early 1960s, organized a walk through the Deep South with the 1963 Quebec-Washington-Guantanamo Walk for Peace and, with others, was jailed in Albany, Georgia. The real issue for the segregationists was that the walk was integrated. (Lynd: 203) There were at least two direct benefits to the local struggle. African Americans in Albany and throughout the South were strengthened emotionally when they saw an integrated northern group willing to come suffer with them, and the northern media reported on the jailing, which drew attention to the lack of basic civil liberties for good, nonviolent citizens in places like Albany.

In Afghanistan, the US has supported the Northern Alliance and many have warned that they are only another fundamentalist, violent force. There has been little attention given to the pro-democracy forces on the ground, such as the Revolutionary Association of the Women of Afghanistan. RAWA's website contains photos of the dire conditions they have been resisting, nonviolently, since long before 9.11.01. (RAWA: online) Founded during the 1980s by Meena, a young Afghan woman murdered in 1987 at age 30, RAWA created clandestine schools for girls that bravely continued to meet even through the nightmarish Taliban years. While RAWA has won some human rights awards, it has received no support from the US, has been cut out of post-Taliban talks, and in fact Meena's assassins were likely funded by the US. (Hilton: 69)

end support for autocracies

Creating an autocracy within the borders of the US by reducing our civil liberties while maintaining support for the repressive regimes in the Mideast and Central Asia seems sadly consistent. Wouldn't the protection of US civil liberties and assistance to those indigenous nonviolent, pro-democracy movements elsewhere be a model of a more positive consistency? Certainly those who are waging struggle selflessly are not as concerned with their own civil liberties, since they fully understand they have staked out a position opposed to a particular government, but can we long expect to remain friends with a populace if we are the primary supporters of their oppressors?

initiate cultural exchanges

Cultural change is the fastest way to initiate systemic change; when appreciation for all cultures is fostered and nurtured on a mass scale, there is less room for objectification and dehumanization. This doesn't mean that sharing TV sitcoms or soft porn with al-Qaeda will predispose them to like the US and not hurt us; we are rather interested in improving culture even as we share it. Certainly there are still almost no US individuals who have any appreciation for Pashtun culture, even though it's ancient and rich.

promote sustainable tourism

Like cultural exchanges, people exchanges in greater and greater numbers serve as an innoculant against aggression and violence. When Henry Stimpson—Truman's Secretary of War—was told that Kyoto was a prime target for the first atomic attack, he vetoed that plan because he and his wife had honeymooned there. Robert Fuller, past president of Oberlin College, has called for a "mo-tzu" model—sending people to visit other places and thus make violent attack on those places less likely. Honeymoon the world.

Empires and nonviolent resistance

Liberty and democracy become unholy when their hands are dyed red with innocent blood.

—Mohandas K. Gandhi (Merton: 55)

Some invading forces are so large and care so little for the coöperation of the citizenry that noncoöperation by those indigenous victims seems ineffectual. For example, China invaded Tibet in 1959, sending the 14th Dalai Lama and approximately 100,000 Tibetans into exile. Chinese settlers were sent in; China wanted native Tibetans either compliant or out of the country and China has historically been so insular and so self-supporting that nonviolent economic sanctions have been essentially irrelevant. What hope have the Tibetans under such circumstances?

Recognizing that all empires end and that preparation for the dissolution of the Communist rule in China will facilitate Tibet's independence some day is the first hopeful step. If Tibet doesn't remain alert to the timing possibilities, she may miss her chance.

The Dalai Lama has, of course, continued his path of nonviolent struggle toward a day of national liberation for his land and people. Noting that, the Nobel Committee awarded him their annual Peace Prize in 1989. He is a world hero and that raises hope.

Tibetan Mahayana Buddhism, recognized by more as a religion of peace and nonviolence as practiced by the Dalai Lama, is spreading globally, helping to bring Tibetan nonviolence around the world, full circle back to the Chinese. (Cabezón: 184)) The Communist regime can certainly observe and feel the global opprobrium directed their way by a general world population in sympathy with the gentle yet persistent Tibetans. This cost is ineffable yet certain in countless ways. The ongoing Chinese occupation of Tibet is an ongoing accumulation of bad faith and distrust that carries a steep pricetag for China, whether it's discussed or not. When, for example, a Chinese fighter jet collides with a US spy plane, the world yawns at the play for sympathy made by both sides. No one feels too sorry for bullies and the US and China fall into that category for many of the peoples of the world.

This is not to say that Tibetan Buddhism's primary goal is the liberation of Tibet; it is not. Tibetan Buddhists themselves clearly reject any attempt to define their religion as either social activism or self-absorbed spirituality. (Cabezón: 185) Nevertheless, given current conditions and historical traditions, the practitioners of a religion associated with nonviolent resistance to invasion are emphatically called upon to lead those who choose to follow, and more are making that choice.

When a colleague of mine attended the Global Summit in Rio in 1993, she reported that the conferences were abuzz every time the Dalai Lama attended any event, every time he uttered a word and anytime he avoided attendance or utterance. It is patently clear that, with Tibet's adherence to nonviolence, they have become heirs to the mantle of global moral leadership formerly worn by such nations as India. The world looks for such exemplars and Tibet currently offers them; this will be the basis for Tibet's independence some day.

violence within nonviolent struggles for national liberation

The world generally considers the transition of power within South Africa to have been "peaceful." This is, of course, a relative term. It was peaceful compared to all-out civil war. But it was probably unnecessarily violent—a redundant term—due to the inability of the Afrikaner government to hold onto minority power without violence and due to the creative failure of much of the African National Congress to envisage a liberation process that didn't involve violent struggle—a failure nearly impossible avoid under a regime as tyrannical and terrorist as the apartheid government, but a failure nonetheless.

The violence of the white minority government was extreme and the conditions of political repression were severe, so after 50 years of peaceful opposition to white-only rule, the leadership of the ANC became understandably drawn to armed insurrection as the only recourse remaining. But those who believe the ANC was essentially nonviolent are mistaken.

Beginning as early as June 1953, Nelson Mandela began to call for the use of armed revolution. He told a public gathering in Freedom Square in Sophiatown that the time for passive resistance and nonviolence was over, and that it was time for violence. He even pointed to police and named them as enemies immediately after calling for the destruction of the enemies of black freedom by violence. Shortly thereafter, ANC official Walter Sisulu traveled to both the Soviet Union and China, seeking help in the armed struggle to overthrow the whites-only government of South Africa. If not for Chief Albert Luthuli—who only believed in and practiced nonviolence—the drift toward the armed rebellion might have been faster in South Africa. (Meredith: 112) As it was, the Special Branch—the state security apparatus in white South Africa—personalized its retaliation for Mandela's remarks in Sophiatown; in September of 1953, Mandela was served with an order under the Suppression of Communism Act. The order specified that he was to resign from the ANC, restricted him to Johannesburg, and forbade his attendance at public meetings for two years. Even talk of violence—the ANC had yet to commit a single act of violence at that time—is enough to retard a social struggle.

This is delicate territory. A. J. Muste, a coalition-builder and leader of disparate groups said, "I've always tried to keep communication open between radicals and non-radicals, between pacifists and nonpacifists. It goes back to something very fundamental in the nonviolent approach to life. You always assume there is some element of truth in the position of the other person, and you respect your opponent for hanging on to an idea as long as he believes it to be true. On the other and, you must try very hard to see what truth actually does exist in his idea, and seize on it to make him realize what you consider to be a larger truth." (Hentoff: 251)

During one radio talk show, I was presenting what I observed about the intifada and expressing how I hoped that the uprising leadership would someday be able to try mass nonviolence, while an Iranian and a Palestinian each shook his head and commented on the emotional impossibility of that. The Palestinian fellow went further, saying that nonviolent methods had been tried.

He was correct, of course, and yet, as always, the issue was not so much whether one tactic had been tried or not, but rather what might work, what might be effective, what might cause fewer casualties for the people who were being violated by unjust rule—as, I think, most critically thinking people would agree is the case in what even Secretary of State Powell calls the Occupied Territories. The pain and rage seems both endless and fruitless and guarantees more casualties on all sides, and sympathy for the Palestinian people evaporates each time a suicide bomber kills another crowd of civilians. That Hamas, for example, is not thinking even remotely rationally is sadly and sharply evident in a 13 December 2001 announcement by them that they began putting dangerous chemicals in their suicide bombs. (Wall: A1) Whatever efforts might have been generated to support a nonviolent intifada—and they might have been significant in Israel and in the West—are exploded into bits with the hate-filled acts and pronouncements that no one can possibly relate to as justified. That three-quarters of the mortalities suffered in the current uprising are Palestinians is not even enough to engender the active support needed because—to be blunt—raw hatred is alienating, no matter how justified.

sources:

Abramovitz, Janet N., ***Unnatural Disasters.*** (Worldwatch Paper 158).
    Washington DC: Worldwatch Institute, 2001.
Abu-Nimer, Mohammed, ***Dialogue, Conflict Resolution, and Change: Arab-***

Jewish Encounters in Israel. Albany NY: State University of New York, 1999.

Abu-Odeh, Adnan, ***Jordanians, Palestinians, & the Hashemite Kingdom in the Middle East Peace Process.*** Washington DC: United States Institute of Peace Press, 1999.

Ackerman, Peter and Christopher Kruegler, ***Strategic Nonviolent Conflict: The Dynamics of People Power in the Twentieth Century.*** Westport CT: Praeger Publishers, 1994.

Assefa, Hizkias, "The meaning of reconciliation," in: ***European Centre for Conflict Prevention, People Building Peace: 35 Inspiring Stories from Around the World.*** Utrecht, The Netherlands: European Centre for Conflict Prevention, 1999.

Bartolf, Christian, ***The Breath of My Life: The Correspondence of Mahatma Gandhi (India) and Bart de Ligt (Holland) on War and Peace.*** Berlin: Gandhi-Information-Zentrum, 2001.

Blalock, Jr., Hubert M., ***Power and Conflict: Toward a General Theory.*** Newbury Park CA: Sage Publications, 1989.

Boyle, Francis A., email, 18 October 2001 (from lecture)

Cabezón, José Ignacio, "The UNESCO Declaration: A Tibetan Buddhist perspective," in:

Carnegie Commission on Preventing Deadly Conflict, ***Preventing Deadly Conflict.*** Washington DC: Carnegie Corporation of New York, 1997.

Congressional Quarterly, ***The Middle East, Ninth Edition.*** Washington DC: CQ Press, 2000.

Dao, James, "U.S. is expecting to spend $1 billion a month on war," *New York Times*, 12 November 2001. http://www.nytimes.com/2001/11/12/national/12PENT.html?todaysheadlines

Deming, Barbara, ***We Are All Part of One Another: A Barbara Deming Reader.*** Philadelphia PA: New Society Publishers, 1984.

Fisk, Robert, "Hypocrisy, hatred and the war on terror," *Independent*, 8 November 2001.

Gregg, Richard B., ***The Power of Nonviolence***, second revised edition. NYC: Schocken Books, 1966 (original 1935).

Hallock, Daniel, ***Hell, Healing and Resistance: Veterans Speak.*** Farmington PA: The Plough Publishing House, 1998.

Hentoff, Nat, ***Peace Agitator: The Story of A.J. Muste.*** NYC: A.J. Muste Memorial Institute, 1982 (original The Macmillan Company, 1963).

Hersh, Seymour, "What went wrong: the CIA and the failure of the American intelligence," *The New Yorker,* 8 October 2001 (34-40)

Hilton, Isabel, "The Pashtun Code," *The New Yorker.* 3 December 2001. (58-71)

Homer-Dixon, Thomas F., ***Environment, Scarcity, and Violence.*** Princeton NJ: Princeton University Press, 1999.

Huffington, Arianna, "Patriots, stop revving your engines," *The Sunday Oregonian*, 18 November 2001. (F5)

Idinopulos, Thomas A., ***Weathered by Miracles: A History of Palestine from Bonaparte and Muhammad Ali to Ben-Gurion and the Mufti.***

Chicago: Ivan R. Dee, 1998.
Interfaith Homeless and Housing Coalition, email, 8 October 2001.
Jeffrey, Paul, "Nicaragua: planting seeds of nonviolence in the midst of war," in: McManus, Philip, and Gerald Schlabach, editors, *Relentless Persistence: Nonviolent Action in Latin America*. Philadelphia PA: New Society Publishers, 1991.
Kegley, Jr., Charles W. and Gregory A. Raymond, *How Nations Make Peace*. NYC: St. Martin's/Worth, 1999.
Kriesberg, Louis, *Constructive Conflicts: From Escalation to Resolution*. Lanham MD: Rowman & Littlefield, 1998.
Lederach, John Paul, *Building Peace: Sustainable Reconciliation in Divided Societies*. Washington DC: United States Institute of Peace Press, 1997.
Loeb, Vernon, "The man who pulls the terrorists' strings," in: Schechterman, Bernard, ed., *Violence and Terrorism 99/00*. Fifth ed. Guilford CT: Dushkin/McGraw-Hill, 1999.
Lynd, Staughton and Alice, *Nonviolence in America: A Documentary History*. Maryknoll NY: Orbis Books, 1995 2nd edition).
Lyttle, Bradford, conversation, 3 November 2001.
Merideth, Martin, *Nelson Mandela*. NYC: St. Martin's Griffen, 1997.
Merton, Thomas, editor, *Gandhi on Non-Violence: A Selection from the Writings of Mahatma Gandhi*. NYC: New Directions Publishing, 1964.
National Conference of Catholic Bishops (USA), "The Just War criteria," in: Ringler, Dick, ed., *Dilemmas of War and Peace*. Madison WI: University of Wisconsin-Extension, 1993.
Newsweek staff, "War on terror: perspectives," *Newsweek*, 15 October 2001 (21).
The New York Times, "A travesty of justice," editorial, 18 November 2001. http://www.nytimes.com
Partnoy, Alicia, *The Little School: Tales of Disappearance and Survival*. San Francisco: Cleis Press, 1998. (original 1986)
Perlez, Jane, "Again, Afghan's Flight Matches His History With His Country's," *New York Times*, 24 October 2001. http://www.nytimes.com/2001/10/24/international/asia/24REFU.html
RAWA: http://rawa.false.net/dec00-ph.htm
Reeve, Simon, *The New Jackals: Ramzi Yousef, Osama bin Laden and the Future of Terrorism*. Boston: Northeastern University Press, 1999.
Rigby, Andrew, and Nafez Assaily, "The Intifada," in: Anderson, Shelley and Janet Larmore, eds., *Nonviolent Struggle and Social Defense*. London: War Resisters' International, 1991.
Roodman, David Malin, *Still Waiting for the Jubilee: Pragmatic Solutions for the Third World Debt Crisis* (Worldwatch Paper 155). Washington DC: Worldwatch Institute, 2001.
Rothman, Jay, *Resolving Identity-Based Conflict in Nations, Organizations, and Communities*. San Francisco: Jossey-Bass Inc., 1997.
Roy, Arundhati, *The Cost of Living*. NYC: The Modern Library, 1999.
Said, Edward, *Peace & Its Discontents: Gaza-Jericho 1993-1995*. London: Vintage, 1995.

Spencer, William, *The Middle East*. Global Studies 6th ed. Guilford CT: Dushkin Publishing Group/Brown & Benchmark Publishers, 1996.
Toobin, Jeffrey, "Suing bin Laden," *The New Yorker* 1 October 2001 (40-41).
Wall Street Journal staff, "Palestinian attacks kill 10," *Wall Street Journal*, 13 December 2001. (A1)
Walter, Eugene Victor, *Terrorism and Resistance: A Study of Political Violence*. NYC: Oxford University Press, 1969.
White, Jonathan R., *Terrorism: An Introduction*. 2nd edition. New York: West/ Wadsworth Publishing, 1998.
Wilkie, Alan, "Dr. Moonie's moment of truth," *Speed the Plough*, 12 November 2001. (7)

CHAPTER NINE

Defense of Creation

The Governments of the United Sates of America, the United Kingdom of Great Britain and Northern Ireland, and the Union of Soviet Socialist Republics, hereinafter referred to as the "Original Parties,"

Proclaiming as their principal aim the speediest possible achievement of an agreement on general and complete disarmament under strict international control in accordance with the objectives of the United Nations which would put an end to the armaments race and eliminate the incentive to the production and testing of all kinds of weapons, including nuclear weapons,

Seeking to achieve the discontinuance of all test explosions of nuclear weapons for all time, determined to continue negotiations to this end, and desiring to put an end to the contamination of man's environment by radioactive substances,

—opening of the *Partial Test Ban Treaty Banning Nuclear Weapons Test in the Atmosphere, in Outer Space and Under Water*, 5 August 1963 (World: 193)

A source of hope lies in the capacity for social learning of individuals, families, grassroots groups, old and new faith communities, NGOs, and of institutions of governance, including states and intergovernmental bodies.

—Elise Boulding, Peace Research scholar, sociologist, mother of five, Norwegian, historian, past chair WILPF (Boulding: 257)

Elise Boulding dreamt up the United States Institute for Peace. She cofounded the International Peace Research Association. She chaired the sociology department at Dartmouth. She devised the *Imaging a World Without Weapons* workshops that so many of us have taken and benefited from. She did—and does—much more.

She performed this hyperactivism while writing seven books and raising her five children; why is it that so many people seem stuck trying to do just one worthy thing in their lives? How can one woman—not rich, not powerful politically, not royalty, not a popular culture celebrity—achieve so much?

Wrong question. Rather, how much can *I* achieve if I focus on doing all I can to further nonviolence and justice? Elise Boulding is brilliant, yes, but no more intelligent than hundreds of thousands of women currently focused on improving their financial picture in corporate America. Elise Boulding demonstrates principled priorities, not a self-absorbed stance to the world. Defending Creation will require more of us than a devotion of our talents to personal gain. Dr. Boulding might be called one of our best models of life choice behaviors; our ethical and lifestyle "supermodel." She would shrug off the sheroic mantle, but she is an exemplar nonetheless.

weapons of mass destruction

Creation is indeed under attack, and the war system is the perpetrator. Without the weaponry of the Pentagon and other militaries, justice could not be denied to vast numbers of people in the poorest nations worldwide. Without nuclear bombs, atomic waste would be a vastly smaller problem. Without the desire to destroy the other's living room, anti-Earth weapons such as HAARP could not be built—a beam so powerful it disintegrates the ionosphere, upon which life depends. (Begich: 187)

What, we wonder, could scientists be thinking? At times, even for those of us who do not profess belief in the doctrine of a particular sect of organized religion, we wonder if there is indeed some general Good and some essential Evil struggling for the soul and spirit of humankind. We are often a loss otherwise to explain the very existence, for example, of arsenals of thousands of nuclear weapons, thousands of biological bombs, thousands of chemical warheads. What, apart from raw yet sophisticated Evil, could drive humans to push Creation to the precipice with such annihilatory machines poised to commit mass murder? The teleological implications continue to prick at any easy answers with powerful doubts. After all, the consequences of ever using the nuclear arsenal are well known, which makes the possession of even a single nuclear weapon a premeditated crime with intent to kill untold mass numbers of humans putatively protected, a violation of the most elemental legal protections of civilians under international law—and yet weaponeers walk the streets and meet in suites whilst nonviolent nuclear resisters sit in jail cells. Politicians who vote for Trident submarines do so in the name of national security—while the very core of all our security is threatened by an environmental destruction far faster and much worse than global warming. Even those elite individuals we generally credit with supreme self-interest and rock-ribbed pragmatism—corporate heads—will tell it plainly if they decide to be honest. "I'm absolutely positive that the arms race and nuclear weapons are very, very bad for business," said Ted Turner. "The only way out is certain death, because sooner or later, there will be a Chernobyl of nuclear weapons, like the Soviet nuclear Polaris-type submarine that had technical problems and sank off Bermuda not long ago, and our missile in Arkansas a few years ago that went a couple hundred yards and fortunately didn't explode when it took of accidentally." (Krieger: 82)

Almost a century ago, in 1906, Bertha von Suttner noted that we continue to make laws about how we annihilate each other, not whether we ought to do so. She challenged us to move beyond codification of such methods to the development of new methods entirely, that begin from the premise that we cannot kill fellow humans. (von Suttner: 217) We are still struggling to enforce the laws she shook her head at so long ago.

It is now literally years into the new millennium, yet approximately 32,000 nuclear weapons still remain on Earth—more than in 1963, when the high-flown rhetoric issued forth from assembled and dissembling governments who pompously pronounced their alleged desire to rid the Earth of all weapons, not just nuclear weapons, in the Partial Test Ban Treaty quoted above. As a minimal second step—a step they were all so "determined" to take—the nations of the world would declare an end to the test explosions of nuclear weapons. Not only have the governments of the world failed to do so, the US has failed to ratify the Comprehensive Test Ban Treaty, a document that was handed to the US Senate on a golden platter and which was voted down by the smallest minds and most shriveled souls imaginable in 1998, some 35 years after the body declared itself so poised to act positively. As a direct result of the failure of the superpowers to adhere to their promises of that treaty and the Nuclear Nonproliferation Treaty of 1969—in which they promised to disarm atomic and thermonuclear weapons in exchange for the rest of the world foreswearing development of more such weapons—other nations have felt obliged to build nuclear arsenals, including Pakistan, India and Israel.

> *Nuclear Weapon is not for human hands.*
> *It is God's weapon.*
>
> —Mordechai Vanunu, former nuclear technician, in

> prison for revealing existence of Israel's Dimona secret nuclear arsenal. (Vanunu: 18)

In the movie *Dr. Strangelove*, the world is poised at the edge of nuclear war between the US and SU. The US generals and politicians are gathered in the War Room and a Soviet negotiator is secreted in. He tells them that his nation has a doomsday weapon that will end life on Earth if the SU is attacked. Enraged, the US general demands to know why the Soviets haven't told anyone, since that might have deterred certain US actions. It is obvious the Russians hadn't quite thought through the implications or purpose of their technological "breakthrough."

Mordechai Vanunu has been imprisoned in Israel since 30 September 1986. His only "crime" was to suffer a crisis of conscience. He turned over documents to the press showing that Israel has a nuclear arsenal, thereby enraging and activating the Israeli government. The Strangelovian aspect to that particular situation is that Vanunu did the Israeli government a major favor; keeping a nuclear arsenal secret defeats its putative purpose, which is to deter another nation from attack because of fear of reprisal. Deterrence doesn't work well if the other side has no idea that such weapons exist. Announcing them by their use is suicidal, especially in the crowded Middle East, where any nuclear attack is done as a last act of a nation in its death throes. If Israel ever goes nuclear it will be the equivalent to the largest suicide bombing in human history. The use of violence in this case has been carried to the *reductio ad absurdum* limit, not only arming for mutual annihilation, not only making that more likely by doing so clandestinely, but imprisoning a nonviolent man for 18 years (Vanunu's sentence, affirmed by Israel's Supreme Court) for doing what the Israeli head of state ought to have done in the interest of *realpolitik* many years ago. It is a case of governmental insanity and the stakes are existential for millions.

> *Nuclear weapons are the ultimate weapons of state-sponsored terrorism and no other government spends as many of its resources on those instruments of terror.*

—Tom Howard-Hastings (Howard-Hastings: 4)

Nukes are the 800-pound gorilla in the living room; we cannot have a fruitful discussion about reduction of terrorism, enhancing egalitarian access to life's necessities, achieving global justice, encouraging democracy and stopping the ecological destruction of this beautiful planet until we deal with the largest nuclear arsenal on Earth, that of the US.

We can see with pellucid clarity that disarmament, systemic change, and basic defense of Creation will come up from the people, not down from the governments. The responsibility may appear to be with the weapon-holding nation-states, but it falls, by default of perpetual nation-state failure, to the people. We fail and we die along with Creation, which is not a viable option, quite literally. We are called, compellingly, to replace the war system with a peace system, and we will begin soon or we will fail to achieve it.

food fights: feast, famine and conflict

*How to start from the beginning and learn how little I really **must** have, if it means harm to someone else?*

—Juanita Nelson (Nelson: 21)

When is state policy and economic policy violent? Clearly, when state policy consists of an order to shoot people or to bomb them, that's violence. But when do other state and economic policies cross the line into violent actions? If a government protects corporate interests that are causing people to go hungry, and if those people occasionally die of malnutrition, is that violence? If a government policy denies health care to those in need, and if those people suffer and die, is that violence? When a corporate Chief Executive Officer gets a paycheck that is literally 300 times more money than a hardworking maintenance person—and literally 3,000 times more than an exploited very hard worker for his firm's overseas production plant—and those workers either get sick and can't afford medicine or they simply cannot afford enough food and clothing for their families, is that violence? If corporate influence—usually in the form of highly profitable economic arrangements for the local decisionmakers—causes leadership in so-called developing nations to ignore environmental laws that cost the corporations money for compliance, and if, say, a local manufacturing plant simply dumps chemical waste instead of disposing of it properly, and when the local children begin to sicken and die from drinking the water, is that violence?

All this happens, and it happens on a more pervasive scale than do the highly visible, dramatic wars. When a child is cut down by gunfire or blown up by a bomb, that is instant, tragic, objectionable. But when a child quietly perishes after an agony of starvation or hideous disease, that is just how life has been lived by various groups since the beginning of history, and it's sad, but it's not as gripping to the average citizen. Until we think about it. When the bombs fly, some of those killed are soldiers. But when starvation hits a land, the soldiers eat first and die last. "Macroparasites," is how historian William McNeill refers to members of the military; they produce nothing and take the best. The structural violence can, when viewed from the standpoint of the demographic of the victims, look more violent than even hot flying steel.

So, if we are to address this structural violence, are we then called to feed the hungry or to work to effect systemic change so that hunger isn't a daily, inevitable effect of official policy? Yes. The answer is yes to both. Ministering to the immediate needs of those in misery is an act of nonviolent love. Sitting in the road blocking chemical waste trucks bound for some Native American reservation is another act of nonviolent love. They are equally important and commendable if the goal is to lessen the impact of violent policy. And thousands of other examples of such valuable action are done daily and have effected change in public policy, and economic policy, and environmental law enforcement.

When the Civil Rights Act of 1964 and the Voting Rights Act of 1965 were passed due to in-the-streets nonviolent campaigns waged by African Americans, the system enforced the measures of the law that we might call low-cost or no-cost. Integrated schools and lunch counters are nice, wrote Dr. King, but it was time to enforce the sections of the law that would make real change in people's economic and lifestyle realities. It was time, he wrote, for the systemic changes that would bring better jobs, better housing and all the other fundamental conditions that would "require money for their solution, a fact that makes those solutions all the more difficult." (King: 321) When King began to make these connections, when he began to see the systemic problems and to devise systemic solutions, he was cut down. Coincidence or not, he was assassinated just as he began to enunciate the connections between waging war and imposing systemic violence. He made the linkage between the war in Vietnam and the lack of programmatic funds for poverty mitigation in the US. And then he made the connections between peoples as he built the emerging coalition of poor whites, blacks, Hispanics and others that became Resurrection City, his last major project. His nonviolent plans for basic change in how the US treated its own poor and how it treated foreign human beings were stopped by a bullet. If enforcing oppression is ultimately done by the credible threat of violence, then the threat must be carried out occasionally in order to remain credible. If a person or a movement emerges that threatens to upset the bedrock arrangements that tilt the field for the rich and against the poor, that person or that movement is both dangerous to those who feel they must have the most—and that person or that movement is in danger as well. Was King's assassination a result of a conspiracy on behalf of a war system or was it the wicked work of a demented racist? The question is moot in the sense that those who benefited from the loss of the most eloquent peace and justice spokesperson on Earth were the rich and powerful; it made no real difference if they or their representatives ordered King's killing. They were relieved and their basic set-up was not as threatened as a direct result of our loss.

When we ponder the casualties of structural violence and wonder how best to end that violence—and when some argue that violence is necessary in order to achieve that structural change—we are then drawn to analyze the problem and crunch the numbers. If, say, 1,000 children die each month in a certain nation because of economic policies, and 100 children die each month from state-inflicted or sponsored violence, then 900 more children are lost monthly from structural violence than from shooting violence. If a nonviolent campaign to alter that formula is undertaken that results in an additional 10 children killed each month from state-inflicted or sponsored violence, that makes nonviolent action look dysfunctional and dangerous, especially if those fundamental changes aren't made and the 1,000 children still die each month from starvation or lack of health care. Assuming that the nonviolent campaign will ultimately work and there will be an end to the loss of those lives due to structural violence, then the total losses over a period of time are the question. In other words, if it takes five years to wage a successful nonviolent campaign that results in an end to losses due to structural violence, then 60,600 lives were lost during that time period. If, by contrast, an additional 1,000 children are killed each month during a one-year civil war that brings about systemic change that stops that same structural violence, then "only" 24,000 children were lost to a combination of structural and state-inflicted violence over the entire five-year period and one could argue that violent revolution is clearly the moral and practical choice. One could make the case that nonviolence caused the deaths of 35,400 children in this poor nation and that it was the choice of murderously stupid leaders. Indeed, that exact argument has been used repeatedly against those who advocate for nonviolent opposition to a government or consortium of governments whose policies are so oppressive that children die as a result of them.

But, in reality, the formula usually shows that nonviolence is by far the most effective life-saving method. Violent revolutions usually take much longer and result in many more casualties. Nonviolent revolutions are often effected quite quickly, provided there are enough participants prepared to sacrifice in order to assure that victory—exactly the requirements of a violent victory. One soldier cannot wage a revolution; it will be done by the people or it will fail. Just so with nonviolent revolution; it will be done by the majority or it will never work. Violence only stiffens the resolve of the oppressor—and justifies his violent suppression of dissent—and usually guarantees a longer struggle with higher human costs. At the end of the day, at the bottom of the lines of calculations, we can only guess and my guess is that nonviolence saves lives in the immediate sense, in the short run, and in the long run. It stands a greater chance of effecting systemic change because it changes the very methodology of change from a war system, arms-based method to a people-based peace system, thus removing the profit motive even more from the equation and changing the political pollution inevitable in the arms trade, when so-called liberation fighters become more clients than partners, more customers than inspirational leaders. The huge arms merchants love violent revolution; they make money on all sides. They hate nonviolent campaigns; fewer guns are sold and the oppressor needs no upgrades from the arms merchant. The revolutionists use no costly matériel or ordnance and they make no deals for missiles. They cannot be so easily owned, led, corrupted or coöpted.

food as a weapon

Starving warriors by cutting off their food supply until they surrender is one weapon of war that is arguably relatively humane, if we are comparing it to shooting, bombing, stabbing or otherwise violently ending their lives. After all, you can't bomb an individual to death until he surrenders, but there is hope for those hungry warriors who cannot march on empty stomachs and instead choose to become nonviolent, if defeated. History is replete with examples of warriors who have returned to lives in losing nations, only to be successful or at least reasonably happy in their remaining years. Violent attacks, by contrast, take away all remaining years.

Starving civilians when they are sheltering the warriors—as, for instance, in an ancient walled city under siege—is a tactic of war that is less soldierly. After all, the attacking warriors know that those warriors under siege will almost invariably requisition the most and best food for themselves, and that, if anyone is to perish by malnutrition or outright starvation, it will be the babies, the infants, the elderly, the sick—in short, the "protected" populations long understood to be off-limits to honorable warriors with any decent code.

Starving the people of another land by military-enforced policies that cut off food—sanctions, blockades, scorched earth, weather modification, poisoning, diversion of needed resources, boycotts—is generally disdained by warriors with any kind of code, yet is practiced in a *de facto* sense by many of the sanctions undertaken by diplomats and politicians, especially in the post Cold War geopolitical transition period. Nations which engage in such behavior are usually regarded as nationalistic and xenophobic, since the trade-off they are working with is usually the danger level to their own warriors versus the lives of the vulnerable civilians of the other country. It is never the leadership who suffers; Saddam never missed a meal because of US-initiated sanctions against Iraq.

Widely regarded as the worst example of the inhumanity of using famine as a weapon of war is the application of such policies designed to bring an ethnic population under control within a nation, or, even worse, to actually attempt to kill groups of people by starvation because of their identity—e.g., ethnicity, religion, tribe, political affiliation.

> *It is perplexing why the tactic is still used after all these centuries. Ultimately, it is a failure. All the great military strategists, from Carl von Clausewitz to North Vietnamese General Vo Nyien Giap, have said that*

Defense of Creation 221

> *making war on the civil population solidifies the opposition and stiffens its resolve. Few, if any, wars have been won by starving the enemy's civilians. Those bearing arms will always be the first to receive food.*
>
> —Fred Cuny, disaster relief practitioner and researcher (Cuny: 139)

Many factors contribute to the starvation of civilians during war; they often are in flight with little or no food. They usually rely on trucked-in supplies that cannot survive the destruction of roads, or the dangerous highways that scare away drivers. Food supply systems swiftly grind to a halt, even without genocidal intent. Worse, since the advent of child soldiers with lightweight automatic weapons—an estimated 300,000 in the field as of this writing—international aid workers are much more likely to be attacked, since the children usually have no warrior code, no value system that we recognize as coherent or even somewhat mature. Indeed, famine relief practitioner and researcher Fred Cuny himself disappeared and is presumed dead in the very nation responsible for the invention and widespread dissemination of those very lightweight weapons that make child soldiering so possible—he was lost in 1995 in Chechnya as it battled for its independence from Russia. For the first time in history, international aid workers are routinely coming under attack and that directly affects the ability to feed millions of war refugees still living in war zones.

A wide variety of strategies and tactics can mitigate or even prevent such disasters.

- Proper military training, including study of international rules of warfare, will introduce a deterrent in the minds of soldiers determined to be upright in waging war.
- Cross-cultural communications and sensitivity opportunities help to make it socially objectionable to use starvation as a weapon.
- Better training of international relief workers can make them less vulnerable to the attacks of soldiers—often irregulars—who themselves have no training but who may be reachable on a human level by some communicative means.
- Policies that tend to *flood* conflict areas with food instead of cutting off that food will reduce the perception of scarcity and its concomitant resource-capture environment.
- Infusions of income-earning opportunities for refugees living in or near conflict zones will re-ignite very local economies and keep food and other essentials more available in many situations. (Cuny: 142)
- Paired villages have had some success, whereby relief workers aid displaced peoples in forming a symbiotic economic and workforce relationship with locals living near the refugee camps. While this often leads to exploitation,

that is preferable to death. (Cuny: 142)
- Cross-border feeding operations—usually involving negotiations with all conflictual parties to determine who can be regarded as a neutral allowed to assess and provide—have worked in Ethiopia and other places. (Cuny: 144)
- Get the US on board and the UN to enforce the child soldier law.
- Work on more small arms trade reductions and elimination. Support those (e.g. Nobel Laureate Oscar Arias) who are leading this effort.

Using nonviolent methods of creative confrontation and communication, then, individuals can make a difference in the most hopeless of situations. Often the lone emissary can achieve what the armed unit cannot. It is risky, and growing more so, but the need is also greater. *Increase the peace*, say those who operate in the inner cities of North America, by which they mean do whatever it takes to reduce tension and bring about justice, jobs and a better living. This small-step, incremental, each-person-do-what-she-can approach can even work on a global scale.

identity conflict is bad for our world

> *I know God has other worlds and probably wonderful beings are managing it better than we do, to preserve it from the absurd super-sensitivity and pride that start us grumbling and pitying ourselves and resenting (what a damnably dangerous habit that is!) and it eventually leads to the murder and tortures of children via war.*
>
> —Muriel Lester, ambassador to the world from the Fellowship of Reconciliation, written to her friend, about the war in Vietnam, one-half hour before her death at age 83 in 1968. (Deats: 222)

The corporate owner reprimands upper management, singling out one fellow who is in charge of production costs. That humiliated executive reams out the lead foreman, who threatens the point person on the section of production line that slowed down the previous month. That point person curses out three offending workers, one of whom goes home and beats his wife on some flimsy pretext. The poor woman brutalizes two of her six children, and they in turn torture the dog, who escapes and attacks the corporate owner as he is jogging the next morning. In the most foul of moods, the owner will probably chew out one of his sycophantic vice-presidents at the early afternoon meeting and the systemic conflict cycle continues. What other such systems exist globally?

One such system of rippling and cycling violence is control of oil, so crucial to how our current world works. Oil has been an issue since the early

Defense of Creation

20th century, as it was discovered in country after country. One subsystem of oil and group conflict is found in the Kurdish question.

As we know, oil was found in the Kurdish region of Iraq in 1927 and has been an influence on conflict there ever since. While conflict in the region certainly preceded the discovery of oil, that has served to contaminate the air, water, soil, and political relations of everyone in the region since 1927, and has exacerbated external influence. The Brits lorded over the natives, burning hatred of the West into hearts across the region. The proposed creation of Kurdistan—a logical nation that would require territory of five Mideastern nation-states, all in possession of areas with Kurd majorities that should be part of such a nation—was anathema to outside interests for three reasons. One, the concentration of vast oil reserves in a larger Mideastern nation might upset the balance of power that so judiciously serves the US and Europe. Two, some of those states—Turkey, in particular—are vital to US and European interests and simply could not be approached about such an idea. Three, nation-states cannot systemically countenance much flexibility regarding ethnic claims on territory, since there are about 10,000 ethnic groupings on Earth and only 191 nation-states. Precedent lies with the hegemonic political establishment every time except the notable Cold War enemies, the SU, and then their "little Slav brothers," the Serbs. In those cases, with the understanding that this was highly irregular and not meant to establish a pattern, the SU was allowed to disintegrate into what humorist Dave Barry called "postage-stamp-sized countries." So was Yugoslavia.

In the 1970s, Elise Boulding explored ethnic conflict and found that, of 159 states she surveyed, only four were monocultural, just 24 were monolingual, and 91 states had between 100-3,000 ethnies. (Boulding: 167) The system is inherently, ethnically unstable. Kurdistan is not going to happen anytime soon.

The Kurds in Iraq and Turkey were mercilessly pounded by the governments of both nation-states, yet the UK and US warplanes that patrolled the no-fly zone supposedly protected the Kurds in Iraq, while the terrorism inflicted on Kurds in Turkey was supported because Turkey is a crucial NATO nation. (Arnove: 12) Another bitter irony to the Kurds is that the US supplied Iraqi with components and know-how for its chemical weapon attacks of 1988, then floated by Bush the Elder's regime as a human rights reason to wage the Gulf War. (Aruri: 24) At the conclusion of the Gulf War, Kurds rose against Saddam Hussein, logically accepting US assurances of help. They were brutally crushed by Iraqi forces so then-recently defeated by the US-led UN forces, with no interference at the time, no help from the most mighty military on Earth.

The nesting of conflict within a war system fuels bitter and brutal identity battles in many of the world's hottest conflict zones. Without the externals, some identity conflict would still happen, of course, but the cascading effect pours the worst onto those at the bottom, time and after time. The systemic problem is left unaddressed except by a systemic solution, beginning with a nonviolent alternative, moving to growth of alternatives to the demand side (oil replacement), bringing in good mediation and massive aid with an eye to local self-reliance.

War on Mother Earth: military attacks planet

> *In recognition of the possible increased need for training as a result of the September 11 terrorist attacks, the settlement allows the Army to conduct limited live fire training during the preparation of the EIS.*
>
> —Environmental News Service

The militaries of the world are waging an undeclared war on the environment, on human health, on Creation. The largest single consumer of fossil fuel on Earth is the United States Department of Defense, a tremendous consumption rate during peacetime that increases by a factor of between five and ten during wartime. The US Pentagon's industries—from the producers of battleship gray paint to the creation of chemicals "needed" to maintain the nuclear arsenal—are responsible for more Superfund sites than any other sector of the economy. And, as is seen in the very small but typical example from the Environmental News Service above, these countless little acts of environmental degradation and destruction are advanced with little or no question during times of war.

This is not to claim that the US military is worse than other nations' militaries; it is not, except in sheer scale. Indeed, while the US military is more responsive to environmental concerns on a case-by-case basis than most militaries, the vast number of such cases means that the annual damage is tremendous.

One person can make a difference.

Laura Olah, a housewife, found out that wells in her neighborhood in rural Wisconsin were contaminated by a local military ordnance production facility. She organized other residents and successfully shut down that base and is getting it turned over to both the state of Wisconsin and the Ho-Chunk tribe. Olah simply refused to give up, refused to accept that city hall, the state regulators, or indeed the United States armed forces were more powerful than aroused mothers. She learned, she agitated and she won.

Indeed, the model of the lone housewife taking on the industrial giant corporations, the government regulators and the mass media all at once became the norm during the period 1978-1980. Beginning with Lois Gibbs at Love Canal in New York and spreading to Sue Greer in Wheelot, Indiana, "people now felt they had to defeat attempts to bring wastes into their communities." In 1976, less than half the toxic facility operators said public opposition was a problem; by 1979, virtually all said that public protest of their operations was a major problem. (Szasz: 71)

A small group of US young men who fled to Canada during the Vietnam War—rather than participate in that unjust, imperialist and high-tech war against barefoot peasants—started a little group called Greenpeace in 1971 in Vancouver, British Columbia. Their first political involvement was to sail a small boat into waters reserved for the United States military as it prepared to detonate a series of nuclear test explosions at Amchitka, an Alaskan island. The most powerless people—kids who were branded deserters, who had lost their citizenship, who had nothing and no political power whatsoever—proposed to stop the most powerful military in the world from the most powerful country on Earth in one of its planned military activities.

Which they did.

Public outcry is what moved the US military off Amchitka and that island is now a wildlife sanctuary. Some Alaskan natives thanked Greenpeace and called them Rainbow Warriors; the name stuck. (Buenfil: 83) The organization has a million or more dues-paying members and is involved in many policy debates, winning some, losing some, doing public outreach and education and acting on behalf of nonviolence and for the Earth with daring acts of nonviolent confrontation. The combination of savvy media work and high commitment activism has been their strategy and it gives power to small groups or individuals willing to take risks in little rubber boats confronting huge military ships—or a climber or two willing to scale a polluting smoke stack in order to drop a banner that is then photographed and offered to the media for broadcast. It also gives power to huge groups of individuals who donate so that this work can go on. Our contributions to Greenpeace might be regarded as a voluntary tax to fund the nonviolent navy and a scansorial disarmy habitually climbing bridges, stacks, corporate highrises and Big Trees. Greenpeace is the grandmother organization behind all the high-risk treesits and other nonviolent climbing actions—even when the current treesitters are not aware of that history—so the model is finding new creative manifestations and the power of the powerless is felt to the extent that it remains both bold and nonviolent. Rainbow warriors have been beaten, arrested and one—Fernando Pereira—was even killed by agents of the French government in 1985 when the Greenpeace flagship *Rainbow Warrior* was bombed and sunk at the express orders of French president Francois Mitterand. But the counterfactuals tell the story, even using just one example, the original issue at Amchitka.

What if they hadn't acted? At the least, the environment of that island would be ruined and radioactive.

What if they would have chosen violent opposition? They would have been crushed.

The Rainbow Warriors—a group of average citizens who answered to a special call and decided to risk their own safety for the general good—chose the most pragmatic and most idealistic response and succeeded completely. There is no guarantee of safety, nor of success, but the record of impressive victories is long. Greenpeace can teach us much.

weapons of mass instruction

> *Now would I give a thousand furlongs of sea for an acre of barren ground–long heath, brown furze, any thing. The wills above be done, but I would fain die a dry death.*
>
> —Gonzalo, "The Tempest," Act One, Scene One, William Shakespeare

Afloat on the seas of war in a military ship, we are drowning in weapons and violence. Nonviolence offers an acre of heath, so to speak, one in which our souls are not drenched in the blood of others. The oceans of arsenals and death-by-hot-steel are looking less and less like an expedient path. Risky nonviolence offers a better chance, and it is to those likely to volunteer to risk that we should generally direct our analysis.

Successful practitioners and promoters of CBD will heed the examples of King, Chavez and Gandhi, who may have occasionally spoken to the opponent, but who spent their time talking to their colleagues, to the citizens who were going to be doing the risk-taking, the action, the hard work. When Ann Braden spoke on the steps of the Lincoln Memorial to a large crowd intending to risk arrest in opposition to the funding of contra forces in Nicaragua, she urged those who engaged in the act to understand to whom they were speaking. "People are going to tell you that the President and Congress didn't hear you. That's right. But you're not talking to the President and Congress. You are here talking to the American people." (Braden) Similarly, philosopher Arne Naess noted, "Gandhi is here talking to all of us, not mainly to politicians whose power is dependent on the opinions of others." (Naess: 8)

Students and academicians are called to continue to educate themselves and each other; each time we study the methods of peace we make the study of war less necessary, less desirable, less useful, more obsolete. "The key to habitual obedience," writes Gene Sharp, "is to reach the mind." (Sharp,

Power: 12) And then to activate the conscience and the feet, hands and hearts.

Aside from the moral questions, we again wrestle with effectiveness when we suggest that we learn to defend ourselves with nonviolent power. Hughan turns the question around and asks how effective war has been. In her 1942 essay, she tallies the war dead from World War I for each of six nations and then gives the monetary cost to wage the war, and finally, whether that war was successful or not for each of the six nations. Only one—Britain—was successful, and it still lost a million soldiers while spending $35 billion. France was partially successful and lost more than 1.3 million people, spending some $35 billion (in 1942 dollars) as well. The rest—Russia, Germany, Austro-Hungary, Belgium—were unsuccessful and spent more billions. (Hughan: 318) She doesn't even count the environmental costs, which were considerable. (Hastings, 2000: 40+)

When will the cost-benefit analysis finally become important to belligerent nations? The risks are incredible and the rewards are dubious, especially when the rewards seem to demand a permanent war economy and a permanent willingness to regard the rest of humanity as the enemy. It seems unlikely that the costs of "a general strike raised to the nth power," which is Hughan's civilian-based answer to militarization, would exceed or even approach the total costs of maintaining and using armed forces. Denying coöperation to invaders would be costly; so is war.

Arguably, the Russians did almost exactly that to both Napoleon and Hitler, both of whom foundered against the Russian winter and the absolute refusal of the people themselves to surrender. The citizenry retreated and destroyed anything of value to the invading French and then the invading Germans, exhibiting complete noncoöperation and they eventually won in both cases, not because they held pacifist views dear to their hearts, but because they had no other method of striking back. It is then up to us to imagine how much more effective their resistance might have been if it had been explicitly nonviolent. Might the French have been challenged to disobey Napoleon and changed history? Could the German soldiers have become friends and allies to the Russians, undermining Hitler much earlier in the war? We will never know, but we do know that military action didn't save Russia in either war; rather, it was the iron will of the people, willing to suffer for their nation.

from the war system to a peace system

Nothing should be out of reach of hope. Life is a hope.

—Oscar Wilde, *A Woman of No Importance*, Act One

(Wilde: 64)

> *To be truly faithful to these Buddhist ideals, we must build a system of human security on a global level, a system that needs no recourse to military might or weapons, and consolidate the system by strengthening its moral and spiritual foundations—compassion, control of desires, and mutual trust among people.*
>
> —Yoichi Kawada, Director, Institute of Oriental Philosophy (Kawada: 64)

Dr. Kawada is a practical man, trained as a physician, yet he is calling for a world without weapons, a utopia of compassion, controlled desires and mutual trust. Is his Buddhist viewpoint pragmatic or fantasy?

Elise Boulding says, "Put in the simplest possible terms, a peace culture is a culture that promotes peaceable diversity." (Boulding: 1) Like many who envision a "peaceable Kingdom," (or, in the phraseology of the Catholic Workers, *Kin*dom) Dr. Kawada speaks to the faithful in his particular religion, and in that sense is not accounting for the behavior of the rest of humanity, who, if they continue as they are, will make sure that his faith is not hegemonic and his practices are not the norm. In that sense, his call is a nice vision but not realistic.

On the other hand, when a scholar can go to the wellsprings of a faith and come to the conclusion that a faithful practitioner must strive to become part of building a peace system, that is the kind of incremental and intentional and realistic step necessary toward the ultimate goal of "a system that needs no recourse to military might or weapons."

What, in addition to a massive military, does a war system look like?

- Families teach war is noble and necessary. Warriors are models.
- Schools teach the same and ignore fundamental critical thinking. Patriotism is the highest value, even above respect of life.
- Organized religion lines up with a military model. At times they even fly the flag of the nation-state; at the least, they stand aside when essential ethical questions beg to be addressed. *I'll make a voyage to the Holy Land, to wash this blood off from my guilty hand*, said Bolingbroke of the assassination of terrorist King Richard the Second in the final stanza of Shakespeare's play by that name.
- Media assumes a cheerleader role with little investigative zeal and heavy self-censorship. ("George Bush is my commander-in-chief."—Dan Rather)
- Economic gain is great for those who purvey war products.

Defense of Creation

- Laws protect war goods and weapons manufacturers and punish people who seek to nonviolently block warmaking.
- Political leadership never fundamentally questions war or the preparation for war, which leads them to vote the people's money toward war readiness.

Other sectors of society click into place like parts in a rumbling war tank. The system meets the needs of war profiteers neatly and sacrifices "insignificant" lives, including the poor and including the environment. While thousands of infants died each day around our Earth due to lack of basic nutrition in FY 1998, the top US military corporation raked in well over $12 billion dollars from the US taxpayer. Lockheed Martin, of Bethesda, Maryland, was the recipient of a full 10 percent of all DoD contracts that year and the children of Afghanistan, North Korea and Somalia starved. With that $12.341 billion, all those nations could have fed their starving, still leaving more than $10 billion in that same year for McDonnell Douglas, more than $5.6 billion for Raytheon, and so forth down the pricey line. (Center: 32)

This system is threatening the planet.

> *Up to about 35,000 B.C., for a million or more years our ancestors were upright, relatively highly cultured primates whose impact on the planet differed little from that of baboons.*
>
> —Robert Ornstein and Paul Ehrlich (Ornstein: 26)

The Earth can afford the violence of baboons. The Earth cannot afford the violence of humans. Nonviolence is an ecological priority, a human priority, and thus an entire system needs renovation until it tends toward peace and away from war and preparation for war.

Changing such a system won't be easy, but it will be worth it. Each element, each subsystem, will resist because it has achieved a functional role in the war system. The late but then-imprisoned nonviolent resister Phil Berrigan—former Josephite priest and Roman Catholic to the core—wrote of his beloved church: "We have obviously surpassed the German Church in negligence both moral and criminal. (Resistance to Hitler, for example, meant totalitarian reprisal, which would not quite be the case here.)" (P. Berrigan: 141) In short, noted Berrigan, if the church fails to resist plans to annihilate Creation, and if the church fails to stand institutionally against war, and if that church fails to do so in a society much less repressive than totalitarian Germany under the nazis, how can we cede any moral authority whatsoever to such a church? How can we respect an institution that is a part of a war machine when it would be difficult but certainly not impossible to be the beginnings of a peace system?

What will a peace system look like?

That will be up to collective humanity to design. Each subsystem within the war system meets human needs but meets them allowing for and at times encouraging war. A peace system meets the same needs nonviolently and will require sacrifice to pay for the transition. Currently, the sacrifices for not making the transition are tremendous, so relative costs are the question.

The objects of our conflicts—so often our most precious natural resources—are in the most danger from the very methods we use to engage in the conflicts. Water, for example, presents conflictual problems that flow through ideological and cultural, religious and rational notions of understanding. Whether we analyze violent conflict in terms of bipolar Cold War thinking or multiparty ethnic struggle for basic human rights, water bubbles at the center of many of those pictures. "Water can be a defining factor in the wealth and power—and in the economic and political strength—of a nation. Access to water resources may serve as a focus of dispute or provide a justification for actual conflict." (Gleick: 108) Then, when the bombs fly and the troops travel, the water is polluted, sometimes for generations; in addition, we simply have no more luxury of freshwater waste in the face of a human family that has grown from 2.6 billion in 1950 to more than 6.2 billion just 52 short years later.

Clearly, we are called to replace the model of conflict resolution that leads to the desire for such polluting weaponry. Nonviolence offers us that alternative, especially when synthesized with techniques and thinking associated with conflict resolution. We look to our most dedicated for cues and clues.

Some of our most gifted philosophers and actionists have been taken from us just as they were coming into their power. Martin Luther King, Jr., Dietrich Bonhoeffer and Blaise Pascal were all prematurely snuffed at age 39. The challenge of the evil of violence has been, for some, the risk worth taking, and the commensurate prod to greatness of spirit. King might have lived a long and pleasant life as a parish minister had he not been thrust into a movement just at the moment his skills and spirit were prepared to pick up the baton. About Bonhoeffer it has been written, "The influence of his parents and teachers was great, but it was Adolf Hitler who stimulated the theologian to do and dare what he considered right." (Bailey: 39) One plowshare resister, in federal US prison for 18 years once told me that she felt like the "grocer for whom God had other plans." The mystery in this, according to nonviolent theorist and theologian Daniel Berrigan, S.J.—writing of Bonhoeffer—is made manifest "when a symbolic activity, quite modest and concrete, brings about a meeting of two freedoms: the divine and the human, and the opportunity of creative change in human life, a climate of choice." (D. Berrigan: 6) Indeed, it is the sense of choice that we seek, with nonviolence, to introduce into the set behavior patterns that otherwise militate against

Resource wars

> *Homo sapiens:*
> *over five billion served!*
> *The fabled bison:*
> *fifty million, tops.*
> *A human sea*
> *with an onmidirectional tsunami*
> *headed toward your children,*
> *made up of your children,*
> *headed toward the Earth,*
> *toward every bird,*
> *toward every animal,*
> *toward Life,*
> *overpowering Nature,*
> *destroying it all until it is spent.*
> *Period.*
> —Ecesis Freshperson, Screaming Broccoli (Ecesis: 12)

Peace researcher Michael T. Klare, in his recent books **Resource Wars: The New Landscape of Global Conflict**, and **Blood and Oil: The Dangers and Consequences of America's Growing Dependency on Imported Petroleum**, stresses the role that increasing scarcity will have in conflicts to come. He asks us to imagine a map of the globe with colors that represent the origins of resources; black for fossil fuel deposits, blue for freshwater, white for precious minerals, green for timber, red for strategic minerals.

Most of the color on Earth, then, is in a wide band straddling the equator, which is also where a great deal of ethnic conflict has occurred and is ongoing. Klare says that conflict will increase. This is currently true in oil-rich Colombia and will likely be the case in Venezuela, also an oil exporting nation. The US is the major supplier of arms to Colombia and the guerrilla frequently attack the oil pipelines. (Klare: 215)

The question of the Kurdish identity conflict in the Mideast involves international conflict and water issues. The Kurds are inhabitants of portions of Iraq, Syria, Iran, Turkey (and a small portion of Azerbaijan), and are in rebellion against all, though Syria has lent aid to the Kurd guerrilla—the PKK—as the Kurds battle the government of Turkey. The government of Turkey, in turn, has built the massive Ataturk Dam on the Euphrates river, which rises in the mountains of Turkey and flows then through Syria and finally Iraq before emptying into the Persian Gulf. In October 1989, Turkish president Turgut Özal warned Damascus that he would cut off the Euphrates if Syria continued their clandestine support for the PKK. When Turkey completely shut down the Euphrates river for a month in the winter of 1990, Syria and Iraq were, of course, livid. Assad and Hussein talked of war. Turkey bragged about its superiority and virtually taunted Hafiz al-Assad into continuing his support for the armed Kurdish rebellion against Turkey, which he did, exacerbating ethnic conflict. By the mid-1990s, NATO-supplied Turkish troops had driven hundreds of thousands of Kurds from their homes in a scorched earth ethnic war, more than 30,000 were killed, many were jailed and tortured, and the PKK engaged in a war of terrorist acts in reprisal. By 1998, Ankara had warned of all-out war against PKK camps in Syria and had amassed thousands of troops along the Syrian border. Syria relented, Abdullah Ocalan was deported, and tensions reduced for a while. But the Euphrates issue remains. (Klare: 178+) Thus can internal resource conflict spill over, potentially, into international conflict.

Another locale of ethnic conflict in dynamic relationship to resource scarcity conflict is the Caspian Sea basin, a region rich in untapped oil reserves. The oil is located in the middle of a sea of identity conflict, from Chechnya on the north, Nagorno-Karabakh to the immediate south, Turkey to the southwest, Iran to the south, and Turkmenistan to the east. The US has been busily supplying arms to everyone in the region, totaling some $1.06 billion to a combination of Armenia, Azerbaijan, Georgia, Kazakhstan, Kyrgyztan, Tajikistan, Turkmenistan and Uzbekistan between 1998-2000. (Klare: 96) Identity conflict has periodically erupted into war in the past in all these regions, but the arrival of Western oil companies has only exacerbated these ethnic conflicts. (Klare: 98) There is no path for pipelines in the region that does not pass through disputed territory. (Klare: 101) As the oil begins to flow toward various points—even including an 1,800-mile proposed line to China—all pipelines will be natural targets for armed separatists and other identity conflict forces, and the likelihood of Russian intervention, American involvement and Chinese military presence will increase. Thus the mixed blessing of oil feeds and fosters ethnic conflict and, in several cases, religious conflict, as Islamic forces also rise against Western-style secular governments that use window-dressing democracy as a front to garner more US military aid even as they repress their own minorities.

Some of the tensions in that region are legacies of the Soviet attempts to reduce ethnic conflict within its borders by drawing interrepublic borders that cut across ethnic lines. This was transparent and only lasted effectively as long as the Soviet Union existed, but the old internal borders still exist in many cases and fuel ethnic tensions to this day. Through all this turmoil, the infusion of a Western oil economy has also created new class and income disparities that add tension and bitterness to already divided populations. Part of the end result to all this instability has been shifting and uneasy military alliances in the region, with the possibility for eruption of proxy war a constant. While tension would exist without the influence of Moscow and Washington, the externals make matters infinitely more destructive and carry the seeds of regional or even global conflict. (Klare: 106+) Another historical example of the cross-tribal boundaries is the Durand Line, drawn in 1893 by a cartographer under orders from Sir Mortimer Durand—the foreign secretary of the colonial government of India—in an effort to split the strong and seemingly undefeatable Pashtun tribe, the traditional rulers of Afghanistan. The British empire had tried twice—in 1839 and 1878—to conquer Afghanistan and had twice been driven out. The first attempt was one of the greatest defeats of the British empire, ever. The end result was to attempt to make Afghanistan a buffer between Russia and Britain, controlled by the Pashtun tribes and a kind of no-European-colonialist land. (Hilton: 60) The tragedy for the Pashtuns is that the line officially gave half their territory to what became Pakistan and half to the buffer state, Afghanistan, in that typical divide-and-rule maneuver used so devastatingly across the planet by invaders with big guns. We continue to pay the price for that arrogance today.

> *Natural resources are the building blocks of civilization and an essential requirement of daily existence. The inhabitants of planet Earth have been blessed with a vast supply of most basic materials. But we are placing increased pressure on these supplies, and in some cases we face, in our lifetimes, or those of our children, the prospect of severe resource depletion. If we rely on warfare to settle disputes over raw materials, the human toll will be great. To avoid this fate, and to ensure an adequate supply of essential materials, we must work now to establish a global system of resource conservation and collaboration.*

—Michael T. Klare (Klare: 226)

Connecting to Creation

> *I belong to a Clan of One-Breasted Women. My mother, my grandmothers, and six aunts have all had mastectomies. Seven are dead. The two who survive have just completed rounds of chemotherapy and radiation....Most statistics tell us breast cancer is genetic, hereditary, with rising percentages attached to fatty diets, childlessness, or becoming pregnant after thirty. What*

> *they don't say is living in Utah may be the greatest hazard of all....above ground atomic testing in Nevada took place from January 27, 1951 through July 11, 1962.*
>
> —Terry Tempest Williams, Mormon, naturalist, author, downwinder (Williams: 281+)

Is environmental concern the province of the wealthy elite who simply wish to preserve spots of aesthetic beauty for their own pleasure? If so, we certainly cannot expect nonviolence to be relevant.

Some elements of the environment have been recognized as vulnerable to war and have been protected by law for ages. Indeed, the Koran and the book of Judges in the Bible both proscribe the destruction of fruit trees and fields where crops have been planted. (Boulding: 19) This is not about saving lovely places for the few at the expense of jobs for the many; this is a clear and ancient recognition that war destroys what we are fighting for, our homelands.

It's about our survival, so environmental defense becomes a matter of priority for poor people too. And if sacrificial nonviolence can be used to defend the environment by the poorest, it is even more available to those who can better afford the risks. When women and children from Reni, a remote village in northern India, hugged trees to prevent loggers working for lumber companies from cutting down local trees, they teach us about priorities and possibilities. (Boulding: 207) This "Chipko" method of nonviolent forest defense has been a successful movement in India, where the jobs of loggers are arguably more important to them than are the jobs of loggers (or miners, or oil drillers, or weapons workers) here in the richest nation on Earth. Similarly, we find the poorest per capita incomes and highest unemployment in the US are on some Native American reservations, yet the Anishinabe on Bad River reservation in Wisconsin, and on the White Earth reservation in Minnesota, stopped logging on their reservation nonviolent blockades, thus denying themselves income. (LaDuke: 128) (Hastings, 2002: 142) Just because someone gets paid to do something wrong doesn't justify more of the same behavior. A hired killer is rarely able to convince a jury that such behavior is acceptable because money is involved. Certainly the killer may have children dependent upon the income from the fee for "making the hit," but that has no legal or even moral cache. Why should other bad behavior be allowed because it gains money for engaging in it?

Whether we learn, practice and promote nonviolence because we are concerned with self-preservation, with protecting loved ones, with achieving social change, with protecting the environment, with national liberation or with improving social norms in general—all arguably logical reasons to study and use nonviolent tactics—we ought to do so understanding the risks. Gandhi died for nonviolence, as did King. Many of us have endured beatings, jail and prison. Nonviolence is an eminently practical set of skills for those who wish to prepare for possible moments of self-defense, yet it brings additional dangers to those who use it to seek a role interposing between perpetrators and vulnerable ones. When we volunteer we refocus the risk from others to ourselves. That is when either violence or nonviolence brings additional risk, and keeping the relative possibilities in mind is instructive. Performing risk-benefit analysis will lead more and more to the employment of nonviolent competencies as a matter of clear choice and the time is always at hand to learn more about this Ultimate Weapon in the defense of Creation.

The risks are relative. "As for my readiness to go to prison," wrote Daniel Ellsberg about his consideration of the risks involved in releasing the Pentagon Papers," I'd already risked my life for the war when I had gone to Vietnam. And if I could do that, I could now go to prison if necessary, as the price of opposing it." (Hallock: 316) Warriors understand this relative risk clearly and the best are willing to talk about it. It is one reason Gandhi sometimes bemoaned the lack of warrior attitude amongst his fellow mellow Hindus. As some Christians jokingly refer to the idea of sacrificing, nonviolence and risk, You'd better look good on wood.

This is certainly true collectively. We have risked global annihilation in a half-century of atomic brinksmanship and we have risked—and suffered—environmental contamination from the mere production and testing of these hellish weapons. For 52 years, in fact, the fed government and its corporate contractors dumped radioactivity straight into the Columbia River or knowingly allowed huge vats of radioactive waste to leak into the soil within sight of that mighty, that beautiful, that precious 1,400-mile salmon breeding and well-loved river. (Gerber: 233) The effects of radiation were known in the early 20th century and yet the risks were taken in the name of violent threat power. What risks are we willing and able to take for nonviolence?

Perhaps the most useful perspective tool when contemplating the relative usefulness of violence and nonviolence is the counterfactual. What if Gandhi had advocated and used violence? He might have been killed even younger. Many more Indians might have been killed achieving liberation. Certainly many more innocent ones would have been at risk. What if Martin King had promoted violence and used it? He might have been dead at 29 instead of 39; almost certainly there would have been no Civil Rights Act of 1964 or Voting Rights Act of 1965. There may have instead been a Military Law Act of 1956 if King had urged violence in Montgomery rather than the bus boycott. Civil rights for African Americans could have been retarded instead of advanced. We will never know, but we can mentally extrapolate. When we do, we make more considered choices; some believe that nonviolence is the only logical choice when we take these factors into consideration. Clearly, using nonviolence offers the only true alternative to militarism, since violence demands another form of militarism, even for the so-called "freedom fighters," the guerrilla, who end up donning the mantle of the oppressor when they use such tactics.

When, for example, the Innu peoples of the far north in Canada began to resist the low-level practice bombing flights that Canada allowed NATO to do where "nobody" lived, they found themselves standing up to white people for the first time, using nonviolent occupation of the runways, elders of 80 standing silently in the path of 500-ton warjets. (LaDuke: 58) Most had no culture of resistance, since war against the dominant society was suicide, but they continue to use nonviolence and have had some victories. They are modeling what NATO ought to be using, though NATO seems determined not to learn from the First Nations. The Innu campaign has entered its second decade and serves as inspiration to other native peoples who didn't know there was an alternative to the "choices" of violence or capitulation.

sources:
Braden, Ann, address, April 1985.
Bailey, J. Martin, and Douglas Gilbert, *The Steps of Bonhoeffer: A Pictorial Album*. Philadelphia PA: United Church Press, 1969.
Begich, Dr. Nick, and Jeane Manning, *Angels Don't Play This HAARP: Advances in Tesla Technology*. Anchorage AK: 1995.
Berrigan, Daniel, S.J., *Consequences: Truth and....* NYC: The Macmillan Company, 1965.
Berrigan, Phillip, personal correspondence, 2001.
Boulding, Elise, *Cultures of Peace: The Hidden Side of History*. Syracuse NY: Syracuse University Press, 2000.
Buenfil, Alberto Ruz, *Rainbow Nation Without Borders: Toward an Ecotopian Millennium*. Santa Fe NM: Bear & Company Publishing, 1991.
Center for Defense Information, *1999 CDI Military Almanac*. Washington DC: CDI, 1999.
Cuny, Frederick C., with Richard B. Hill, *Famine, Conflict and Response: A Basic Guide*. West Hartford CT: Kumarian Press, 1999.
Deats, Richard, ed., *Ambassador of Reconciliation: A Muriel Lester Reader*. Philadelphia PA: New Society Publishers, 1991.
Ecesis, (Tom H. Hastings) "Screaming Broccoli," *Mosaic*, Fall 1989.
Environmental News Service, "Army will review impacts of Hawaii training," 5 October 2001.
Gerber, Michele Stenehjem, *On the Home Front: The Cold War Legacy of the Hanford Nuclear Site*. Lincoln NE: University of Nebraska Press, 1997. (original 1992)
Gleick, Peter H., *The World's Water: The Biennial Report of Freshwater*

Resources 1998 1999. Washington DC: Island Press, 1998.
Hallock, Daniel, ***Hell, Healing and Resistance: Veterans Speak***. Farmington PA: The Plough Publishing House, 1998.
Hastings, Tom H., ***Ecology of War & Peace: Counting Costs of Conflict***. Lanham MD: University Press of America, 2000.
———, ***Meek Ain't Weak: Nonviolent Power and People of Color***. Lanham MD: University Press of American, 2002.
Hilton, Isabel, "The Pashtun Code," *The New Yorker*. 3 December 2001. (58-71)
Howard-Hastings, Tom, and Donna Howard-Hastings, ***Laurentian Shield: Nonviolent Disarmament of the Nuclear Navy in Wisconsin***. Maple WI: Laurentian Shield Resources, 1996.
Hughan, Jessie Wallace, and Cecil Hinshaw, "Toward a national defense," in: Sibley, Mulford Q., ed., ***The Quiet Battle: Writings on the Theory and Practice of Non-violent Resistance***. Boston: Beacon Press, 1963. (Hughan's original 1942)
Kawada, Yoichi, "The Earth Charter: a Nichiren Buddhist view," in: Morgante, Amy, ed., ***Buddhist Perspectives on the Earth Charter***. Cambridge MA: Boston Research Center, 1997.
King, Jr., Martin Luther, ***A Testament of Hope: The Essential Writings and Speeches of Martin Luther King, Jr***. NYC: HarperSanFrancisco, 1986.
Klare, Michael T., ***Resource Wars The New Landscape of Global Conflict***. NYC: Metropolitan Books, 2001.
Krieger, David and Frank Kelly, eds., ***Waging Peace in the Nuclear Age: Ideas for Action***. Santa Barbara CA: Capra Press, 1988.
LaDuke, Winona, ***All Our Relations: Native Struggles for Land and Life***. Cambridge MA: South End Press, 1999.
Naess, Arne, ***Gandhi and the Nuclear Age***. Totowa NJ: The Bedminster Press, 1965.
Nelson, Juanita, "What do you believe," in: Farren, Pat, ed., ***Peacework: 20 Years of Nonviolent Social Change***. Baltimore MD: Fortkamp Publishing Company, 1991.
Ornstein, Robert, and Paul Ehrlich, ***New World New Mind: Moving Toward Conscious Evolution*** NYC: Doubleday, 1989.
Shakespeare, William, ***The Complete Works of William Shakespeare***. Glasgow, Scotland: HarperCollins Publishers, 1994.
Sharp, Gene, ***Power and Struggle: Part One: The Politics of Nonviolent Action***. Boston: Porter Sargent Publishers, 1973.
Szasz, Andrew, ***EcoPopulism: Toxic Waste and the Movement for Environmental Justice***. Minneapolis: University of Minnesota Press, 1994.
Vanunu, Mordechai, ***Faith Under Siege: Letters from a Christian Prisoner-of-Conscience***. Samuel H. Day, Jr., ed. Madison WI: U.S. Campaign to Free Mordechai Vanunu, 1998,
von Suttner, Bertha Sophie Felicia, "The evolution of the peace movement," in: Thee, Marek, ***Peace! By the Nobel Peace Prize Laureates: An Anthology***. Paris: UNESCO Publishing, 1995.`
Wilde, Oscar, ***Sayings***. Rome: Demetra, 1998.

Williams, Terry Tempest, ***Refuge: An Unnatural History of Family and Place***. NYC: Vintage Books, 1992.

World Law Fund, ***Current Disarmament Proposals: As of March 1, 1964***. NYC: World Law Fund, 1964.

Bibliography

Abu-Nimer, Mohammed, Dialogue, *Conflict Resolution, and Change: Arab-Jewish Encounters in Israel*. Albany NY: State University of New York, 1999.

Abu-Odeh, Adnan, *Jordanians, Palestinians, & the Hashemite Kingdom in the Middle East Peace Process*. Washington DC: United States Institute of Peace Press, 1999.

Ackerman, Peter and Christopher Kruegler, *Strategic Nonviolent Conflict: The Dynamics of People Power in the Twentieth Century*. Westport CT: Praeger Publishers, 1994.

Ackerman, Peter, and Jack DuVall, *A Force More Powerful: A Century of Nonviolent Conflict*. NYC: St. Martin's Press, 2000.

Ahmed, Mohammed M.A., and Michael Gunter, eds., *The Kurdish Question and International Law: An Analysis of the Legal Rights of the Kurdish People*. Oakton VA: Ahmed Foundation for Kurdish Studies, 2000.

Albert, Michael, *Stop the Killing Train: Radical Visions for Radical Change*. Boston MA: South End Press, 1994.

Aldridge, Robert C., *First Strike! The Pentagon's Strategy for Nuclear War*. Boston: South End Press, 1983.

Alexander, Yonah, and Michael S. Swetnam, *Usama bin Laden's al-Qaeda : Profile of a Terrorist Network*. Ardsley NY: Transnational Publishers, Inc., 2001.

Allport, Gordon W., *The Nature of Prejudice*. NYC: Doubleday Anchor Books, 1958. (original 1954)

American Kurdish Information Network, *The Fast for Peace in Kurdistan and the Freedom of Leyla Zana*. Washington DC: The American Kurdish Information Network, 1998.

Anderson, Shelley and Janet Larmore, eds., *Nonviolent Struggle and Social Defense*. London: War Resisters' International, 1991.

Andregg, Michael, *On the Causes of War*. revised (original 1996) Minneapolis MN: self-published, 1999.

Appleby, R. Scott, *The Ambivalence of the Sacred: Religion, Violence, and Reconciliation*. Lanham MD: Rowman & Littlefield Publishers, 2000.

Arnold, Johann Christoph, *The Lost Art of Forgiving: Stories of Healing from the Cancer of Bitterness*. Farmington PA: The Plough Publishing House, 1998.

Arnove, Anthony, ed., *Iraq Under Siege: The Deadly Impact of Sanctions and War*. Cambridge MA: South End Press, 2000.
Ashmore, Richard D., et. al., eds., *Social Identity, Intergroup Conflict, and Conflict Reduction*. NYC: Oxford University Press, 2001.
Bailey, J. Martin, and Douglas Gilbert, *The Steps of Bonhoeffer: A Pictorial Album*. Philadelphia PA: United Church Press, 1969.
Barash, David, *Approaches to Peace: A Reader in Peace Studies*. New York: Oxford University Press, 2000.
Barash, David P. and Charles P. Webel, *Peace and Conflict Studies*. Thousand Oaks CA: Sage Publications, Inc., 2002.
Bart, Pauline B., and Patricia H. O'Brien, *Stopping Rape: Successful Survival Strategies*. NYC: Teachers College Press, 1993.
Bartolf, Christian, *The Breath of My Life: The Correspondence of Mahatma Gandhi (India) and Bart de Ligt (Holland) on War and Peace*. Berlin: Gandhi-Information-Zentrum, 2001.
Bateson, Mary Catherine, *Composing a Life*. NYC: Plume, 1990. (original: NYC: Atlantic Monthly Press, 1989).
Begich, Dr. Nick, and Jeane Manning, *Angels Don't Play This HAARP: Advances in Tesla Technology*. Anchorage AK: 1995.
Bergen, Peter L., *Holy War, Inc., Inside the Secret World of Osama bin Laden*. NYC: The Free Press, 2001.
Berrigan, S.J., Daniel, *Consequences: Truth and....* NYC: The Macmillan Company, 1965.
———, Love, *Love at the End: Parables, Prayers and Meditations*. NYC: The Macmillan Company, 1968.
———, Whereon to Stand: *The Acts of the Apostles and Ourselves*. Baltimore MD: Fortkamp Publishing Company, 1991.
Berrigan, Philip, *Fighting the Lamb's War: Skirmishes with the American Empire*. Monroe ME: Common Courage Press, 1996.
Blalock, Jr., Hubert M., *Power and Conflict: Toward a General Theory*. Newbury Park CA: Sage Publications, 1989.
Bondurant, Joan V., *Conquest of Violence: The Gandhian Philosophy of Conflict*. Rev. ed. Berkeley CA: University of California Press, 1965.
Boulding, Elise, *Cultures of Peace: The Hidden Side of History*. Syracuse NY: Syracuse University Press, 2000.
Boulding, Kenneth, et alia, *Proceedings of the International Peace Research Association Inaugural Conference*. The Netherlands: Van Gorcum & Comp., 1966.
Boyer, William H., *Education for the Twenty-first Century*. San Francisco: Caddo Gap Press, 2002.
Brisard, Jean-Charles, and Guillaume Dasquié, *Forbidden Truth: U.S.-Taliban Secret Oil Diplomacy and the Failed Hunt for Bin Laden*. NYC: Thunder's Mouth Press, 2002.
Brogan, Patrick, *The Fighting Never Stopped: A Comprehensive Guide to World Conflict Since 1945*. NYC: Vintage Books Edition, 1990.
Browne, Angela, *When Battered Women Kill*. NYC: The Free Press, 1987.

Buenfil, Alberto Ruz, *Rainbow Nation Without Borders: Toward an Ecotopian Millennium*. Santa Fe NM: Bear & Company Publishing, 1991.

Bussey, Gertrude, and Margaret Tims, *Pioneers for Peace: Women's International League for Peace and Freedom* 1915-1965. London: WILPF, 1980. (original 1965)

Butler, C.T., and Keith McHenry, *Food not Bombs*. 2nd ed. Tucson AZ: See Sharp Press, 2000. (original 1992)

Butler, Richard, *The Greatest Threat: Iraq, Weapons of Mass Destruction, and the Growing Crisis of Global Security*. NYC: Public Affairs, 2000.

Byrne, Sean and Cynthia L. Irvin, *Reconcilable Differences: Turning Points in Ethnopolitical Conflict*. West Hartford CT: Kumarian Press, 2000.

Carawan, Guy and Candie, *Sing for Freedom: The Story of the Civil Rights Movement Through Its Songs*. Bethlehem PA: A Sing Out Publication, 1990.

Carnegie Commission on Preventing Deadly Conflict, Preventing Deadly Conflict. Washington DC: Carnegie Corporation of New York, 1997.

Carter, Jimmy, *Talking Peace: A Vision for the Next Generation*. NYC: Dutton Children's Books, 1993.

Casey, Helen Marie, and Amy Morgante, eds., *Women's Views on the Earth Charter*. Cambridge MA: Boston Research Center, 1997.

Center for Defense Information, *1999 CDI Military Almanac*. Washington DC: CDI, 1999.

Center for the Study of Human Rights Columbia University, *Twenty-five Human Rights Documents*. NYC: 1994.

Chadda, Maya, *Ethnicity, Security, and Separatism in India*. NYC: Columbia University Press, 1997.

Chappell, David, editor, *Buddhist Peacework: Creating Cultures of Peace*. Boston: Wisdom Publications, 1999.

Chatfield, Charles and Ruzanna Ilukhina, *Peace/Mir: An Anthology of Historic Alternatives to War*. Syracuse NY: Syracuse University Press, 1994.

Chomsky, Noam, *Fateful Triangle: The United States, Israel, and the Palestinians*. Cambridge MA: South End Press, 1999.

Cobban, Helena, *The Israeli-Syrian Peace Talks: 1991 and Beyond*. Washington DC: United States Institute of Peace Press, 1999.

Coles, Robert, Dorothy Day: *A Radical Devotion*. Reading MA: Perseus Books, 1987.

Conway, M. Margaret, et al., *Women & Political Participation: Cultural Change in the Political Arena*. Washington DC: Congressional Quarterly Inc., 1997.

Congressional Quarterly, *The Middle East*, Ninth Edition. Washington DC: CQ Press, 2000.

Cooney, Robert and Helen Michalowski, *The Power of the People: Active Nonviolence in the United States*. Philadelphia: New Society Publishers, 1987.

Coover, Virginia, et al., Resource *Manual for a Living Revolution: A Handbook of Skills & Tools for Social Change Activists*. Philadelphia

PA: New Society Publishers, 1977.
Coy, Patrick G., ed., *A Revolution of the Heart: Essays on the Catholic Worker*. Philadelphia PA: New Society Publishers, 1988.
Cortright, David, and George Lopez, *The Sanctions Decade: Assessing UN Strategies in the 1990s*. Boulder CO: Lynne Rienner Publishers, 2000.
Creighton, Allan, and Paul Kivel, *Helping Teens Stop Violence*. Alameda CA: Hunter House, 1992.
Cuny, Frederick C., with Richard B. Hill, *Famine, Conflict and Response: A Basic Guide*. West Hartford CT: Kumarian Press, 1999.
Daniels, Steven E., and Gregg B. Walker, *Working Through Environmental Conflict: The Collaborative Learning Approach*. Westport CT: Praeger, 2001.
Day, Samuel H., *Crossing the Line: From Editor to Activist to Inmate—a Writer's Journey*. Baltimore MD: Fortkamp Publishing, 1991.
Dellinger, David, *More Power Than We Know: The People's Movement Toward Democracy*. Garden City, NY: Anchor Press/Doubleday, 1975.
Deutsch, Morton, and Peter T. Coleman, eds., *The Handbook of Conflict Resolution: Theory and Practice*. San Francisco: Jossey-Bass Publishers, 2000.
Downton Jr., James, and Paul Wehr, *The Persistent Activist: How Peace Commitment Develops and Survives*. Boulder CO: Westview Press, 1997.
Dyson, Freeman, *Weapons and Hope*. NYC: Harper Colophon Books, 1984.
Egan, Eileen, *Peace Be With You: Justified Warfare or the Way of Nonviolence*. Maryknoll NY: Orbis Books, 1999.
Ehrlich, Anne H and John W. Birks, editors, *Hidden Dangers: Environmental Consequences of Preparing for War*. San Francisco: Sierra Club Books, 1990.
Eitzen, D. Stanley and Maxine Baca Zinn, *In Conflict and Order: Understanding Society*. Eighth edition. Boston: Allyn and Bacon, 1998.
Elhance, Arun P., *Hydropolitics in the 3rd World: Conflict and Coöperation in International River Basins*. Washington DC: United States Institute of Peace, 1999.
Erikson, Erik H., *Gandhi's Truth: On the Origins of Militant Nonviolence*. NYC: W.W. Norton & Company, Inc., 1969.
Eschle, Catherine, *Global Democracy, Social Movements, and Feminism*. Boulder CO: Westview Press, 2001.
European Centre for Conflict Prevention, *People Building Peace: 35 Inspiring Stories from Around the World*. Utrecht, The Netherlands: European Centre for Conflict Prevention, 1999.
Everett, Melissa, *Breaking Ranks*. Philadelphia PA: New Society Publishers, 1989.
Farren, Pat, ed., *Peacework: 20 Years of Nonviolent Social Change*. Baltimore MD: Fortkamp Publishing Company, 1991.
Feiveson, Harold A., ed., *Nuclear Turning Point: A Blueprint for Deep Cuts and De-Alerting of Nuclear Weapons*. Washington DC: Brookings

Institution Press, 1999.
Fisher, Roger and William Ury, *Getting to Yes: Negotiating Agreement Without Giving In*. NYC: Penguin Books 1981, 2nd edition, 1991.
Fisk, Larry & John Schellenberg, editors, *Patterns of Conflict: Paths to Peace*. Peterborough, Ontario: Broadview Press, 2000.
Fitzell, Susan Gingras, Fre*e the Children! Conflict Education for Strong & Peaceful Minds*. Gabriola Island BC: New Society Publishers, 1997.
Forcey, Linda Rennie, and Ian Murray Harris, *Peacebuilding for Adolescents: Strategies for Educators and Community Leaders*. NYC: Peter Lang, 1999.
Forest, Jim, *Love Is the Measure: A Biography of Dorothy Day*. Maryknoll NY: Orbis Books, 1997. (original 1986)
Fox, Helen, *"When Race Breaks Out": Conversations About Race and Racism in College Classrooms*. NYC: Peter Lang, 2001.
Gallagher, Michael, *Laws of Heaven: Catholic Activists Today*. NYC: Ticknor & Fields, 1992.
Gandhi, Mohandas K., *Autobiography: The Story of My Experiments with Truth*. NYC: Dover Publications, Inc., 1983. (original Public Affairs Press, 1948)
Gandhi, Mohandas K, *The Essential Gandhi: An Anthology of His Writings on His Life, Work and Ideas,* Fischer, Louis, ed., NYC: Vintage Books, 1983 (original 1962).
Gerber, Michele Stenehjem, *On the Home Front: The Cold War Legacy of the Hanford Nuclear Site*. Lincoln NE: University of Nebraska Press, 1997. (original 1992)
Gioseffi, Daniela, ed., *Women on War: Essential Voices for the Nuclear Age from a Brilliant International Assembly*. NYC: Touchstone, 1988.
Gleick, Peter H., *The World's Water: The Biennial Report of Freshwater Resources 1998 1999*. Washington DC: Island Press, 1998.
Glenny, Misha, *The Fall of Yugoslavia: The Third Balkan War*. Third ed. NYC: Penguin Books, 1996.
Glossop, Ronald J., *Confronting War: An Examination of Humanity's Most Pressing Problem*. Jefferson NC: McFarland & Company, Inc., 1987.
Glossop, Ronald L. *Confronting War: An Examination of Humanity's Most Pressing Problem*. 4th ed. Jefferson NC: McFarland & Company, 2001.
Gonzalez, Gaspar Pedro, *A Mayan Life.* Rancho Palos Verdes CA: Yax Te' Press, 1995.
Goodson, Larry P., *Afghanistan's Endless Wars: State Failure, Regional Politics, and the Rise of the Taliban*. Seattle: University of Washington Press, 2001.
Gowan, Susanne, et al., *Moving Toward A New Society*. Philadelphia PA: New Society Press, 1976.
Greene, Matthew W., *Learning about School Violence: lessons for educators, parents, students, & communities*. NYC: Peter Lang, 2001.
Gregg, Richard B., *The Power of Nonviolence,* second revised edition. NYC: Schocken Books, 1966 (original 1935).

Greider, William, *One World, Ready or Not: The Manic Logic of Global Capitalism*. NYC: Simon & Schuster, 1997.
Groves, Denise, *Rebuilding the Future: Child Soldiers and Sustainable Disarmament*. Washington DC: Center for Defense Information, 2000.
Grusky, David B., *Social Stratification: Class, Race, & Gender in Sociological Perspective*. 2nd ed Boulder CO: Westview Press, 2001.
Halberstam, David, *The Children*. NYC: Random House, 1998.
Hallock, Daniel, *Hell, Healing and Resistance: Veterans Speak*. Farmington PA: The Plough Publishing House, 1998.
Hanh, Thich Nhat, *Being Peace*. Berkeley CA: Parallax Press, 1987.
Handicap International, *Antipersonnel Landmines: For the Banning of the Massacres of Civilians in Time of Peace*. Second ed., Lyon, France: Handicap International, 1997.
Harak, S. J., G. Simon, ed., *Nonviolence for the Third Millennium: Its Legacy and Future*. Macon GA: Mercer University Press, 2000.
Hastings, Tom H., *Ecology of War & Peace: Counting Costs of Conflict*. Lanham MD: University Press of America, 2000.
———, *Meek Ain't Weak: Nonviolent Power and People of Color*. Lanham MD: University Press of America, 2001.
———, *52 Stories of Nonviolent Success*. NYC: War Resisters League, 2002.
Hawkley, Louise and James C. Juhnke, Nonviolent America: History Though the Eyes of Peace. North Newton KS: Bethel College, 1993.
Henderson, Michael, *All Her Paths are Peace: Women Pioneers in Peacemaking*. West Hartford CT: Kumarian Press, 1994.
Hentoff, Nat, *Peace Agitator: The Story of A.J. Muste*. NYC: A.J. Muste Memorial Institute, 1982 (original The Macmillan Company, 1963).
Herr, Robert and Judy Zimmerman Herr, eds., *Transforming Violence: Linking Local and Global Peacemaking*. Scottsdale PA: Herald Press, 1998.
Hersey, John, *Hiroshima*. NYC: Bantam Pathfinder, 1966. (original 1946)
Holbrooke, Richard, *To End a War*. NYC: Random House, Modern Library, 1999.
Holmes, Robert L., *Nonviolence in Theory and Practice*. Belmont CA: Wadsworth Publishing Company, 1990.
Homer-Dixon, Thomas F., *Environment, Scarcity, and Violence*. Princeton NJ: Princeton University Press, 1999.
———, The Ingenuity Gap. NYC: Alfred A. Knopf, 2000.
Hopkins, Jeffrey, ed., *The Art of Peace: Nobel Peace Laureates Discuss Human Rights, Conflict and Reconciliation*. Ithaca NY: Snow Lion Publications, 2000.
Howard-Hastings, Tom, and Donna Howard-Hastings, *Laurentian Shield: Nonviolent Disarmament of the Nuclear Navy in Wisconsin*. Maple WI: Laurentian Shield Resources, 1996.
Idinopulos, Thomas A., *Weathered by Miracles: A History of Palestine from Bonaparte and Muhammad Ali to Ben-Gurion and the Mufti*. Chicago: Ivan R. Dee, 1998.
Ingram, Catherine, *In the Footsteps of Gandhi: Conversations with Spiritual

Social Activists. Berkeley CA: Parallax Press, 1990.
Karrass, Dr. Chester L., ***Effective Negotiating: Workbook and Discussion Guide***. Santa Monica CA: KARRASS, 1991.
Kegley, Jr., Charles W. and Gregory A. Raymond, ***How Nations Make Peace***. NYC: St. Martin's/Worth, 1999.
Kempton, Murray, et al., ***Trials of the Resistance***. NYC: The New York Review, 1970.
Kennedy, Paul, ***The Rise and Fall of the Great Powers: Economic Change and Military Conflict from 1500 to 2000***. NYC: Random House, 1987.
King, Jr., Martin Luther, ***A Testament of Hope: The Essential Writings and Speeches of Martin Luther King, Jr***. NYC: HarperSanFrancisco, 1986.
Kivel, Paul, and Allan Creighton, ***Making the Peace: A 15-Session Violence Prevention Curriculum for Young People***. Alameda CA: Hunter House Inc., Publishers, 1997.
Klare, Michael T., ***Resource Wars The New Landscape of Global Conflict***. NYC: Metropolitan Books, 2001.
———, ***Blood and Oil: The Dangers and Consequences of America's Growing Dependency on Imported Petroleum***. NYC: Metropolitan Books, 2004.
Krieger, David and Frank Kelly, eds., ***Waging Peace in the Nuclear Age: Ideas for Action***. Santa Barbara CA: Capra Press, 1988.
Kriesberg, Louis, ***Constructive Conflicts: From Escalation to Resolution***. Lanham MD: Rowman & Littlefield, 1998.
Kyi, Aung San Suu, ***The Voice of Hope***. New York: Seven Stories Press, 1997.
LaDuke, Winona, ***All Our Relations: Native Struggles for Land and Life***. Cambridge MA: South End Press, 1999.
Lederach, John Paul, ***Preparing for Peace: Conflict Transformation Across Cultures***. Syracuse NY: Syracuse University Press, 1995.
———, ***Building Peace: Sustainable Reconciliation in Divided Societies***. Washington DC: United States Institute of Peace Press, 1997.
Lewis, Bernard, ***The Multiple Identities of the Middle East***. London: Weidenfeld & Nicolson, 1998.
Lewis, John, ***Walking with the Wind: A Memoir of the Movement***. San Diego: Harcourt Brace & Company, 1998.
Lerner, Michael, and Cornel West, ***Jews & Blacks: Let the Healing Begin***. NYC: G. P. Putnam's Sons, 1995.
Lulofs, Roxane S. and Dudley D. Cahn, ***Conflict: From Theory to Action***. Boston MA: Allyn and Bacon, 2000.
Lynd, Staughton, ***Living Inside Our Hope: A Steadfast Radical's Thoughts on Rebuilding the Movement***. Ithaca NY: Cornell University Press, 1997.
Mahony, Liam and Luis Eguren, ***Unarmed Bodyguards: International Accompaniment for the Protection of Human Rights***. West Hartford CT: Kumarian Press, 1997.
Marine, Gene, Th***e Black Panthers: Eldridge Cleaver, Huey Newton, Bobby Seale***. NYC: Signet Books, 1969.
Maslow, Abraham H., ***Toward a Psychology of Being***. 2nd ed. NYC: Van

Nostrand Reinhold Company, 1968.
McAfee, John, *The Secret of the Yamas*. Woodland Park CO: Woodland Publications, 2001.
McAllister, Pam, *This River of Courage: Generations of Women's Resistance and Action*. Philadelphia PA: New Society Press, 1991.
McCarthy, Colman, *All of One Peace: Essays on Nonviolence*. New Brunswick NJ: Rutgers University Press, 1994.
McCourt, Frank, *Angela's Ashes*. NYC: Simon & Schuster, 1996.
McManus, Philip, and Gerald Schlabach, editors, *Relentless Persistence: Nonviolent Action in Latin America*. Philadelphia PA: New Society Publishers, 1991.
Mencken, H. L., *H. L. Mencken on Politics: A Carnival of Buncombe*. NYC: Vintage Books, 1960.
Merideth, Martin, *Nelson Mandela*. NYC: St. Martin's Griffen, 1997.
Merton, Thomas, editor, *Gandhi on Non-Violence: A Selection from the Writings of Mahatma Gandhi*. NYC: New Directions Publishing, 1964.
Mertus, Julie A., *War's Offensive on Women: The Humanitarian Challenge in Bosnia, Kosovo, and Afghanistan*. Bloomfield CT: Kumarian Press, 2000.
Morgante, Amy, ed., *Buddhist Perspectives on the Earth Charter*. Cambridge MA: Boston Research Center, 1997.
Moser-Puangsuwan, Yeshua, and Thomas Weber, *Nonviolent Intervention: Across Borders, A Recurrent Vision*. Honolulu: Spark M. Matsunaga Institute of Peace, 2000.
Naess, Arne, *Gandhi and the Nuclear Age*. Totowa NJ: The Bedminster Press, 1965.
Nagler, Michael, *Is There No Other Way? The Search for a Nonviolent Future*. Berkeley CA: Berkeley Hills Books, 2001.
Nesaule, Agate, *A Woman in Amber: Healing the Trauma of War and Exile*. NYC: Penguin, 1995.
Northrup, Jr., Jim, *Frags and Fragments: A Collection of Vietnam Poetry*. Sawyer MN: self-published, 1990.
O'Leary, Daniel E., *Global Directory of Peace Studies and Conflict Resolution Programs*. Fairfax VA: Consortium on Peace Research, Education and Development, 2000.
Oregon Public Policy Dispute Resolution Program, *Collaborative Approaches: A Handbook for Public Policy Decision-Making and Conflict Resolution*. Salem OR: Oregon Dispute Resolution Commission, 2000.
Ornstein, Robert, and Paul Ehrlich, *New World New Mind: Moving Toward Conscious Evolution*. NYC: Doubleday, 1989.
Partnoy, Alicia, *The Little School: Tales of Disappearance and Survival*. San Francisco: Cleis Press, 1998. (original 1986)
People's Commission of Inquiry into the Solution to the War in Vietnam. Minneapolis: People's Press, 1971.
Powers, Roger S., and William B. Vogele, eds., *Protest, Power, and Change: An Encyclopedia of Nonviolent Action from ACT-UP to Women's*

Suffrage. NYC: Garland Publishing, Inc., 1997.
Queen, Christopher S., *Engaged Buddhism in the West*. Boston: Wisdom Publications, 2000.
Rai, Milan, *War Plan Iraq: Ten Reasons Against War on Iraq*. London: Verso, 2002.
Reeve, Simon, *The New Jackals: Ramzi Yousef, Osama bin Laden and the Future of Terrorism*. Boston: Northeastern University Press, 1999.
Ringler, Dick, ed., *Dilemmas of War and Peace*. Madison WI: University of Wisconsin-Extension, 1993.
Roberts, Adam, and Richard Guelff, *Documents on the Laws of War*. Third Ed. Oxford UK: Oxford University Press, 2000 (original 1982).
Roodman, David Malin, *Still Waiting for the Jubilee: Pragmatic Solutions for the Third World Debt Crisis* (Worldwatch Paper 155). Washington DC: Worldwatch Institute, 2001.
Rothman, Jay, *Resolving Identity-Based Conflict in Nations, Organizations, and Communities*. San Francisco: Jossey-Bass Inc., 1997.
Roy, Arundhati, *The Cost of Living*. NYC: The Modern Library, 1999.
Ryan, Charlotte, *Prime Time Activism: Media Strategies for Grassroots Organizing*. Boston: South End Press, 1991.
Said, Edward, Peac*e & Its Discontents: Gaza-Jericho 1993-1995*. London: Vintage, 1995.
Saunders, Doris E., ed., *The Day They Marched*. Chicago: Johnson Publishing Company, 1963.
Schechterman, Bernard, ed., *Violence and Terrorism 99/00*. Fifth ed. Guilford CT: Dushkin/McGraw-Hill, 1999.
Schell, Jonathan, *The Fate of the Earth*. NYC: Avon Books, 1982.
Schwartz, Stephen I., ed., *Atomic Audit: The Costs and Consequences of U.S. Nuclear Weapons Since 1940*. Washington DC: Brookings Institution, 1998.
Shah, Sonia, ed., *Between Fear & Hope: A Decade of Peace Activism*. Baltimore MD: Fortkamp Publishing Company, 1992.
Sharp, Gene, *Power and Struggle: Part One: The Politics of Nonviolent Action*. Boston: Porter Sargent Publishers, 1973.
———, *The Methods of Nonviolent Action: Part Two: The Politics of Nonviolent Action*. Boston: Porter Sargent Publishers, 1973.
———, *The Dynamics of Nonviolent Action: Part Three: The Politics of Nonviolent Action*. Boston: Porter Sargent Publishers, 1973.
Shelden, Randall G., et al., *Youth Gangs in American Society*. 2nd ed. Belmont CA: Wadsworth, 2001.
Sibley, Mulford Q., ed., *The Quiet Battle: Writings on the Theory and Practice of Non-violent Resistance*. Boston: Beacon Press, 1963.
Smith, Perry M., *How CNN Fought the War*. NYC: Birch Lane Press, 1991.
Smith-Christopher, Daniel L., ed., *Subverting Hatred: The Challenge on Nonviolence in Religious Traditions*. Maryknoll NY: Orbis Books, 1998.

Spencer, William, *The Middle East. Global Studies* 6th ed. Guilford CT: Dushkin Publishing Group/Brown & Benchmark Publishers, 1996.
Starkey, Brigid, et alia, *Negotiating a Complex World: An Introduction to International Negotiation*. Boston: Rowman & Littlefield, 1999.
Stoessinger, John G., *Why Nations Go to War*. Eighth ed. Boston: Bedford/St. Martin's, 2001.
Szasz, Andrew, *EcoPopulism: Toxic Waste and the Movement for Environmental Justice*. Minneapolis: University of Minnesota Press, 1994.
Tabb, William K., *The Amoral Elephant: Globalization and the Struggle for Social Justice in the Twenty-First Century*. NYC: Monthly Review Press, 2001.
Terkel, Susan Neiburg, *People Power: A Look at Nonviolent Action and Defense*. NYC: Lodestar, 1996.
Thee, Marek, *Peace! By the Nobel Peace Prize Laureates: An Anthology*. Paris: UNESCO Publishing, 1995.
Ting-Toomey, Stella, and John G. Oetzel, *Managing Intercultural Conflict Effectively*. Thousand Oaks CA: Sage Publications, Inc., 2001.
True, Michael, *To Construct Peace: 30 More Justice Seekers, Peace Makers*. Mystic CT: Twenty-Third Publications, 1992.
———, *An Energy Field More Intense Than War: The Nonviolent Tradition and American Literature*. Syracuse NY: Syracuse University Press, 1995.
Tucker, Judith E., *In the House of the Law: Gender and Islamic Law in Ottoman Syria and Palestine*. Berkeley CA: University of California Press, 1998.
Umbreit, Mark S., *Mediating Interpersonal Conflict: A Pathway to Peace*. West Concord MN: CPI Publishing, 1995.
Ury, William, *Getting Past No: Negotiating with Difficult People*. NYC: Bantam Books, 1991 (2nd edition).
———, *Getting to Peace: Transforming Conflict at Home, at Work, and in the World*. NYC: Viking, 1999.
Van Slyke, Erik J., *Listening to Conflict: Finding Constructive Solutions to Workplace Disputes*. NYC: AMACOM, 1999.
Vanunu, Mordechai, *Faith Under Siege: Letters from a Christian Prisoner-of-Conscience*. Samuel H. Day, Jr., ed. Madison WI: U.S. Campaign to Free Mordechai Vanunu, 1998.
Wallis, Jim, ed., *Waging Peace: A Handbook for the Struggle to Abolish Nuclear Weapons*. San Francisco: Harper & Row, Publishers, 1982.
Walter, Eugene Victor, *Terrorism and Resistance: A Study of Political Violence*. NYC: Oxford University Press, 1969.
Weber, Thomas, *Gandhi's Peace Army: The Shanti Sena and Unarmed Peacekeeping*. Syracuse NY: Syracuse University Press, 1996.
Weil, Simone, *The Iliad or The Poem of Force*. Wallingford PA: Pendle Hill, 1956.
Weiner, Neil Alan, Margaret A. Zahn, and Rita J. Sagi, *Violence: Patterns,*

Causes, Public Policy. Orlando FL: Harcourt Brace Jovanovich, Publishers, 1990.

Weiss, Thomas G., *Military-Civilian Interactions: Intervening in Humanitarian Crises.* Lanham MD: Rowman & Littlefield Publishers, Inc., 1999.

Weiss, Thomas G., and Cindy Collins, *Humanitarian Challenges & Intervention.* 2nd ed. Boulder CO: Westview Press, 2000.

Whaley, Rick and Walter Bresette, *Walleye Warriors: An Effective Alliance Against Racism and for the Earth.* Philadelphia PA: New Society Publishers, 1994.

White, George Abbott, *Simone Weil: Interpretations of a Life.* Amherst MA: University of Massachusetts Press, 1981.

White, Jonathan R., *Terrorism: An Introduction.* 2nd edition. New York: West/ Wadsworth Publishing, 1998.

Wilde, Oscar, *Sayings.* Rome: Demetra, 1998.

Williams, Mary, ed., *Why Is the Middle East a Conflict Area?,* San Diego CA: Greenhaven Press, 2000.

Williams, Terry Tempest, *Refuge: An Unnatural History of Family and Place.* NYC: Vintage Books, 1992.

Wood, Julia T., *Gendered Lives: Communication, Gender, and Culture.* 2nd ed. Belmont CA: Wadsworth Publishing Company, 2001.

World Law Fund, *Current Disarmament Proposals: As of March 1, 1964.* NYC: World Law Fund, 1964.

Yarn, Douglas H., *Dictionary of Conflict Resolution.* San Francisco: Jossey-Bass, 1999.

Yost, Jack, *Planet Champions: Adventures in Saving the World.* Portland OR: BridgeCity Books, 1999.

Ziegler, David W., *War, Peace, and International Politics.* Second ed. Boston: Little, Brown and Company, 1981.

Zinn, Howard, *A People's History of the United States.* New York: Harper & Row, 1980.

———, *The Zinn Reader: Writings on Disobedience and Democracy.* NYC: Seven Stories Press, 1997.

———, *The Future of History: Interviews with David Barsamian.* Monroe ME: Common Courage Press, 1999.

Zunes, Stephen, Lester R. Kurtz and Sarah Beth Asher, *Nonviolent Social Movements: A Geographical Perspective.* Malden MA: Blackwell Publishers, 1999.

Index

Abejas, 82
accompanier; accompanying, 181
active-duty, 155, 165
ad hoc nonviolence, 157
adjudicated youth, 26
Afghanistan, 9, 11, 17, 27, 51-53, 61, 66, 89-90, 93, 101, 122, 137, 165, 186-188, 194, 197, 202-203, 205, 229, 234
Africa, 54, 61, 74, 84, 89, 99, 112, 126, 143, 166, 196, 208
African American, 32-34, 55-56, 58, 75, 86, 131, 205, 218, 236
aggression, 30, 139, 174, 176, 206
AK-47s, 187, 203
al-Assad, Hafiz, 232
Albert Einstein Institution, 160
al-Din, Khayr, 5
Aldridge, Robert, 99, 105
Alinsky, Saul, 34, 150
Alternative Minimum Tax, 165
altruism, 78, 83
American Civil Liberties Union; ACLU, xvii, 34
American Civil War, viii
Amundson, Amber, 125
anarchist, 29, 85, 129, 186
Anglo-Persian Oil Company, 62
Anishinabe, 66, 88, 132, 165, 235
Ankara, 233
Anti Defamation League, ADL, xvii, 56
anti-Semitism, 56
Appleby, R. Scott, 60, 66
Arabs, 30, 62, 93, 193, 197
Arias, Oscar, 10, 203, 222
Armenia, 233
America, 29, 101, 103, 108, 115, 213-214, 222
arms trade, 197, 203, 220, 222
assertion, vii, xiii, xv, 6, 28, 38-39, 50, 53, 102, 163, 176
Ataturk Dam, 232
Atwood, Margaret, 36

Auschwitz, 76
Austro-Hungary, 227
Azerbaijan, 232-233
Badshah Khan, 53, 137, 164
Barash, David, 54, 75, 125, 159
Bateson, Mary Catherine, 5
Belgium, 102, 227
Belgrade, 3, 202
Ben Tre, 75-76
Berne, Eric, 63
Berne, Switzerland, 85, 103
Berrigan, Daniel, 50, 57, 231
Berrigan, Phillip, dedication, 109, 122, 230
bin Laden, Osama, 51, 89-90, 92-93, 101, 159, 193, 197, 199-200
black Americans, see African Americans
blowback, 5
Bolingbroke, 229
Bondurant, Joan V., 144-145, 163
Bonhoeffer, Dietrich, 231
Bosnia, 9, 14, 40, 77
Boulding, Elise, 8, 29-31, 72, 78, 81, 104, 114-115, 127-128, 131, 136, 213-214, 223-224, 228-229, 235
Boulding, Kenneth, 72, 81, 103
boycott, 99, 112, 140, 145, 147, 150, 156, 165, 167, 220, 236
British Aerospace; BAe, xiv, 100
British empire, 144-145, 184, 234
Brous, Devorah, 159
Bulgaria, 165
Bulletin of Atomic Scientists, 133
burnout, 2
Cairo Declaration on Human Rights, 11
Cakars, Maris, 166
Canada, Canadian, 166, 225, 236
Caspian Sea, 233
Catholic Worker; CW, xiv, 4, 19-20, 77, 80, 88, 109, 118, 129, 132, 138, 229
Cedras, Raoul, 11
Chaney, James, 55

Chavez, Cesar Estrada, 149-150, 227
Chechnya, 77, 221, 233
Chiapas, 77, 82
China; Chinese, 37, 60-61, 63, 115, 128, 132, 206-208, 233
Christ, Jesus, 56, 65, 109, 159
Christian Peacemaking Teams, CPT, xvii, 76-78, 83
Christianity,Christians, 5, 10, 28, 36, 51-52, 54, 56, 62, 76-78, 93, 108, 113, 129, 136, 138-140, 196, 236
Christopher, Warren, 14
Cicero, 159
civilian-based defense; CBD, xvii, 158, 160, 162-168, 227
Civilian-Based Defense Association, 160
civil intervention, 80
civil resistance, 78, 85, 132, 173
Civil Rights Movement, 1, 8, 32, 87, 113, 143, 147, 165, 169
civil strife, 71-73, 80, 85-87, 92-93
civil war, 72-73, 79, 83-84, 91, 144, 148, 181, 208, 219
Clan of One-Breasted Women, 234
Clark, Jim, 7
Clement of Alexandra, 159
Code of Hammurabi, 9
Colombia, 78, 204, 232
Columbia River, 236
Columbia University, 194
communication, 3, 6-7, 13, 18, 24, 30, 79, 84-85, 103, 168-170, 177, 179-180, 208, 221-222
Community Service Organization; CSO, vii,150
conflict: contributory factors, 81
Conflict Resolution, 3, 18, 21, 23-25, 37, 46-47, 62, 71-72, 80, 83, 92, 99, 112, 114, 158, 163, 168-169, 170, 178, 203, 231
Congress, 3, 32, 64, 75, 99, 112, 122, 147, 165, 187, 189, 198, 201, 203, 208, 227
Congress of Racial Equality; CORE, 147
consumer choices, 74, 158
contra forces, 227
corporate lobbies, 165
Costa Rica, 10, 155
Council on Peace Research in History, 8
cruise missiles, 203
Damascus, 232
Day, Dorothy, 20, 65-66, 77, 88, 118, 129, 138
Day, Sam, 132-133
dehumanizing, 75
Dellinger, David, 87
Department of Defense; DoD, xvii,165, 224, 229
Desai, Narayan, 76, 160
deterrence through terror, 28
disarmy, 31, 76, 143, 156, 163, 204, 226
divide-and-rule, 234
domestic violence, 5-6, 36, 40
Druze, 136-137, 164
Duckwitz, Georg, 140
Durand Line, 53, 233
Durand, Sir Mortimer, 233
Dworkin, Ronald, 128
Dyson, Freeman, viii
Ecesis, 232
Economic Community of West African States, 84
ego, 45, 56
Ehrlich, Anne, 117
Ehrlich, Paul, 230
El Salvador, 78, 91, 144, 188
England, 90, 116, 164
enslaved Africans, 165
Equilibre, 79
ethnic conflict, 68, 76, 79, 110, 223, 232-233
Euphrates, 232-233
fair trade, 74, 204
Farrakhan, Louis, 56
Federal Employment Practices Commission; FEPC, xvii, 147
Ferguson, Adam, x
Fifth Commandment, ix
fight nonviolently, 25
Final Solution, 38
Fisk University, 1
Ford, 165
Forest, Jim, 138, 149
forgiveness, 62-66, 189
Foster, Sister Rita, 19
France, 67, 130, 142-143, 145, 191, 227
free trade, 126, 129, 204
functions of violence, 160
Galtung, Johan, 12
Gandhi, Mohandas K., 2, 12, 50, 53, 65-66, 74, 76, 82, 104, 106, 108, 113, 115, 127-128, 131, 137, 143-145, 155, 160, 163, 184, 204, 206, 227, 235-236
gender, 3, 5, 23, 35-36, 52, 58, 84, 86
gendered violence, 35
genocide, 11, 38, 75, 110, 135, 164
Georgia (state), 87, 116, 205
Georgia (nation-state), 239
Germany, 67, 116, 139-140, 142, 165, 188, 191, 227, 230
Girl, Interrupted, 4
globalization, 105-106
Glover, Danny, 150

index 253

Gonzalez, Gaspar Pedro, 27, 49
Good Friday Peace Accord, 90
gooks, 75
Gould, Stephen Jay, 2
Green Fire Productions, 18
Guatemala, 28, 40, 78, 91, 106, 144, 186, 188
guerrilla, 21, 91, 97, 144-145, 181, 202, 204, 232, 236
gutter religion, 56
Haiti, 11, 77
Halberstam, David, 1, 7, 15, 88
Hamas, 159, 191, 209
Harris, Arthur, 8
Harris, Rabia, 53
Hartland, Vermont, 17
Hebron, 77
Hennacy, Ammon, 89, 159
Hersey, John, 64
Heschel, Rabbi Abraham, xi
Heyerdahl, Thor, 4
high-frequency active auroral research project; HAARP, xiv, 214
Highlander Folk School, 157
Hindu Killers, Hindu Kush, 53
Hiroshima, 64, 76, 116-118, 186
The Hitchhiker's Guide to the Galaxy, 138
Hitler, Adolph, Hitlerism, 13, 30, 57, 67, 82, 108, 129, 138-140, 142, 145, 164, 188, 191, 228, 230-231
Hoffman, P.J., 167
Holbrooke, Richard, 14
Holy Disobedience, 54
Homer-Dixon, Thomas, 71, 81, 190
homicide, 42
Homo Negotiator, 159
hope, hopeless, 2-3, 6, 18, 23, 40, 46, 48, 59-60, 71, 77, 80-81, 93, 103, 108-109, 112-115, 126, 139, 142, 148, 150, 157, 159, 164, 170, 174, 175, 183, 192-193, 207, 209, 213, 220, 222, 228
Hope Community, 19
humanitarian intervention, 11-12
humanizing; humanize, dehumanize, dehumanizing, 5, 37, 39-40, 63, 75 177, 206
human resources, 157
humor, 132-134, 221
Hymietown, 56
hyperconsumerism, 157
id, 56
identity conflict, 3, 8, 32-33, 46-47, 49, 52, 54, 56-57, 60-61, 67, 75, 110, 131, 179, 222 224 232-233
I Have a Dream, 148

"I" messages, 179
indigenous leadership, 81, 189
Industrial Areas Foundation, 150
Ingram, Catherine, 86
Institute for Defence Studies & Analyses; IDSA, xvii, 49
Institute of Oriental Philosophy, 228
inter arma silent legis, 159
internalized self-oppression, 177
International Court of Justice; ICJ, xvii,197, 201-202
International Criminal Court; ICC, xvii,197, 200-201
International Fellowship of Reconciliation; IFOR, xiv, 115
international peace force, 76
International Peace Research Association, 8, 214
intrastate conflict, 76
Ippy, 93
Iran, Iranian, 51, 60, 62, 73, 90, 130, 188, 209, 232-233
Iraq, 11, 27, 62, 66, 73, 77, 99, 111-112, 121, 125, 188-189, 191, 193, 199, 220, 223-224, 232
Irish Catholics, 57
Islam, Islamic, 5, 10, 15, 36, 50-55, 61-62, 68, 103, 136, 159, 188-189, 233
Islamic fundamentalism, 52
Islamic Jihad, 159
Israeli Defense Force; IDF, xvii, 57, 137, 159, 191, 200
Jackson, Jesse, 56, 165
Jainist, Jainism, xi
Japanese-Americans, 63
Jewish-Black relations, 56
Jews-as-Christ-killers, 56
jihad, 50-51, 53
Judaism, 56
Just War doctrine, 159
Kabul, 52, 61, 187
Kawada, Yoichi, 228-229
Kazakhstan, 233
Kennedy, John, 120, 141
Kennedy, Paul, 61,145
Kennedy, R. Scott, 137
Kennedy, Robert, 150
Khan, Abdul-Ghaffar; Badshah Khan, 53, 137, 164
Khan, Sarfraz, 51
Khan, Wali, 75
Khana, 192
Kindom, 229
King Richard the Second, 229
Kissinger, Henry, 9

Klare, Michael T., *89, 232-234*
Korean War, *75*
Kosovars, *12-13*
Kosovo, *3, 12*
Ku Klux Klan, *66*
Kurdish identity, *232*
Kyrgyztan, *233*
Lakey, George, *164*
law enforcement, *9, 28, 136, 185-186, 196, 202, 218*
Laws of Manu, *10*
Lawson, James, *1*
Le Chambon, *142-143*
legitimate targets, *159*
Leninism, *131*
Lerner, Michael, *54, 56*
Lewis and Clark College, *192*
Lewis, Bernard, *62*
Lewis, John, *7-8, 148*
Lincoln Memorial, *87, 227*
Lockheed Martin, *229*
Lulofs, Roxane S., *3, 6, 13, 35, 37, 59*
Lysistrata, *130*
MacArthur, Douglas, *158*
Madigan, Sister Char, *19*
Marx, Karl, *50*
mass noncoöperation, *156*
massive demonstrations, *74*
Matthew, *40, 99*
Maurin, Peter, *77, 138*
McAfee, John, *27*
McCarthy, Colman, *34*
McCarthy Era, *114*
McCourt, Frank, *45*
McDonnell Douglas, *128, 230*
Mead, Margaret, *2, 115, 135-136*
Mecca, *53*
mediation, *18, 21, 23, 46-48, 103-104, 114-115, 158, 169, 180, 196-197, 202-203, 224*
Medina, *53*
Meena, *205-206*
Mencken, H. L., *146-147*
Mexican-Americans, *149*
Mexico, *78*
Michigan, *165*
Mideast, Middle East, *3, 30, 34, 60-62, 89, 93, 104, 126, 136, 188-189, 193, 205, 216, 223, 232*
mientzu, *37*
migrant farm workers, *165*
Miller, Andrew, *78*
Milošević, Slobodan, *9, 12, 67-68, 200, 205*
Minneapolis, Minnesota, *19, 55, 121*

Mir Sada, *79*
Mogul Empire, *61*
Mohawks, *77*
Montgomery, Alabama, *99, 147, 150, 157, 167, 236*
Mosaic Law, *9, 28*
Moser-Puangsuwan, Yeshua, *160*
Mothers of the Disappeared, *40*
Movement for a New Society; MNS, *87, 110*
Muslim Peace Fellowship, *53*
Muslim practices, *52*
Muslims, *5, 51-53, 57, 61, 68, 75, 89, 92-93, 103, 137, 159, 188-190, 195, 200*
Muste, A.J., *54, 208*
Nagorno-Karabakh, *233*
napalm, *10, 75*
Napoleon, *145-146, 191, 228*
Nash, Diane, *65-66, 85-86*
Nashville, Tennessee, *1, 86, 169*
National Association for the Advancement of Colored People; NAACP, *xvii, 147, 157*
National Farm Workers Association; NFWA, *150*
nongovernmental organization; NGO, *74, 84, 98, 100-103,112,115, 196, 203, 205, 213*
North Atlantic Treaty Organization; NATO, *11-12, 68, 224, 232, 236-237*
negotiations, *14, 91, 158, 197, 202-203, 213, 222*
Nelson, Wally, *frontispiece*
Newton, Huey, *33*
Nicaragua, *184, 190, 202, 227*
non-antagonistic language, *179*
noncombatants, *97, 144*
nonviolence, *1-5, 7, 9, 11-12, 14, 17-18, 20-24, 26-29, 32-33, 35-36, 39, 43, 45-47, 50, 53-54, 57-59, 61-63, 65-66, 72, 76-78, 80-83, 86-88, 91-93, 98, 104-108, 117, 127-128, 131-132, 136-138, 140, 142-147, 149-151, 155-162, 164, 166, 168-171, 173, 175, 181, 183-185, 191-192, 196, 199, 202, 204, 207-209, 214, 219, 224-227, 230-231, 234-237*
nonviolent conflict management, *5, 23, 29, 31, 77, 92, 110, 170*
nonviolent success: contributory factors, *2-3*
nonviolent direct action, *158*
nonviolent history, *151*
nonviolent interposition, *76, 80-81, 148*
Nonviolent Peaceforce, *76, 79-80, 163*
Noriega, Manuel, *9*
North American Free Trade Agreement; NAFTA, *xiv, 82*
Northern Alliance, *52, 90, 205*
Northern Ireland, *46-47, 63, 68, 90, 204, 213*
Northrup, Jr., Jim, *97*
North Vietnam, *91, 221*

index

Northwest Frontier of Pakistan, 53
Notre Dame, University of, 60
nuclear, 3, 10, 15, 19, 27, 40, 64-65, 80, 105, 108, 116-120, 131, 167, 178, 181, 194-195, 202-203, 213-216, 224-225
nutrition, malnutrition, 215, 220, 229
oath of nonviolence, 157
obedience, 54, 227
oil pipelines, 232
oil reserves, 223, 233
Oka, 77
Oregon Peace Institute, 17
Organization of American States; OAS, xvii, 11
Ornstein, Robert, 230
pacifism, pacifist, 109, 116, 129-131, 138, 159, 208, 228
Pakistan, 52-53, 75, 137, 144, 186, 194, 215, 234
Palestinians, 11, 56-57, 65, 187, 190-194, 209
Parks, Rosa, 150, 157
Pascal, Blaise, 231
Pashtun, 51, 53, 75, 137, 206, 234
passive-aggressive, 166
Pathans, 53, 164
patriotism, 198, 229
pax, 11
Pax Americana, 71
Pax Britannica, 71
Pax Christi, 20
Pax Islamica, 53
peace, frontispiece, vii, viii, x, xiii, xv, 3, 8-12, 14, 17-21, 26, 28-32, 34, 42, 46-47, 50, 53-54, 61, 67, 71-72, 75-76, 78-80, 82-84, 87, 90-92, 98-107, 109-111, 113-115, 117, 125-132, 135-136, 145-146, 149, 155-156, 158-159, 163-164, 167, 174, 178, 185, 190-196, 198-199, 202, 204-205, 207-208, 213-214, 217-218, 220, 222, 224, 225-230, 232
Peace Brigades International; PBI, 78, 167
peacekeeping, 75
Peace Now, 79
Peace Studies, 3, 31, 47, 71, 84, 99, 111, 158
peace system, 30-31, 34, 78, 103, 105, 115, 136, 156, 159, 163, 217, 220, 228-230
Pearl Harbor, 64, 101, 199
Pentagon, 34, 76, 87, 93, 105, 110, 142, 156, 165-166, 178, 183, 203, 214, 224, 236
Persian Gulf, 60, 117, 232
personalism, 177
police violence, 35
political will, 166
power relations, 81

Prayer of the Vindicated, 50
principled negotiation, 178
protective accompaniment, 80
Quebec, 77, 205
Quebec provincial police, 77
racial discrimination, 165
racism, 32, 34, 75-76
Raj, 53
rape, 3, 36-39, 57, 175
Rather, Dan, 229
Raytheon, 230
Reagan, Ronald, 90, 112, 117, 131, 198
rebellion, 32, 72, 82, 140, 166, 208, 232
reconciliation, 62, 66, 68, 197, 203
redirecting; redirection, 4, 136, 181
Reeb, James, 88
religion, 5, 36, 46, 50, 52, 54-57, 60-62, 72, 82, 98, 103, 127, 129, 143, 156, 207, 214, 221, 229
religious extremism, 60
resolve conflict, 26, 72, 143
resolve (determination), 118, 145, 177, 184, 219, 221
Resource Wars: The New Landscape of Global Conflict, 232
Revolutionary Association of the Women of Afghanistan, 205
right to err, 163
Rothman, Jay, 47-48, 203
Roy, Arundhati, 100, 194-195
Royal Ulster Constabulary; RUC, xiv, 57
Russia, 10, 52, 120, 144-145, 187, 216, 221, 227-228, 233-234
Rwanda, 11
Ryder, Winona, 4
sacrifice, 32-33, 63, 155, 157, 163, 167, 187, 189, 219, 229-230
satyagraha, 115, 127, 144, 163-164
satyagrahis, 143, 155, 160, 164, 184
Saudi Arabia, 89, 92-93, 188, 199
Schwartzkopf, Norman, 117, 158
scofflaw nation, 202
scorched earth, 220, 232
secrecy, 163-164
security, insecurity, 7, 10, 29, 49, 77, 89, 104, 109, 112, 121, 142, 151, 158, 162, 166, 208, 215, 228
Sejr, Arne, 139-140
Selma, 7-8, 28, 88
September 11, 2001; 9.11.01, 90, 92-93, 101, 120, 122, 125, 165, 199-200, 205, 224
Servants of God, 53, 137
Seville Statement, 135, 143
sex object, 5

Shah of Iran, 188
Shakespeare, 226, 229
Shanti Sena, 76, 79, 115, 163, 204
Shanti Sainiks, 76
Sharp, Gene, 160, 162-166, 227
Sheats, Ladon, frontispiece
Sierra, Katie, 29, 122
Sierra Leone, 73-74
Silk Road, 51, 61
Silone, Ignatzio, 126
Sin, Cardinal, 148
Sino-Soviet relations, 60
skinhead, 56
slaveowners; slavery, 32, 74, 98, 113, 143, 165, 172
Slovenia, 67
social change, 23, 31, 50, 76, 114, 121, 127, 138, 157-158, 235
soldiering, 156, 221
Somalia, 11, 27, 229
South Africa, 99, 112, 126, 131, 143, 166, 198, 208
Southern Christian Leadership Conference; SCLC, xvii, 147
Soviet Union, 17, 52, 89, 110, 140, 188, 208, 233
Sri Lanka, 68, 78-80
Starbucks, 74
statuary, 52
Stoessinger, John H., 98
Student Nonviolent Coordinating Committee; SNCC, xiv, 120, 147, 169, 175
suicide bombing, 50, 57, 90, 159, 200, 216
Sunni Islam, 52
Syria, 30, 106-107, 136-137, 232-233
Tacitus, 100
Tajikistan, 233
Tajiks, 53
Taliban, 10, 52, 90, 93, 186, 188, 205
teaching tolerance, 76
Ten Commandments, 140, 159
Terry, Jennifer, xiii, 195
Thucydides, 89
Tibet, 132, 166, 206-207
Tikkun, 56
Timorese, 100, 110
Training for Change, 164
treaty rights, 66, 132, 165
tribal leadership, 202
True, Michael, 141, 164
Turkmenistan, 233
Turks; Turkey, 51, 61-62, 223-224, 232-233
UN, 11-12, 74-75, 84, 100, 103-104, 112, 137, 190, 201, 203-204, 222, 224

union leader, 157
United Farm Workers; UFW, xiv, 150, 165, 167
Universal Declaration of Human Rights, 9
Unnithan, T.K.N., 83
UN peacekeeping, 75
US, 9-11, 14, 17, 20, 26, 30-32, 34, 37, 46, 51-57, 60, 63-65, 67-68, 73, 75, 79, 85-87, 89-93, 101, 103, 106, 108-110, 112-114, 121-122, 126, 130, 138, 142-144, 146-150, 156-157, 159, 161, 165, 172, 184-191, 193-194, 197-207, 215-216, 218, 220, 222-225, 229, 231-233, 235
US American military, 93, 126, 149, 156-157, 165, 189, 197, 225, 229, 233
USS Georgia, 116
utopia, 78, 159, 228
utopia of compassion, 228
Uzbekistan, 233
Uzbeks, 53
Venezuela, 232
Vietnamese, 75, 90, 142, 221
Vietnam War, 75, 225
Virgil, 73
von Suttner, Bertha, 98, 103, 135, 215
Wahab, Zahir, 194
Waging Peace, 155
Wallis, Jim, 155
war dead, 83, 227
War Resisters League, 88
war system, 29-30, 32, 34, 67-68, 75-76, 78, 99, 105, 113, 115, 128-129, 136, 156, 159, 214, 217-218, 224, 228-230
war taxes, 157
water, 40, 51, 73, 106-107, 113, 190, 213, 217, 225, 230-232
weapon, weapons, weaponry, 3, 8-10, 12, 36, 40-41, 45, 57, 63, 65, 67, 73-74, 78, 81, 84, 89-90, 99-100, 103, 105, 108, 115-122, 136, 138, 142, 157-158, 167, 170, 181, 187, 202-204, 213-217, 220-221, 224, 226, 228-229, 231, 235-236
weapons of mass destruction, 3, 116, 119, 136, 214
weapons merchants, 81
Wellington, Duke of, 146
West Africa, 61, 74, 84, 111
West, Ben, 86
West, Cornel, 54, 56
West Indies, viii
Wilde, Oscar, 228
Wisconsin, 40, 87, 114, 132, 165, 225, 235
Witness for Peace, 132
A Woman of No Importance, 228
work object, 5

World Court, 201
World War I, 8, 62, 73, 114, 117, 227
World War II, 63-64, 105, 108, 114-115, 117, 130, 142, 145, 147, 183, 186, 193, 199
X, Christian, 139, 141
X, Malcolm, 55
xenophobia, xenophobic, 11, 52, 116, 220
Yoder, John Howard, 166
Young, Nigel, 31, 131
Zahn, Gordon, 20, 141
Zapatistas, 82
Zazen, 41
Zinn, Howard, 2, 67, 118, 120-121, 135, 165
Zionist, 51, 55, 193